Power and the Social

Power is a theme that is central to an understanding of a wide range of sociological topics. In this text, the author looks at the different ways power has been theorised, from Hobbes to Giddens, and at the ways in which the theories have been applied. Within key areas of sociological concern – including race, gender, class, sexuality, the spatial and the visual – the processes and structures of power are analysed, as well as the ways in which power relations underpin everyday life. Areas of discussion include:

- A brief history of power
- Racialised power
- Class and power
- Engendered power
- Power and sexuality
- Visual and spatial power
- Re-inventing power

This book considers a wide range of cases from across the globe, including the 'underclass' in Britain; the power of the military in Latin America; gender and politics in India; and the visual politics of consumption and the media. By bringing together theory and substantive analysis, *Power and the Social* provides a clear and imaginative account of power and power relations and will prove an invaluable text for students.

Sallie Westwood is Professor of Sociology at the University of Manchester.

Power and the Social

Sallie Westwood

London and New York

First published 2002
by Routledge
11 New Fetter Lane, London EC4P 4EE

Simultaneously published in the USA and Canada
by Routledge
29 West 35th Street, New York, NY 10001

Routledge is an imprint of the Taylor & Francis Group

Typeset in Times New Roman by
Prepress Projects Ltd, Perth, Scotland
Printed and bound in Great Britain by
MPG Books Ltd, Bodmin

British Library Cataloguing in Publication Data
A catalogue record for this book is available
from the British Library

Library of Congress Cataloging in Publication Data
Westwood, Sallie.
  Power and the Social / Sallie Westwood.
    p. cm.
  Includes bibliographical references and index.
HM1256 .W47 2001
303.3–dc21   2001019962

ISBN 0–415–16287–4 (hbk)
ISBN 0–415–16288–2 (pbk)

Contents

Acknowledgements

I have accrued many debts during the course of the work that has informed the pages of this book. To the many people with whom I have worked and whose patience and good humour has facilitated the research process, I offer my gratitude and warm thanks. Research requires a material base, and I am indebted to the Economic and Social Research Council, which made so much of my research possible. I would also like to thank my colleagues in Sociology who have supported my efforts, James Fulcher, Anthony Giddens, Syd Jeffers, Nick Jewson, Annie Phizacklea, John Scott, Peter van der Veer, and the many students with whom I have enjoyed working on issues of power relations. My thanks also to Robert Ash, Ian Jamie Goodchild and Mark Maynard for technical support.

Mari Shullaw, my editor, has been a model of encouragement and patience and I am very grateful for her contribution. Finally, I owe very special thanks to Rashpal Singh, to whom this book is dedicated.

Sallie Westwood
July 2001

Introduction

This book is an extended essay on the theme of power. It began life as a lecture course in which students were offered the opportunity to consider writings by specific authors on power. The book moves forward from the theoretical and philosophical concerns with power to provide an alternative account linking theoretical and substantive concerns. This is not an easy undertaking, and I am sure that as a reader you will bring different understandings to the discussion that follows. This is to be welcomed; the complexities and twists and turns in the stories of power and power relations are much more likely to generate discussion and debate than any simple consensus. Indeed, the aim of the book is to generate debate and dissent, and I very much hope that the book will be used in this way.

Debates around power and power relations are the mainstay of television drama and documentaries and, of course, news coverage such as the US Presidential Election in 2000, which provided an account of the minutiae of the democratic process and the relationship between political and judicial powers. More routinely, television programmes, watched by millions, dramatise power relations within families, between women and men and between the forces of law and order and criminality. Although the dramatic and visual tensions of power plays provide entertainment, one channel, Channel 4 in the UK, has tried to explore power in a more systematic way. A series of programmes was constructed as televisual seminars in which the participants were given the task of constructing a 'power list'. Economic power and the power of multinational corporations figured strongly in the initial 'power list'. As a prelude to these power lists, there was some discussion of the key question, 'What is power?' Like sociologists, the contributors to these programmes, who included political figures, scientists like Susan Greenfield, and people from private industry and the media, were very exercised by this question. In part, the answer around which their discussions coalesced is also of major import for sociological accounts. Power was viewed as a capacity within which is contained the ability to intervene in the lives of others. This introduces the first important distinction when considering the analysis of power: that between an understanding of power as a 'thing', usually signified by the notion of capacity, and the exercise of power, which is necessarily relational. However, although we can see the relational aspects of power in interpersonal situations, it is much more difficult to 'see' the power of Rupert Murdoch to impress upon our lives. Importantly, the exercise of power constantly invokes the relational and implies agency, and the ability of one person to impose their will or authority on another. This is, of course, the Weberian model of power and power relations that has been so influential in sociology, and continues to underpin much of the empirical work carried out by social and political scientists. Studies of political power often treat power as a goal, and emphasise the instrumental rationality that underlies routes to this goal. Although this often produces fascinating accounts of strategies, it does not begin to unpack the notion of power itself. Power plays are conceptualised as part of a game that is rule bounded, like football, but too often it seems as though capturing the ball is more important than winning the game. Perhaps, for sociologists, cricket is a better model. Favoured by British politicians as a model of two-party representative democracy, it offers a series of nuances and requires strategic acumen, especially in relation to spatial relations. This is not to deny, of course, the importance of spatial relations in football.

It is clear from the above that in an attempt to answer the question 'what is power?', a number of additional questions are raised. Power as capacity linked to the imposition of one person's will on another is a favoured answer, but there are alternative ways in which to conceptualise power. A whole new impetus to our understanding of power was provided by the work of Michel Foucault, who returned to the work of Nietzsche and an account of power as productive. This book takes off from this insight and seeks ways in which to provide a sociological reading of power.

Foucault (1978: 94) wrote: 'Power is not something that is acquired, seized or shared, something that one holds on to or allows to slip away: power is exercised from innumerable points, in the interplay of non-egalitarian and mobile relations'. Foucault's account, which will be explored throughout the pages that follow, offers a new direction; one in which power is not treated as a capacity outside and beyond social relations but is constitutive of social relations. It is everywhere and always present rather than a thing to be fought for and over. Power is imminent is a shorthand for the way in which power is conceived in this analysis. The idea of the diffusion of power through all social relations, and the sense that power is everywhere is also intelligible at a commonsense level as an account of day-to-day interactions. Sociology, however, uses a different language, and wishes to make the commonsense world problematic and strange as a means to theorising power and the social realm.

Thus, the major concerns of the chapters in this book are sociological and seek to tease out the relationship between power and the social. The social and the ways in which sociology has defined, conceptualised and constructed the idea of the social remain central to the discipline. It was one of the major ways in which sociology was called into being, and actually defines the subject as being conceptually based rather than empirically based. Every study of work or communities, for example, has within it an implicit notion of the social, which is re-inscribed through the research design. Through this constant reinvention of the social, sociology has built, over time, a complex account of interpersonal relations, groups and institutions within specific social formations. My argument is that power is imbricated in all of these accounts, but it is de-centred. Power is not located in one place, institution or person but, like the social, is constantly reinvented through the accounts generated from the research process. Conceptualising power in this way is creative, but it does not mean that power is free-floating. I want to suggest through the structure and discussion in this book that we can excavate power through the consideration of what I will call *modalities of power* and *sites of power*. Modalities are the different forms in which power is exercised, the qualities or attributes of different forms of power and the manner in which power is enacted. Sites are social spaces, locations for the exercise of power. These two, *modalities* and *sites*, provide the key axes around which the discussion takes place.

The chapters that follow elaborate within specific sites the modalities of power, but I am not claiming that this is an exhaustive account. On the contrary, this is the beginning of an elaboration of power: one way in which it is possible to examine the articulation of theoretical and substantive issues. This is realised through the use of examples and cases, many of which are developed from my own research and my concern with the ways in which we now live our lives within a globalised world. The attempt is to move beyond the European and North American worlds, and to integrate accounts from different societies with which I am familiar as a counter to the understanding of sociology as geographically located in the metropolitan world.

The book opens with a discussion of the ways in which power has been conceptualised using a wide range of sources, and concentrating on the discourses that have been important within sociological accounts of power. The chapters that follow this opening account are constructed in relation to specific sites of power. These *sites of power* are: *racialised power, class and power, engendered power, sexualised power, spatial power* and *visual power*. Each chapter details the ways in which forms of power are central to the theorisation of race, class, gender, sexualities, space and the visual. These sites of power privilege different modalities of power. The *modalities of power* are: *repression/coercion; power as constraint; hegemony and counter-hegemony; manipulation and strategy; power/knowledge; discipline and governance;* and *seduction and resistance.* The interaction between the specific themes of the chapters and the different modalities developed from the overview in Chapter 1 allows for an analysis of power that is not located simply with a homogeneous view of power but with its multiplicities.

Linking forms of power and the enactments of power plays with specific sites enables the discussion of the social and the ways in which the social has been conceptualised in sociological discourses. The argument rests upon an understanding of the social as de-centred, in process and, thereby, constituted and reconstituted in a variety of sites. This is a transformative social, no longer simply understood as part of the binary nature/social, virtual/social but fashioned and re-fashioned through the play of powers that are elaborated throughout the book. The final chapter of the book brings together the arguments of the preceding chapters and the ways in which the social may now be constituted in sociology as a myriad of socials, some with continuities and others that are discontinuous. This suggests a creative sociology not bound to one specific model of the social or of power relations but able to create accounts of social life that are textured and nuanced in keeping with the traditions of the discipline, yet reframing those in relation to the changing world that they seek to explain. I begin this narrative with 'a brief history of power', which provides an introduction to the modalities of power and how they have been thought of through time.

1 A brief history of power

Power is the shadow of freedom and, as an Arab proverb says, one cannot jump outside one's own shadow. We can certainly free some social possibilities but only at the price of repressing others. The relationship between power and freedom is one of permanent renegotiations and displacement of their mutual frontiers, while the two terms of the equation always remain. Even the most democratic of societies will be the expression of power relations, not of a total or gradual elimination of power.

(Laclau, 1996: 52)

Power still rules society; it still shapes, and dominates, us.

(Castells, 1997: 359)

...the principles of general sociology should be concluded with the proposition: all social relations are relations of power.

(Touraine, 1981: 33)

The attempt to theorise and define power has consistently been one of the major areas of concern in sociological analysis. Similarly, constituting the social as the object of sociological enquiry has been an ongoing problem, which has recently been foregrounded in work on the body, sexualities and the re-visioning of the binaries natural/social, virtual/real. This book is an intervention in these debates in the light of the recent revival of interest in the theorisation of power and the ways in which work on gender and 'race', for example, has brought the issue of the relationship between the natural and the social into sharp relief. This chapter, as the title suggests, provides a brief history of the ways in which some theorists have conceptualised power, beginning with very early accounts from Aristotle and Plato and then providing a more detailed analysis of the work of pre-modern theorists like Hobbes and Machiavelli who are considered to be central to the sociological account of power. Moving via Marx towards the sociological imagination, the chapter then considers the work of Foucault and the important distinction between power and violence. The overview presented in the pages that follow is then re-ordered as a series of modalities of power, the primary modes of the exercise of power that are explored in the later chapters of this book.

However, theorising power as the philosophers in this chapter have done, although in part defining the sociological imagination, is not the preserve of sociology and the social sciences more generally. Importantly, sociological accounts of power are only one set of discourses within a vast literature in which power is a central motif. The classical Hindu texts, the *Ramayana* and the *Mahabharata*, told and re-told as tales and through the medium of television, are in themselves constructions from a largely oral tradition, which as van der Veer (1993: 40) notes: '...resulted from the interaction between the orientalist production of "Ur"-essences and Brahminical ideology' which produced 'a "history", established by modern science..' and available as a narrative of a 'glorious Hindu past' disturbed by the Muslim invasion. The narratives are interwoven with issues of morality, of duty, honour, renunciation and spiritual redemption, and the thread that binds these accounts together is the discourse on power, its varieties and manifestations, in the relations between human beings and the deities and between human beings themselves. The *Mahabharata* recounts the epic battles of Krishna and Arjuna, and the struggles between brothers, father and son and their forms of resolution in relation to the strategic acumen of Arjuna, whose periods of exile involve a multitude of adventures with the gods and 'men'. The enduring popularity of the epic lies not only in its revival for latter-day political ends but in the passion, seductions, dilemmas and conflicts between individuals and across generations, ending ultimately in violence and death. The compelling quality of these narratives and the struggles that unfold are bound to the notion that, like Greek tragedies, the Old Testament stories and Shakespeare, the reader or viewer is reading the mysteries of the 'human condition'. These are in the structuralist sense the binaries of human existence, good versus evil, duty versus freedom, etc., that make a connection between the reader of today and the characters as embodiments of the great struggles of life for all human beings. The essentialism of this construction is, in fact, tempered by the understanding that the 'human condition', understood in this way, is social-bound to the spaces between individuals and, of course, the gods or destiny. Further, this understanding suggests that the 'spaces of the social' are not empty spaces but filled with the power plays, strategic encounters, passion and violence of the epics. At a commonsense level, we come to understand the indivisibility of the social and power. Power is the invisible architecture of the social. But, as this book elaborates, power and the social are neither transparent nor homogeneous. How then are we to understand their indivisibility and their complexity? As the pages of this book attest, this is not a new question, but one which has exercised philosophers, political and social theorists since the inception of an understanding of the distinction between the social and the natural. But, the notion of the 'human condition' suggests that the natural and the social are constantly interwoven, and a slippage between the natural and the social is very common. Both the distinctiveness of the natural versus the social and the bridge between the two are explained in relation to moral categories in the pre-modern period, and notions like the inherent qualities of human beings are still in circulation today. The relationship between the natural and the social is important for the analysis of power relations because the distinctions allows us to make the substance and exercise of power in social relationships transparent rather than assuming that excessive use of power, for example, is just one part of human nature or the human condition. Instead, it is our task to excavate the forms of power and social context in which power is exercised.

Aristotle (384–322 BC) wrote on a huge variety of subjects including biology and, in relation to our concerns with power, followed and criticised Plato (*c.* 428–347 BC) in his attempt to delineate the forms of government necessary for order and well-being. Aristotle, like Plato, viewed such discussions as the means whereby ethics and politics were brought together. For Aristotle, as well as Plato, the overriding concern was to promote stability and harmony. This was to be achieved for Plato in his famous text *The Republic* by the prolonged training of a special cadre who would form the ruling elite. There was no impulse to democracy within Plato or Aristotle and, indeed, Aristotle was not impressed by the idea of an intellectual elite as the ruling guardians of society. Both were committed to hierarchy and notions of natural aptitudes that translated into social positions including enslavement, which was viewed as socially useful. Plato, in particular, was concerned with governance and the mode of authority best suited to order rather than democracy. Plato's discussion of democracy in the Greek city state was romanticised by Hegel and nineteenth-century philosophers and poets as the model of democracy. But, it was a democracy organised around an exclusionary notion of the citizen who was male, not enslaved and lived in Athens.

Some centuries later, but similarly concerned with issues of harmony and stability in social life, the historian Ibn Khaldun (1332–1406), in a monumental work, sought ways in which to explain the decline of North African societies. The answer, he suggested, was to be found in an understanding of solidaristic ties that constitute the social as communitarian and encourage social stability. Larger social units are an unstable form of the social without the power of cohesion necessary to survival and reproduction. The issue of power and power relations was central, but subsumed in a discourse on authority, the city state, or forms of social change, bound in Ibn Khaldun's model to universal laws of change. There is no doubt, however, of the importance of the fourteenth-century Arab writer to sociological discourses as they developed. His concern with modes of authority, social order, urban forms and laws of social change pre-empted many of the preoccupations of the later 'founding fathers'.

Precursors to the modern period

Debates on the nature of power in sociological discourses usually turn initially to the work of Hobbes (1588–1679), Locke (1632–1704) and Machiavelli (1469–1527) as precursors to the modern period. Later writers have emphasised one or other of these early theoreticians: Clegg (1989) uses the differences between Hobbes and Machiavelli to trace distinctively different accounts of power, whereas Hindess (1996) uses Hobbes and Locke in relation to a more Parsonian account of power as capacities. What is of concern here is not only the differing approaches and definitional emphasis within and between Hobbes, Locke and Machiavelli, but the ways in which for each of these writers there was an account of power in relation to a construction of the social. In part, I would argue this is, indeed, what marks the work of these three philosophers as precursors of modernity and sociological enquiry. The writings of Hobbes, Locke and Machiavelli were not concerned with simply defining power, but addressing the issues raised by the exercise of powers, the relations between state and 'people', governance and, most importantly, the moral questions bound to the exercise of power, responsibility and freedom. Hobbes and Locke struggled, most especially, with the key conundrum for latter-day sociologists, i.e. the relationship between subjectivities and the social, presented in their writings, in the distinctions between nature and passions, 'man' as social and part of a collectivity or social formation.

Sociologically, it was Hobbes, writing in the seventeenth century, who directed attention to the problem of order, and who suggested that all subjects exchange a degree of personal power for social stability in a social contract with the sovereign. This was the alternative to the famous life of man as, 'nasty, brutish and short'. Macpherson (1962) has characterised Hobbes' views as those attuned to the then developing capitalism of Europe in which his deliberations on the nature of 'men' and 'selfish' morality were, in effect, a theory of 'possessive individualism', well suited to the specific phase of capitalist development. Although there is no simple correspondence between discourses and economic development, Macpherson's reading of Hobbes is still cogent, and relates well to Hobbes as a social philosopher trying to think through the upheavals, political, economic, social and religious, of his time. Hobbes was a radical, a self-professed atheist, at a time when religious sentiments were not questioned, apart from which camp an individual belonged to. Here was Hobbes, ruminating on the nature of human life, its passions, loves and the role of reason. Thus, in his work, a notion of the social is elaborated against the war of all against all. The social here is identified not simply with the sovereign and the problem of order but also with the notion of civil society. The idea that barbarism rules without civil society has been re-visited recently by Keane (1996) in his *Reflections On Violence*. Equally, as Clegg (1989) suggests, the Hobbesian tradition has strong moral overtones but a mechanistic notion of power, and one which is very much part of the 'modern' accounts of nations, states and institutional frameworks. Thus, Durkheim (1858–1917) raised the problem of social order and sought ways to re-define the Hobbesian solution, looking instead to the division of labour in society as the basis for a new moral order and the generation of consensus.

Clegg (1989) contrasts Hobbes' account of power with that of Machiavelli, wrongly cast as the villain of the piece, in the way in which the notion of 'Machiavellian' has come into common usage. In fact, it is not so far removed from Machiavelli's fascinating account of power plays and strategies. Writing in *The Prince* (1513), Machiavelli offers us an ethnography of power as it is constituted and re-constituted in the network of relations in the palace. Power is not an absolute, nor is it vested in the Prince or sovereign. Power is simply the effectiveness of strategies for generating a wider scope of action, *vis-à-vis* other people who must then operate within these arenas. Machiavelli uses military metaphors, suggesting a keen awareness of the role of violence in the exercise of power. For Machiavelli, there are effective and failed strategies; the judgments are not moralistic but based on efficacy in relation to the goal of the Prince, which was to stay in power.

Hindess (1996), writing more recently, appears to offer little credibility to Machiavelli as a theorist of power, and dismisses him more as a lieutenant to the powerful Prince. Instead, Hindess concentrates on the Hobbes of *Leviathan* and the work of John Locke as an alternative account of freedom and responsibility, suggesting that although Locke introduces a series of complexities in the account of power and its exercise, these are ultimately based on the notion of consent shared with Hobbes and the idea of a dispersal of powers as regulatory mechanisms in society. It is this consensus that is at issue for Foucault (Hindess, 1996: 140). The Hindess thesis is, however, hampered severely by his emphasis upon power as capacity and power as right, which ties his account to the discourses of liberal theory as they developed through the latter part of the nineteenth century and into the twentieth century, in the era of state formation. In his attention to these facets of the debates around power, the discourses that turned 'natural man' into 'social man' for Hobbes, Machiavelli and Locke are noticeably absent. The importance of these distinctions lies in their groundwork for the development of a sociological space in which the social could be thought and theorised as distinctive.

Among these thinkers, what is noteworthy is the way in which the emphasis upon instrumentalism in human affairs defines 'rational' actors (cf. Hobbes, 1650, *Human Nature*, p. 90) which coincide with conceptions of the person (Hobbes, [1651] 1968: 106). The strategist and the person are separated from nature by reason, and it is reason that is the invisible thread of the social. Hobbes, the atheist, lived within a material world which, although he acknowledged the power of love, gave precedence to reason. However, this materiality was also an embodied world in which corporeality was not separated from the social in the way that it came to be in later attempts by sociologists to define the social. Thus, Hobbes could discuss the strategic deal done between the subjects and the sovereign in which subjects exchanged freedoms for security, but also implicit in Hobbes' account was the ever-present threat of violence as both an aspect of the human condition and the state of nature.

Although, as Hindess (1996: 141) suggests, Hobbes recognised the variability of power and its heterogeneity, he did not recognise the significance of this for the theorisation of both power and the social. It was only much later, after Nietzsche, that Foucault could expand this notion to the point where the general, all inclusive notion of power became superfluous. In terms of a conception of the social, however, these three writers are crucial. Hobbes, with his notion of a social contract, conceived a collectivity that could be thought beyond the individual, whereas Machiavelli, with his ethnography of power, placed the individual in relation to others. Locke, more importantly, conceived a notion of laws, rights and responsibilities (as did Hobbes) that placed a premium on a conception of the social good, eventually turned into the 'felicific calculus' of Benthamite social philosophy. These philosophers were, of course, empiricist and the precursors to one variant of the developing concern with the social that eventually, two centuries later, produced sociology. These concerns were historically placed in the time and space of merchant capitalism and the growing urbanisation of parts of Europe. Within this context, these theorists of power could differentiate forms of power. Locke, for example, elaborated a distinction based on legitimation that produces tyranny when absent. Equally, there are different forms of legitimation that may invoke paternal control and power when dealing with minors or those who are incapacitated.

Unfortunately, I can dwell only briefly on the complexity and richness of the works of Hobbes, Locke and Machiavelli, but their importance for this text is in part their insistence on the complexities of power, its differentiations and nuances. Equally, their texts demonstrate the ways in which, from the earliest attempts to theorise power, power has been bound to theorisations of the social. This has occurred, in part, in relation to the separation natural/social and in the construction of 'social man' against 'natural man'. However, in the latter case, conceptions of human nature as violent, in the case of Hobbes, or 'wicked', in the case of Machiavelli, have persisted to the present day alongside a commitment to the cause of reason and rational man. It was this latter cause that became the hallmark of the ensuing Enlightenment both in France and in Scotland.

The modern project

The importance of the Enlightenment in European thought has been rehearsed many times, and I want to only briefly emphasise again the major motifs of the shift in worldview that occurred. The first of these, as I have suggested, was the foregrounding of reason as a way of being and knowing the world, but as Hawthorn (1987: 9) writes: 'Hence the insistence on supplementing the much vindicated faculty of reason by experience and experiment.' It was this combination that provided the impetus for sociology and a conception of the social as intelligible through laws, measurement and empirical verification. However, French intellectual life was less wedded to empiricism, and this persists today. The different philosophical traditions produced the different emphases in the developing states of France, England and Germany; whereas, in Scotland, the importance of the social was writ large in the work of Millar (1735–1801), Ferguson (1723–1816) and Smith (1723–90) (see Swingewood, 1980; Rattansi, 1982).

In part, the importance of the social as distinctive and intelligible was related to the opposition between natural/social set up by the writers of the time. How, and through which mechanisms, the social was to be constituted and man's natural tendencies curbed because of the defects with human nature was the issue explored in Montesquieu's *The Spirit of the Laws* published in 1784. Law was the embodiment of reason, but as Hawthorn (1987: 15) suggests, '...what was rational was held to be natural and what was natural was held to be rational'. This suggested a notion of natural justice and a universality to the law. However, Montesquieu (1689–1755) was equally aware that law interacted with specific cultures and customs, thus it was also specific. These specificities were related to the somehow innate characteristics or sensibilities of specific groups or nations. This was, of course, a very common feature of writing at the time, whether the speculations in a proto-anthropology or the musings on mental health and illness.

For Montesquieu it was the *esprit* in each country that should be honoured and to which reason brought stability and relevant laws. He did not have a conception of a developing continuum for societies – they were different and should remain so. Equally, the notion of a human nature was bound to society because individuals did not exist outside of the nexus of relations of power within society, whatever the type. Contradictory and conservative, the laws emphasised the immutability of 'national' characteristics and located politics with ethics and the fit between reason, ethics and cultural specificities.

In opposition to Montesquieu, Rousseau's (1712–78) writings suggest a romanticisation of the 'state of nature', the opposite of the Hobbesian nightmare. He also adopted a more evolutionary view of the development of societies through a conception of stages. Although all was well for 'natural man', the answer to the ills of the world lay not in nature but in society. Man enters the moral universe through society which, of course, also introduces notions and practices which are evil and reprehensible. The task lies in creating moral man and 'the best' of human beings and in generating the 'best' form of government, including the issue of order and the role of the law in society. For Rousseau, the answer lay in 'the social contract', which was a trade of liberty for the individual against the security of the general will. It is within these conditions that the moral individual is created and sustained. Thus, the twist in the tale, as Hawthorn (1987: 26) adds, is that Rousseau had not so much solved the problem of the individual versus society but that he had re-framed the definitions of individual and society in a modern way.

Power in these accounts lay with reason and science, and their coming together in the rational ordering of human affairs. Although the forms of government were not necessarily at issue, there was the enormous impact of the French Revolution and the growing sense that a social contract had to be sought between governors and governed in the interests of stability and order. There were, in effect, contradictory messages of optimism and a new sense of control in relation to the natural world, coupled with a view of a moral universe that was changing ever more quickly. Also changing were the economic and political relations within Europe as capitalism was consolidated, cities took shape, and the sense of turmoil and change infected the political and intellectual spheres. At the same time, wars continued and governments grew more interventionist and moved into modernity.

Modernity, born of the Enlightenment, suggests the importance of science and rationalisation but also, as Touraine (1995: 11) insists, the notion that both of these were revolutionary. 'Reason takes nothing for granted; it sweeps away social and political beliefs and forms of organisation which are not based upon scientific proofs.' Thus, the appeal to nature was not a simple naturalistic one but a foundational one in which nature stands for truth. Thus, the search for truths had new tools, science, reason and empirical verifications, which would unite man and the world. For Rousseau, for example, this unity is 'the general will', which is both society and those who compose society, not one section against another. As Touraine (1995) suggests, this predates the Durkheimian conception of the collective consciousness and offers a view of the social located with reason. For the Scottish Enlightenment philosophers, this is civil society. As Touraine (1995: 22) notes, 'It would be a mistake to transform Rousseau into a romantic, as in the interval separating *The Social Contract* and *Émile* he introduces the theme of the construction of the social "We" that transcends the individual and raises him to a higher level.' Similarly, Kant provides an ethics akin to Rousseau's politics in which the higher good is duty or a part in the social/universal and the duty is to know: 'Dare to know! Have the courage to use your own understanding' (cited in Cassirer, 1932: 163).

This modernising project generated forms of global domination summed up by Touraine (1995: 30), 'The triumph of modernity meant the suppression of eternal principles, the elimination of all essences and of artificial entities such as the Ego and cultures in favour of a scientific understanding of biopsychological mechanisms and of the unwritten and impersonal rules that govern the exchange of commodities, words and women' and 'It paved the way for the invasion of the classical order of modernity by the violence of power and the diversity of needs' (ibid.: 31).

Touraine sees the attempt to generate a rational society as a project doomed to and, indeed, ending in failure, in part, because 'social life, far from transparent and governed by rational choices, proved to be full of powers and conflicts...' (ibid.). However, he does acknowledge the sense of liberation that also marked modernity so well expressed by Berman (1983: 15). Modernity 'promises us adventure, power, joy, growth, transformation of ourselves and the world – and, at the same time, threatens to destroy everything we have, everything we know, everything we are'. The contradictory, paradoxical legacy of modernity currently fuels the preoccupations of our times and our futures. Central to these concerns are the main axes of this text, the relationship between the social and powers, the individual and society, the relationship between the natural, the virtual and the social.

Marx and the Marxian legacy

Marx (1818–83), the early socialists in France and later sociologists struggled with these issues again but within the context of developing modern capitalism, imperialism and nationalisms. Marx, influenced both by Hegel (1770–1831) and the political economists, set out with a scientist's verve to uncover the laws of motion of capitalism, including an understanding of the mechanisms of accumulation and, as he begins Capital, the role of the commodity. But, as we know, Marx was philosopher, economist and inspiration to revolutionary movements, which learned from Marx conceptions of power that led to revolutionary programmes. Marx wrote much on power and its exercise through economics, but he also had a notion of the power of ideologies and of collective subjects to act on the world. In his writings, Marx emphasised the revolutionary nature of capitalism itself and the ability of the powerful, the bourgeoisie, to act on the world in their own interests with initiative and a power base to enable transformations. But, capitalism was bifurcated and held within itself the revolutionary potential of the growing proletariat – it contained its own critique and modes of organisation that turn critique into action in specific circumstances.

Marx understood the power of coercion and the state, and the ways in which violence is part of every nation-state, available to those in power through the military. But, while this provides a backcloth to struggles within and against the state, there are other forms of power in play – the necessities of life, the organisation of capitalist production, the power of poverty and the power of ideas and representations expressed in the language of ideologies. Lefebvre (1995: 170) notes that during the early period (1840–45) 'Marx's thought produces a concept of modernity. This concept is primarily but not exclusively a political one'. The subtleties of Marx's analysis were lost in the development of authoritarian regimes and communist parties dedicated to statist versions of the socialist future. The relevance of Marx's writings for the analysis and conceptualisation of power is one issue, but also within the context of the development of sociology the history of the subject is often characterised as a debate with Marx. The social in Marx's work is expressed within the frame of capitalist development in which social, economic and political elements are constantly articulated. It is this articulated social that provided the basis for a re-reading of Marx away from the economic determinism of earlier understandings. Instead, the articulations between the political, economic and ideological spheres generated the space of the social in which collectivities could secure gains. In part, this re-reading, inspired by structuralism, was heavily dependent upon the work of Antonio Gramsci.

Gramsci (1891–1937) fought a long and lonely battle against the crude economism of the developing communist parties, suggesting instead that the state and civil society are indeed separate but interacting, and that the latter is also a space of political action. Equally, the ideological sphere is crucially important to the fate of political action and programmes. Gramsci understood the power of cultures as lived practices, and the ways in which power blocs from the ruling classes could generate a consensus in society through the processes of ideological hegemony. This did not mean simply that people were duped, but that the ideological spaces were both actively embraced and resisted by people in relation to a vast array of messages and signs mediated by the life circumstances of individuals.

Gramsci's work has been vitally important in recent sociological debates, especially in relation to the role of the media and the generation of ideological forms. It has overturned many of the earlier accounts of ideologies, which often emphasised Marxist notions of 'false consciousness' or the all-embracing power of the media. Instead, writers like Stuart Hall and the development of cultural studies have generated a much more nuanced account of the role of the media in the seductions of capitalism. These accounts introduce the notion of desire and the investments that subjects have in consumption as a crucial part of global modernities.

Equally, Gramsci's work has inspired a variety of interpretations and re-interpretations of state/civil society relations in both sociology and political science. The growing volume of material on social movements has drawn on the importance of civil society, the modes of representation of politics and the development of collective subjects, especially in Latin America after the resurgence of democracy in the eighties (Escobar and Alvarez, 1992).

Skocpol's (1979) comparative analysis of France, Russia and China attempts to analyse the specificities of revolutionary moments in relation to the importance of the state, not as an analytical category or absence, but as an organisational structure responsible for policing, the military, and securing the conditions for economic development. In this sense, her work is separated from more thoroughly Marxist accounts, which place the state in relation to economic and political forms, but are less concerned with the historical development and geo-political place of different states within global political and economic structures. Her emphasis is 'realist' and comparative, and the states with which she is concerned are not directly comparable in the sense of present day economic situations – especially at the time her book was published. Historically, however, these are states with powerful and wealthy agrarian bases in which a crisis within the state was exacerbated by rebellion from below and pressures from without, 'The revolutionary outcome in each instance was a centralised, bureaucratic, and mass-incorporating nation-state with enhanced great-power potential in the international arena.' (Skocpol, 1979: 41). Skocpol admits readily that this realist form of analysis is not a substitute for theoretical work, but offers an explanatory framework in which social revolutions can be theorised. Skocpol actually produces a historical and comparative analysis closer, in effect, to the work of Weber in sociology.

Weber, Simmel and modern times

Weber (1864–1920) worked with the central motifs of the Enlightenment project, developing an account of the rationalisation and bureaucratisation of modern societies. He understood more than many other writers the sense of disenchantment that prevailed in the West. His comparative studies sought ways in which to analyse the distinctive development of Western modernity, and his concerns ranged from religion to music. In relation to his studies of power, he distinguished legal–rational power from traditional and charismatic forms of authority in relation to the presence or absence of the state. These forms of authority were separate from the issue of individual power, very simply understood as the will to effect changes in another actor's behaviour, context or view of the world. Thus, power was central to Weber's understanding of the processes of rationalisation. As Beetham (1991) notes, the issue in relation to bureaucracy for Weber was not so much efficiency as the way in which power is exercised and developed through bureaucratic forms. Power, conceived both institutionally and individually, is constructed by Weber in a negative sense and as a capacity, linking Weber to Hobbes and those before him. Weber did not doubt the importance of economic factors, but consistently inserted the social in the guise of ideas and ideologies, as in his famous *The Protestant*

Ethic and the Spirit of Capitalism (1904–5). Unlike Marx, Weber did not develop a theory of exploitation in relation to class; instead he sought to understand class forms through the notion of status and market situation. It is many of these notions that have been incorporated into the main body of both empirical and theoretical sociology. Weberian sociology did not seek to elaborate 'social facts' in the way that Durkheim sought to do as the way in which to create the object of study of sociology. Weber, from a different philosophical tradition, emphasised instead a theory of social action and the power of *verstehen* – understanding. This suggests a social that is not external to the subject, but the two are one and the same. However, following his Enlightenment forebears, Weber's social actors were rational actors and, consequently, the social was constituted within the realm of reason and morality. Clearly, this has echoes of the French rationalists and Hobbes and Locke.

Therefore, for Weber, unlike Durkheim, there were no social facts, no collective consciousness and no re-building of solidaristic ties through a re-figured division of labour that would allow for a moral social space. Weber's vision, as is well known, was altogether more gloomy, and based on the rise and rise of bureaucratic forms of power that stretched out as a vast network through society, generating forms of individuation and alienation not located, as they were for Marx, with capitalist production but with, what Foucault later termed, governmentality and the management of populations. For Weber, these forms were a special form of power tied to rationalisation and bureaucratic procedures, and separated from charismatic power, which was secured through the person.

Unlike Weber, Simmel (1855–1918) revelled in modernity and became, as Frisby (1984) suggests, the true sociologist of modernity, making the link between the developing forms of urbanisation, city life, the role of intellectuals and artists, and the importance of money. For Simmel, the cultural and social, and the practices of everyday life were bound into each other and not separated as Weber separated science and culture, locating the former with progress and the latter with a life of its own. It was this relative autonomy that was so fascinating for Simmel. Again, for Simmel unlike Weber, there was no looking backwards to history but, instead, a delight in the new and an attempt to understand the new mentalities of urban life, bringing together the subjective and the social in, as he notes, 'the dissolution of fixed contents in the fluid element of the soul' (Frisby, 1984: 46). Simmel, the social theorist, was also the poet of the new modernity, trying to make sense of, and elucidate, the transience of life in the cities and the shake out it implied for ties of kin and culture. Disruptions of social and cultural ties were part of the ways in which commodification forged an increasing separation between the subjective and objective realms expressed through the power of money, so central to capitalist forms and relations. But Simmel held on to the notion that money, as a medium of exchange, was separated from the social actors in the transactions. Equally, commodities were everywhere, and displayed in the fairs and trade exhibitions, but this realm was not encompassed only by the economic. These were social spaces, alive with social relations and pleasures, in contradiction to the stultifying production relations that had produced the commodities.

Simmel, therefore, is very much the sociologist of consumption and metropolitan life, and a forerunner of much that came to be understood as cultural studies and the cultural turn in sociology. Simmel did not seek to separate a social from the realm of the individual psyche or the economic; his insight was to see that for modern living, the world of capitalism, consumption and production was deep in the psyche and part of the times. For Simmel 'Modern Times' expressed it beautifully. Power within Simmel's frame of understanding is a much more nebulous notion, implicit in the economic relations of capitalism, in the capitalist labour process and in the power of consumption. Simmel understood the seductions of capitalism and the ways in which power does not stand above or outside individuals, but requires an active engagement. Thus, like Gramsci, Simmel could articulate the ideological hegemonies bound to consumption as much as the imperatives of production relations.

The sociological imagination

The developing sociological imagination in Germany and France was not matched in Britain, and this was not only a consequence of the traditional university but, and I paraphrase Hawthorn (1987), the sense that sociological discourses were everywhere else in the concerns of 'the general liberal and socialist-liberal consciousness' (Hawthorn 1987: 170). This was not enough, however, to generate and sustain a more searching account of the social and the role of power in society. Instead, the development of sociology imported the founding fathers: Marx, Weber and Durkheim and followed Charles Booth, a social reformer, into a form of social research and a passion for class studies and class analysis. Theoretical importations continue today, in part, a mark of the different status and role that intellectuals are accorded in France and Germany compared with the UK. Thus, if we look to the development of contemporary accounts of the social and the theorisation of power, it is to the work of Habermas and the tradition of critical theory and the Althusserians, to Ulrich Beck and Michel Foucault, the work of Touraine and, in the UK, to the work of Anthony Giddens and Zygmunt Bauman, both deeply influenced by writers from beyond the UK.

Although Habermas consistently describes himself as a Marxist, it is a Marxism influenced deeply by Weber and the Frankfurt school, developing into the critical theory that takes its departure from Simmel. Habermas has a project, and that is to understand modernity in relation to the limitations of rational scientism within a grounding of philosophy. Habermas continues to be a political writer, but sees the sociological and the political as more separated than his avowed Marxism would suggest. Outhwaite (1994) calls him a Weberian Marxist, occupying a position not unlike that of Weber, experiencing in many ways the same sense of disenchantment with the outcomes of modernity while maintaining a constructively critical relationship with Marxism. Although Habermas is wedded to the development of the modern project, it is seen by him to be an unfinished project rather than one which is superceded by a post-modern project.

Habermas, like Weber, is concerned with the issue of action in relation to rationality, but he sets his discussion within a political frame. He distinguishes instrumental and strategic action, and provides a critique of the promise of emancipation through rationality. He seeks an alternative account of the social sciences from that within scientism, which cannot offer the discourses necessary for a critical sociology. Consistently, Habermas is concerned to develop an account of the public sphere and, throughout his writings, issues of power and the ways in which power is transformed in modern societies are crucial.

Although critical of Foucault, Habermas also analyses the ways in which the growth of specific regulatory discourses come to bear upon citizens in modern societies. However, he is more concerned to analyse the legal process and the role of the law in democratic societies. Consequently, Habermas maintains the importance of the state, distinguishing between two different forms of state power. The first is the administrative power of the state and the second, following Hannah Arendt, communicative power located with collective action, often of course, against the state. Habermas criticises Foucault's work because collectivities in struggle are absent from the analysis. However, Habermas also sees this communicative power in less literal ways in the 'subject-less communication circuits of forums and associations. Only in this anonymous form can its communicatively fluid power bind the administrative power of the state apparatus to the will of the citizens' (Outhwaite, 1994: 143). What is at issue here is the generation and sustenance of consent in liberal democracy and the relationship between civil society and the state, and how this relationship can be more emancipatory and participatory. Habermas's concern with communicative action is one part of the way in which he seeks to theorise the relationship between the subject and the social, overcoming the structure/action dichotomy, and locating the social with communicative acts within a frame that encompasses the rational, the political and the ethical. In this sense, his work focuses our attention once again on issues of morality and state power, the role of civil society and the citizen, major themes for Hobbes, Locke and the Enlightenment philosophers, especially Kant. But, Habermas seeks consistently to radicalise this vision by his attention to Marxist categories and the role of collective subjects.

The work of Giddens has also sought ways in which to delineate the social, and overcome the division between structure and action through his theories of structuration. This also has a relationship to Giddens' account of modernity and, most importantly, his conceptions of power, authority, domination and violence. For Giddens (1984: 14) 'An agent ceases to be such if he or she loses the capability to "make a difference", that is, to exercise some sort of power'. Power is part of all social relations, and defines the actor and agency. However, as Giddens emphasises, power is not one thing but many, from the transactional level wherein power is constituted as transformative capacity, to the state and institutional level wherein domination is inscribed in institutions and the state. Giddens notes, according to the theory of structuration, 'Power is intrinsic to all interactions...' (ibid.). Thus, emancipation is a flawed project in so far as there is no social space beyond authority. Instead, the best to work for is 'the achievement of rationally defensible forms of authority' (Cassell, 1993: 228). In his critique of Foucault,

Giddens also emphasises what is important in his own theory of power. Thus, while acknowledging that history generally has no subject, he confirms the view that knowledgeable subjects are making history even if they do not choose the conditions under which they do so. Equally, Giddens sees the importance of Foucault's account of discipline, but regards it as over written in relation to modern societies more generally. The prison is not the factory although there may be similarities; the systems of surveillance and those involved are distinctive. The network of powers that come to bear upon subjects under capitalist relations are not all one way, especially in relation to liberal democracies where the gains that have been exacted from the state and within civil society need to be acknowledged: 'Liberalism is not the same as despotism, absolutism or totalitarianism and the bourgeois ethos of national, universalised justice has the same double-edged character as prisons and their reform' (Cassell, 1993: 234). The final problem to which Giddens alerts us is the now well-known problem of the absence of the state in Foucault's writings, which leaves an analytical chasm that needs to be filled both practically and theoretically in relation to the politics of democracy in states around the world.

In his own work on the nation-state and global order, Giddens is acutely aware of the importance of violence and its relationship to surveillance, and it is these extremes of totalitarianism that deny the reflexivity of individuals, the marker of liberal democracy. Against the enormity of state power and control over the means of violence, Giddens (1991) suggests a life-world where actors have choices and possibilities to act on their own worlds and effect their biographies. Thus, the numbing surveillance of Foucault is re-cast as a series of contradictions that both discipline and emancipate simultaneously. The difficulty, as critics have been eager to point out, is that the possibility of exercising choice and securing outcomes is still bound in capitalism to the refractions of class, gender and racism, which are also crucially bound to the issue of violence and the nation-state.

Nevertheless, Giddens' work is an important reminder of the saliency of context and the ethnographies of power that permeate the social structure. Like Beck, he is more concerned with process and the role of agency within the developing forms of late modernity. For Beck (1992), it is the issue of risk and safety that is a major preoccupation for the middle classes in Western societies (and globally), who set about using their cultural capital and competence to 'insure' themselves against the risk-laden world they inhabit. Risk, of course, is proportional to investment, rather like renunciation – it is not possible if you have nothing. Thus, individuals who have obtained secure jobs, high levels of education and income have to struggle constantly with securing these. This feeds into a sense of the world as risky and without safety which, of course, has been incorporated into the endless surveillance through cctv cameras with which we live, from shopping malls to school buildings. The important thing here is the psychic fix that this generates, which has major implications for commonsense accounts of the social and the place of individuals within the social. The emphasis upon risk management, from insurance policies to home security, generates a binary between the world out there and the subject, de-centring the social and enfeebling the lived experience of the social within the individual. Beck is mindful of this and of the costs of all this security in our lives and how imaginary it can be.

Nietzsche, Foucault and power

This leads us back to Foucault whose work on power, whatever the criticisms, has revived the whole area in sociological theory with a new impetus concentrating upon the fluidity and ubiquity of power. While Giddens' criticisms of this Foucauldian project are well founded, it is also important to present the nuances within the Foucauldian account itself. Following Nietzsche (1844–1900), Foucault (1926–84) regards power not as negative or positive but as omnipresent and productive. However, there are different forms of power, from governance through state organisations and the management of populations to discipline through internal bureaucracies and institutional arrangements that come to bear on all citizens in modern societies. In fact, of course, the constant running battles between citizens and the state belie the efficacy of these modes of surveillance – why else would the 'beat a cheat' hotline be in existence. Crucially important is the Foucauldian notion of 'technologies of the self'; not only are we disciplined from without, but we are constantly in the process of surveillance and punishing ourselves. It is this that marks the lives of modern peoples and into which subjects are carefully inducted through a series of discourses and discursive practices organised, in part, by the state but also through civil society. It is this disciplinary being and society with which Giddens takes issue in his work. Equally, feminist analysis has been critically engaged with Foucault's work on power, areas of concern to be developed further in a later chapter.

Hindess (1996), in his recent book, provides an account of Foucault's conceptualisations of power organised around four major themes: power and domination, government, discipline and pastoral power. Although acknowledging the importance of Foucault's contribution in which he finds echoes of earlier philosophers and the importance of Weber, Hindess provides a constructive criticism within the major area of government. It is in Foucault's writing on government that the sense of the emancipatory project as doomed is clearly found because there are no relations outside government. As Hindess suggests, Foucault uses the term in its widest sense to acknowledge the myriad ways in which the self, family and behaviours are 'governed' and the ways in which government seeks to exercise authority over citizens. Government in the modern era has extended its work to 'the management of populations' through an extensive bureaucratic network, which intervenes morally and practically in all areas of life, from sexuality to voting, collecting data and making laws. This interventionist mode of government is linked with notions of policing, discipline and the construction of citizens as 'obedient subjects of the state'. In liberal democracies, power is exercised through the consent of 'free' individuals who, for the most part, are already attuned to the culture of the collective and their place as citizens. Hindess (1996: 125) suggests that Foucault's later work on government and governmentality offers a much more nuanced account of power relations in modern societies than the cruder and earlier accounts of discipline and policing, which generated much of the early criticism of his work.

Instead, Foucault attempts to build an account of the modern state, working through government and non-government agencies diffused into every area of life. But, in part, its rationality is to produce the free citizens necessary to liberal democracy. Hindess notes the problem this raises in so far as it treats liberalism as a government strategy, as part of the rationalities of government, rather than a much wider discourse on relations between the state and the individual. However, this is not to slip into a social control model, because Foucault's account of power is predicated upon the freedom inherent in the individual and, although this may be refracted through forms of discipline, state powers and the panoply of institutional arrangements in modern societies, it still remains a prerequisite for the exercise of power. What is of concern to Hindess are the implications for political action in the Foucauldian schema. Unlike critical theory, the notion of consent has no place in Foucault's account and neither does the emancipatory project. Thus, as Hindess (1996: 152) notes '…the most that can be expected…is the substitution of one set of powers for another, rather than some apparently universalistic process of emancipation from the effects of power as such.' However, suggests Hindess, Foucault moves between this view and shades of the emancipatory project in which he suggests that powers should be resisted. The contradictions return in later interviews when Foucault seems to raise a rallying cry of liberty over domination in ways that seem to undermine his own analysis. More importantly, Hindess acknowledges the ways in which the fictions of liberal democracy exposed by Foucault are double-edged, in so far as they can be invoked in relation to emancipatory projects or against the state by citizens. In fact, Foucault's attention to local, delineated struggles was part of this facing up to a rhetoric and using this for specific political goals.

Hindess's constructively critical account of Foucault's radical view of power does not detract from what we can acknowledge to be the major rupture that Foucault's work has wrought, and that is his insistence upon the creative and productive nature of power. These notions have entered sociological accounts via Foucault but the roots of these ideas lie in the work of Nietzsche and his extraordinary daring in breaking with so much that was taken for granted at the time that he was writing. I want, therefore, to very briefly introduce some part of Nietzsche's account of power in this chapter, while leaving the development of accounts of Foucault and some of the debates surrounding his work for later chapters.

Nietzsche, as Deleuze (1983: ix) acknowledges, 'is one of the greatest philosophers of the nineteenth century' but has consistently been misunderstood and had a very bad press in the UK and the USA. Against this, he suggests that above all else Nietzsche re-framed the philosophical gaze, and asked a series of novel and profound questions. Some of these were concerned with power and it is in his account of 'the will to power' that he has been most maligned, and that suggestions about his work as a precursor to fascism have been made. Instead, it could be argued that, on the contrary, Nietzsche's work is the poetry of life, the most affirmative of philosophies. Our concern here is with the notion of the creative and productive view of power; of power not as a capacity that will be exercised, sought, desired by the power-hungry, but of a conception more profound in which power '...above all refers to a process and an activity' (Ansell-Pearson, 1994: 48). In this sense, life is concerned with 'self-overcoming', not in the sense of restraint but in the sense of creative emancipation. This is a part of the life-affirming quality of Nietzsche's writings in which the individual moves away from, and beyond, the binary of good and evil, and is not propelled towards power, wanting power as a representation. For Nietzsche, his conception of the will to power is novel and does not relate, as Deleuze (1983: 82) emphasises, to notions of acquisition or most especially to struggle. Nietzsche was, by his own admission 'much too well-bred to struggle' (ibid.). For Nietzsche, the will to power is 'self-overcoming' and the ability to see the whole pattern of human endeavour, as Ansell-Pearson (1994: 49) notes, 'To think "over" and "beyond" oneself is to employ creatively, not morally...the erotic passion, or *pathos,* which is the will to power.' Ansell-Pearson suggests that Nietzsche can be best understood as a philosopher who wanted to generate a new autonomy in which his works should be interpreted by the reader and read in a multi-textual way, and he concludes his book with notes left by the philosopher for a book on the will to power, 'A book for *thinking* nothing else. It belongs to those for whom thinking is a *delight,* nothing else' (Ansell-Pearson, 1994: 205).

We return to Nietzsche in the twenty-first century because he speaks to our age, and this bears out his own view of himself as a philosopher of the future. It is clear from the very brief account above that 'the will to power' is a major departure from the writings of earlier philosophers and, more recently, sociologists who have, in one way or another, sought ways in which to analyse power as a capacity, as intent and action. Nietzsche, it seems, is closer to the conception of power explored in the *Mahabharata* with which we began.

One thing is clear: the revival of interest in Nietzsche's thought through the work of Foucault has also revived an interest in the theorisation of power. Recent books include John Scott's *Stratification and Power,* which provides an extension and development of Weber's work not only on class, status and party but on forms of authority and domination in relation to substantive data on the class structure and its classification. This clear and readable book is set securely within the sociological tradition, whereas another recent volume by Bech Dyrberg is more Foucault-inspired, and uses insights from the work of Laclau and Mouffe and Žižek in relation to the concerns of political science. Dyrberg (1997: 7) begins with the irreducibility of power, 'that power adheres to nothing but itself'. From this starting point, the author is able to provide a re-reading of some of the most important discussions concerned with community power and the political. Instead, Dyrberg concludes that the emancipatory vision of critical theory, in which democracy is seen as a level playing field in which reasonable players play by the rules, is flawed. And he writes:

> Yet this vision, despite its occasional radicality, is blind towards that which in part conditions it, which is not necessarily publicly accessible, and which is not usually conceived as belonging to the political in the first place, namely

the infrastructure of discipline, surveillance, normalization, regulation and so on, from which the political authorization of power takes off.

(Dyrberg, 1997: 251)

Thus, we return to Foucault because his analysis is so compelling, despite the many and varied flaws to which I have drawn attention. In addition, there is one absence that seems to remain outside most of the criticism and analyses using Foucault's work and that is the issue of violence. Thus, before I present the grammar of power towards which we have been working in this chapter, I want to briefly re-visit the issue of violence.

Power and violence

Hannah Arendt (1969), in her classic text *On Violence*, clearly distinguishes between power, authority and violence. Violence, she suggests, is allied with physicality and strength, and is invoked at precisely the moments when power is in jeopardy. Power and violence are allied through the state but the resort to force destroys the power base from which it has sprung. Thus, Arendt concludes that ultimately power and violence are opposites, and while violence can destroy power it cannot create it. More recently, in his book *Reflections on Violence,* John Keane (1996: 8) notes 'Violence is clothed in an aura of strangeness'. Keane's work explores the ways in which barbarism and civility are the contexts within which violence is perpetrated and defined, and these have shifted over time and space. Violence is part of 'uncivil society' and what is required is the generation and sustenance of 'public spheres of controversy', which can be policed in non-violent ways (Keane, 1996: 165). How then, are we to understand violence? Keane is very clear that the notion of residual elements, often called 'primitive', must be dismissed as an explanation, and that we need to look instead to the cultural and institutional nexus that constitutes 'civility' as it has developed. In terms of a definition of violence, Keane (1996: 66–7) notes, 'Violence is better understood as the unwanted physical interference by groups and/or individuals with the bodies of others, which are consequently made to suffer a series of effects ranging from shock…or even death' and he continues, '…violence is a relational act in which the object of violence is treated, involuntarily, not as a subject whose "otherness" is recognised and respected, but rather as a mere object…'. This definition is consistent with the view from Emmanuel Levinas (1987), paraphrased by Werbner (1997: 227), 'Violence denies otherness its legitimate right to exist and be different'. Thus, violence comes to rest on the body and is marked by physical coercion, which may culminate in death. Violence is, therefore, the antithesis of civil society to the point, suggests Keane, where the two cannot coexist, which is why we still inhabit 'uncivil society'.

Indian scholars have also been anxious to unpack the notion of violence in relation to a series of violent events focused upon the temple at Aydodhya, claimed by Hindus to be the birthplace of Ram, a pre-eminent deity, and by Muslims as a mosque. Equally, violence against minorities and the rise of nationalist parties politically has fuelled violence in India. Jawardena and de Alwis (1996), in the collection *Embodied Violence*, consider the rise of fundamentalism and the ways in which women come to act as signifiers of the nation, the honour of specific groups, and because of this become targets for all forms of violence, especially sexual violence. The concern here, as Jawardena and de Alwis (1996: xv) note in the introduction, is not with the act of violence *per se* but with 'the articulation of communal violence within particular nexuses of power'. In this sense, it is power, and especially the understanding of patriarchal power, that provides the context in which forms of sexualised violence are perpetrated. The language of violence in the text moves from 'massacre' to 'pogrom' to rape as part of the ways in which violence is analysed as an intrinsic part of the nationalist agendas in South Asia. Ashis Nandy (1990) takes issue with the prevailing account of violence as an aberrant moment in civil society. Rather, there is a long history of riot and urban disorder, often against the state, and the state is implicated in the ongoing 'communalism' of India. Equally, there is a debate on the role of the crowd and the ways in which it tempers the normal moral space and allows for acts which would not normally be committed. This idea of the crowd working with the unconscious is set against the notion of crowds as agents of change or revolt etc. used by Thompson (1971) to chart the rise of the working class in England. Veena Das (1990: 28) is clear that one of the problems in relation to the theorisation of violence is the lack of empirical work on collective violence. Das's book concentrates attention on the ways in which religion has become the signifier of collectivity, and that it may be understood both as faith and as ideology and these are a heady mixture within the context of state discourses and practices that promote difference but not within a context of tolerance.

Sudhir Kakar is a psychoanalyst trying, as the previous scholars, to understand the relationships between violence, collective action and religious affiliation in the Indian context. He searches within his own biography, which includes the trauma of partition when India and Pakistan were separated, and uses the Hindu–Muslim riots in Hyderabad in 1990 as a case study. Kakar (1996) seeks ways in which to reconstruct not just the events but the ways in which Muslim and Hindu identities are re-fashioned within the context of religious fundamentalism. Through a series of interviews with both Hindu and Muslim victims of the riots and the examination of transcripts of speeches from the leaders of the communities, Kakar builds a picture of a collective identity into which individuals are drawn. These forms of interpellation are deep psychic processes that generate a commitment to a collective identity, which when threatened is defended, increasingly by violence, in the context of Indian politics.

This is a powerful account of the ways in which subjectivities are constructed through the interplay of intimate and societal contexts, both invoking power relations. However, Kakar is clear that identities are not constructed in violence; it is only within specific contexts that violence is their expression. He suggests that it is within the very collective ritual processes, processions, meetings, for example, that the material for violence may be found. Religion, therefore, offers one space in which identifications can be powerfully distorted.

These accounts are concerned with the violence of the mob, the collectivity, and the ways in which what appears to be spontaneous actually has an intelligible history. Similar accounts have been generated of the forms of football violence in the UK, when so-called 'football hooligans' have been shown to be very well organised groups of white men who use football as a theatre of violence. These forms of violence are separated from the forms of institutional violence that marked the Holocaust, explored in Bauman's work on modernity and the machinery of death. Here the state is the purveyor of industrialised death in relation to 'the others' of Nazi Germany: the Jews, the Gypsies, black people, homosexuals and weak and vulnerable sections of the population. Thus, violence, like power, has differential contexts and ways of being organised. The outcomes of death, destruction, maiming, rape and trauma are shared conditions of violent encounters, and reinforce the understanding from Keane of the ways in which violence comes to rest upon the body of those constructed as 'the other' and denied selfhood, through this process becoming violated, spurned and killed. This understanding is distinct from the understanding of violence as cathartic, used by Frantz Fanon in relation to the colonial context.

It is also clear that violence is not a series of aberrant moments when the social is denied, but is both part of and marks the limits of the social, the end of the social. Violence is configured within the ideological, cultural and political moments in social formations, organised through states who are deemed to hold a monopoly on the legitimate use of force by the military, police and state apparatuses but are ever present, especially in situations of social collectivity, which can be mobilised and erupt in seemingly spontaneous ways. In a shorthand, violence is intelligible, it is not born of 'evil' or the left-over marks of pre-civilisation. Looking at the twentieth century, it is hard to believe that anyone, anywhere, could subscribe to these views, but they are part of the commonsense because they distace acts of violence from 'us'. We bear, therefore, no responsibility for these violations. This is less than helpful in trying to analyse violence and develop ways in which violence can be diminished.

After Foucault

Violence is enacted upon, 'otherised' individuals and collectivities, often in spectacular ways – mob violence, riot, war – and these constitute, in one sense, spectacles and performances. This brings the discussion to recent attempts to theorise power from writers like Judith Butler, Ernesto Laclau and Chantal Mouffe. Butler's account emphasises the performative accomplishment of gendered identities, which present as stable and unified, but are actually the outcome of myriad workings on the details of gender. Such a view also allows for the transgressive nature of performance in which the codes and registers can be disrupted. A similar account may be made of the ways in which power operates, whether through linguistic codes, discursive practices or the use of the body in violent ways; these produce performative powers that move through a variety of sites. Laclau and Zac (1994: 27), however, dispute this and note that pure violence cannot be performative.

Like Foucault, Laclau and Mouffe have sought ways in which to theorise the political as relational and as a sphere in which antagonistic power relations are constantly producing the identities of politics. This contrasts with the view that suggests political identities come fully formed into conflict. It is a vital reformation of the notion of politics, expressed in a series of texts that variously emphasise the making of political identities (Laclau, 1994) and issues of citizenship and radical democracy (Mouffe, 1992). In a radical reconstruction, Laclau and Mouffe seek ways to analyse the changing terrain of democracy and the demise of socialist strategies (developed initially in their earlier work) and the move towards a terrain of the political in which power relations and contestations can move towards plurality, active participants and a radical democracy that fuels 'agonistic relations'.

The consequences for the theorisation of power are explored by Laclau and Zac (1994: 17) when they note:

> Power is, in a sense, the source of the social, though one could equally say in another (and related) sense, that it is the very condition of intelligibility of the social (given that the possibility of representing the latter as a coherent entity depends on a set of orderly effects emanating from power).

Power is imbricated in the social but as Bech Dyrberg (1997: 117) insists:

> ...Power has no origin...power has no *telos* and consequently cannot be described as a priori as either functional or dysfunctional for a social order; it is, rather, a conditioning factor...And power is not, strictly speaking, part of a social order in the sense that it cannot be domesticated by it...To perceive power in this way means, on the one hand, that it is immanent in the structuration of social reality, otherwise it could not be relationally constructed; on the other hand, it is outside the social realm by virtue of the fact that it constitutes and negates it.

This book begins with the proposition from the post-structuralist account that power is immanent – there is no social without power. However, in an attempt to pursue this in a sociological discourse, rather than a purely philosophical one, there are ways in which I hope to show it is possible to provide an account of power and the social that is substantively intelligible through the use of examples that demonstrate there is no social without power.

Modalities/sites

Thus far, we have been able to review some of the discourses on power and provide some part of an introduction to the later chapters. The overview of accounts of power suggests a number of ways in which power has been theorised. I want to re-organize these understandings and to suggest that the variety of ways of understanding power constitutes *modalities of power*. I use this term because 'modality' refers to the property of power as it is exercised, and suggests that this property is characteristic of power. Modalities present types of power. Consequently, modalities of power go some way towards answering the questions: What is power? Who has power? How is power exercised? Equally, the forms of power with which this book is concerned are understood as intersectional, and the ways in which they interact construct the social. In order, however, to better understand the constitution of the social it is important to consider key sites through which the social is thought, organised and constituted. Thus, the remaining chapters of the book bring together modalities of power with key sites of the social.

Power, it is clear, can be understood as a capacity used by agents, held by agents and exercised by agents, but the difficulty with this view is that it is analogous to a football match in which two already designated teams compete for possession of the ball. This still means that there is an interactive moment but not that the interaction is *constitutive* of power. This view is the second major view of power in which power is not a frozen attribute contested by two known quantities. Instead, it is the very contestation that generates, shifts and sustains the identities of protagonists. In this sense, power is productive of identities and of the social. This book is much more sympathetic to the second view of power.

Different writers have understood the modalities of power within these two broad frameworks but the understanding can be further refined:

1   This book considers the way in which *repression and coercion* have been understood as modes of power located with a zero-sum view of power in which some are powerful and subalterns are powerless. It is the football game again but with unequal teams. A similar view underpins the notion of power as constraint. This is the negative view of power as diminishing action, ideas, movement and the development of the social.

2   The idea of power as a process re-enters the frame with the work of Antonio Gramsci in the account of *hegemony* and *counter-hegemony*. It is a relational view of power, and one that understands the materiality of power in the commonsense, everyday world of subjects – the very stuff of the social as a lived space. Hegemony is also a notion that is de-centred and generated through the multiple sites of the social. This understanding is developed in the work of Winant (1995) in relation to racialisation, the global and the local. Gramsci's work on counter-hegemony and resistance has also been developed by the subaltern studies groups in India and Latin America who have engaged in the work of recovering the subaltern subject from colonial history.

3   The coming together of process with the zero-sum view can be found in the notion of power as manipulation and *strategy* – the familiar Machiavellian world described in relation to the princely states of the fifteenth century. The ethnography of power that this work detailed could be read via Nietzsche as a form of power as productive, but it is not always possible to provide this type of reading.

4   Nietzsche was a formative influence on Foucault and helped Foucault to re-frame an account of power that was suffused throughout the social, was

productive and organised in a series of ways bringing *power/knowledge* together: *discipline* and *governance* in modern ways appropriate to modern social formations that sought an infinite variety of ways in which to manage populations.

5   The interactional basis of Foucault's understanding is developed in an account of performative power that can produce transgressions and disruptions. Performative power can be expressed most cogently through the final modality of power – *seduction and resistance* – which emphasises both the relational basis of power and power plays, issues of desire and the unconscious. It is also crucial to the understanding of the social as comprising performative selves through action, language and visual signifiers. Both power and the differentiations of the social are written on the body, and this is part of the scripts that contribute to social life, expressed consciously through consumption patterns, especially dress codes, and the importance that is currently attached to style.

Modalities of power as outlined above are one concern in this book, the other relates to key sites both within the social and within sociology that can be understood as spaces of power or power-filled spaces. This is one way in which we can hope to understand the confluence of power/social not as totalities but as part of a de-centred social in which there are specific moments of the social that provide a focus for the interconnections between power and the social.

Thus, a site is constituted as a conceptual terrain, an analytical device that brings together theoretical and substantive material. The first of these is *racialised power*, the second *engendered power* and the third *class and power*. This triumvirate has a key resonance within sociology and social life, but these are not thought of as variables but as modes of understanding that are made equally important through the consideration of three additional sites: *sexualised power, spatial power and visual power*.

The modalities of power could be further enhanced, the terrain in which power relations are negotiated could be expanded, but these key sites do allow for an examination of the meanings and exercise of power in relation to the constitution of the social, as racialised, gendered, sexualised space in which the world of signs and visual images is also part of the social worlds we inhabit.

The discussion as it develops through these modalities of power in the different sites does so by privileging one site rather than another. This is not intended to imply that where there is racialised power, for example, engendered or visual power is absent – nothing could be further from the multi-textured quality of power relations and the social as we now understand it as de-centred, comprising multiple sites of social reproduction. In order to provide a means by which this can be enunciated, the chapters use a series of substantive studies as material for the arguments of the book. This material is based largely on my own fieldwork, which has consistently sought ways in which to understand power relations. The contexts for this work have been many and varied, from studies of class, gender and power in Ghana and the UK to the politics of space, national identities and belonging in Latin America, and the politics of racism in Britain. Hopefully, we can find a coherent route through this complexity and the complexity will not produce obfuscation but intelligibility.

The brief overview contained in this chapter suggests something of the historical understandings of power and the ways in which it has been central to the sociological enterprise of defining the social. Discourses on power present a complex and difficult terrain, and one which is explored further in the chapters that follow in relation to specific areas of concern for sociology.

The book begins with *Racialised Power,* which is a conscious decision in which I wish to emphasise the formative role of racism in the making of the modern world. Whether it is the global capitalist economy or the structures of sexual desire – racism, racialisation and the issue of otherisation are key defining features of the social.

2   Racialised power

Whether we look to the histories of enslavement, the novels of Richard Wright and Toni Morrison or the turmoil of India, Africa or Europe at the end of the twentieth century, racialised power is everywhere and bound crucially to the rise of modernity and the fate of the post-modern world. It is pre-eminent as a site of powers, and it is why this book begins with racialised power in all its hideous manifestations. All the major power themes elaborated in Chapter 1 are present, from repression and the violence of genocide to the seductions of otherness and the myriad forms of resistance that are part of this story (McClintock, 1995; Stoler, 1995). Importantly, it should be clear that racialised power is not separate from class powers, engendered or sexualised powers, spatial or visual powers. In fact, the more we understand racism the more conscious we are of the ways in which these are articulated and embedded one within the other. Thus, the separation is, in part, a convenient fiction, but one which allows the foregrounding of one site of power.

This chapter examines the ways in which race and racism are embedded in modern societies and the forms of racialised power that were a crucial element of imperial and colonial expansion. This is a complex story, which is further elaborated in relation to Foucault's writings and his concern with issues of race and sexualities. But, understandings of race and racism are also constructed by nations and states, and enacted in everyday practices that have an impact on all our lives. This does not go uncontested, however, and sections of this chapter consider the ways in which forms of collective organising and resistance have challenged forms of racialised power.

Race and modernity

Malik (1996) in his recent book starts from the proposition, borrowed from Disraeli, 'All is race. There is no other truth.' and continues, '…the discourse of race lies at the very heart of modern society'. The book is a fascinating exploration of the relationship between discourses around 'race' and the rise of the West and with this the contradiction between the Enlightenment ideals of tolerance, justice and equality and the ways in which race and racism have been re-organised in successive eras, including the current one with its genocidal war in Bosnia.

Reviewing the debates, including the most recent post-structuralist accounts, Malik takes issue with the politics of difference, seeing in this defeat and the acceptance that racial divisions and abuses are part of the life-world. Unfashionably, he returns to the humanitarian ideals of the Enlightenment project and Marxism as the only means whereby the discourse of race can be transcended. More recently, Paul Gilroy has sought ways in which to explore 'planetary humanism' as the basis for progressive politics (Gilroy, 2000). Malik is also conscious of the ways in which raising the issue of race leads immediately to issues of power and the articulation between the natural and the social, which has marked every era of racist discourses. The biological and the cultural move in and out in a mirror dance, which informs and deforms the ideas of 'race'. Equally, the power of race to sustain genocidal violence provides the most graphic example of what constitutes the social and its collapse into barbarism.

For the Enlightenment philosophers the basic optimism of their position related to their belief in the rationality of 'man' and the common humanity shared by all. Thus, Rousseau was able to declare that man is free but everywhere in chains. Like the thinkers before him, the problem was society and the constitution of the social that degraded man, and ways had to be found to overcome this through the social contract or moral principles. Although the Enlightenment philosophers declared the rational and equal essence of humanity, it was also clear that within humanity there was a huge diversity. The beginnings of anthropology were constituted as a way of seeking to understand this diversity, but the signifiers of difference were not necessarily skin colour or facial features at this time. The suggestion from Malik is that Enlightenment universalism did not provide a precursor to later scientific racisms, but that racist discourses actually developed in opposition to Enlightenment universalism. The difficulty here is with the role of science and the processes of objectification that were crucial to the practice of science suggested by Goldberg (1993), for example, who states, 'The emergence of independent scientific domains of anthropology and biology in the Enlightenment defined a classificatory order of racial groupings…along correlated physical and cultural matrices.'

However, Malik takes issue with this view suggesting, instead, a Marxist, historicist account of the undoing of the Enlightenment project of emancipation via the specific historical circumstances of the advance of capitalism and, within that, the rise of property relations, which were a serious limitation to the emancipatory potential of the French Revolution for example. Further, enslavement and its organisation raised the issue of property rights under capitalism to a new level. The problem here is the juxtaposition. The beginnings of transatlantic enslavement pre-date the humanist project and, although suggestive, Malik's account does not negate Goldberg's. We need them both to weave together the complexities of the relationship between the emancipatory and contradictory project of the Enlightenment, one part of which opposed slavery, and the historically specific consolidation of capitalism as a global system in which enslavement played such a crucial role. Equally, Malik suggests that the contradiction between nationalism and universalism marks the tensions between

Enlightenment ideals and particularisms. Ultimately, it was from the degradation of the Enlightenment ideal of humanity and '...this conviction that inequality was natural that the modern concept of race arose' (Malik, 1996: 70). Race was well placed to enter this terrain as a 'natural' explanation for inequalities. Thus, 'The concept of race arose from the contradictions of equality in modern society, but it is not an expression of a single phenomenon or relationship. Rather it is a medium through which the changing relationship between humanity, society and nature has been understood in a variety of ways' (Malik, 1996: 71).

In part, this is a consequence of the Romantics and the post-Enlightenment interplay between the development of the nation and the contestation of universalism written into the post-Kantian account of essences, which solidified around the notion of 'race'. In this was encapsulated the sense of Herderian community and belonging – Malik's discussion emphasises the contradictions between philosophies and the development of capitalism but it suggests, and I paraphrase, that what was going on was a naturalisation of a fiction that turned 'race' into belonging, blood and kin allied through war with territory. It is a materialist reading of the generation of a discourse of race, which was further elaborated with the new tools of science into the scientific racism of the nineteenth century. What was crucial to this development was not that Darwin published his findings and introduced the notion of 'fitness' in 1859, but that this work entered Victorian society replete with inequalities located with class and a commitment to the stability of the social order and the fixity of these divisions. It was easy to see how this combination emerged later as the Eugenics movement, and how race became fixed and gave substance to the notion of a superior ruling class at home and abroad. However, within this, there was dissent expressed in the anti-slavery lobby, which used the Enlightenment discourse, often re-formulated within Christianity, to argue for the humanity of all human beings and their souls.

Despite his attempt to articulate the complexities of the discourse of race, Malik remains tied to a materialist understanding which emphasises the class relations that fuelled racist discourses, rather than provide an analysis of the discourses as discontinuous and having a productive part in the generation of race as a category.

Gilroy (1993: 48) suggests an alternative understanding, using Hegel's account of the master and the slave as a way in which to '...transcend the unproductive debate between a Eurocentric rationalism which banishes the slave experience from its accounts of modernity while arguing that the crises of modernity can be resolved from within' (Gilroy, 1993: 54). The point emphasised by Gilroy, and explored in the work of DuBois, Wright and James, is that enslavement was not an aberrant moment within modernity but an intrinsic part of the constitution of the West, which remains part of the unfinished nature of modernity explored in the writings of DuBois and the novels of Wright and James. These are part of what Gilroy calls a 'redemptive critique', which is as much part of the project of modernity as the emancipation of the working class. It is another unfinished project but in its constitution it makes racial terror and exploitation as salient as capitalist-based class subordination.

In arguing for the centrality of race and racism within the modern project, this suggests the diffusion of racialised power in the development of the West. However, I have also suggested that power is not unitary. Racialised power confronts us in enslavement and genocide and the histories of African and indigenous peoples around the world, in North and South America, Canada and Australia. This is power as coercion, as terror, and the attempt to impose the will of one class of people on another. The trade in peoples of African descent demonstrates the success of terror, fire power and physical coercion but it was, even in these extreme conditions, resisted, and more so in the new world when the enslaved were settled. C.L.R. James' account of the Black Jacobins, the Choco Revolt in northern Colombia, the independent state of Esmeraldas in what is now northern Ecuador are some part of the history of rebellion, revolt and resistance that marked the period. In addition, there are the countless untold stories of resistance to enslavement and brutalisation, claims for recognition and dignity explored in the context of colonialism in the powerful writings of Frantz Fanon.

Whereas in the sixteenth century the Jesuits had used the terrain of religion and the soul to disenfranchise and dehumanise indigenous and African peoples, the development of science and scientism in the nineteenth century laid claim to a different truth with equally denuding consequences. (This so-called 'scientific' racism drew upon the classificatory systems of the West in which the peoples of the world were divided by race, and specific characteristics were attached to these divisions as part of a power/knowledge complex.) But, as Young's work (1995) shows, as soon as the divisions were in place the difficulty of maintaining them became apparent, and a hybrid world born of desire and miscegenation developed and became, in the Latin American context, a new fictive national identity – *mestizo/a*. The classifications of peoples reached new forms of absurdity in India when one anthropologist advocated nose shape with its attendant hierarchy from aquiline/European onwards. India also provided the colonial service with a canvas on which to draw new contours and divisions by way of the sedimentation of the caste system described and annotated in detail. But, again, this did not go uncontested because there was too much at stake. Land was crucial to caste definitions and much contested in Punjab, which refused the British categories, as happened again with the census at the turn of the twentieth century.

The categorisations, classificatory models, developed as part of the discourse we have come to know as orientalism from its elegant elaboration in the work of Said (1978). It is clear that this discourse was not unitary nor uncontested, but its power was derived from the ways that power/knowledge were conjoined and its long-term impact on the Western definition of 'other' worlds. Inden's (1990) account *Imagining India* details the ways in which the colonial and anthropological accounts constructed a view of India and Indians that survives today. But what is also interesting is the way in which these discourses have been both resisted and re-appropriated in relation to the current politics of India. Thus, van der Veer (1993: 40) sums up:

> What orientalism has done is two things. It gave crucial support to the Brahmanical contention that Indian civilisation is a unified whole...Orientalism

also canonised certain scriptures, such as the Bhagavad Gita, which prepared the ground for Mahatma Gandhi to make this Sanskrit work into a fundamental scripture of Modern Hinduism.

Such forms have fuelled the Hindu nationalism of India and the anti-Muslim movement in India while contesting the secular state. The politics of India is framed by the ongoing interaction between orientalist discourses and their re-interpretation for the end of the twentieth century. Again, at the level of colonial discourse this has not gone uncontested and has produced a large and rich literature from subaltern studies, which has re-inserted a knowing subject from within the indigenous populations. In part, this has been the product of work inspired by Gramsci and the attempt to provide a counter-hegemonic account, emphasising active agents in relation to colonial imaginings and practices. A similar work of retrieval has been conducted in the Latin American context. The attempt within this is to contest and break through the discourses that construct the world as comprising of the West and the Other that Foucault's work can be used to explore. But entrapment is raised by the question, 'can the subaltern speak?', a seminal article by Spivak (1993) in which she explores the 'epistemological violence' that the binary West/Other exacts on the world. Concluding that the 'subaltern cannot speak' (op. cit.: 104) is, in part, a response to the subaltern studies attempt at rescue. Spivak refuses both the essentialism of a 'history from below' and the reified subject as well as the all-embracing power of Foucault's analysis, what Said called, 'the captivating and mystifying category of power in Foucault'.

Foucault, race and racism

Despite the power of Foucault to inspire elaborations of the West in relation to the Other – the Other is an absence from Foucault's work. Issues of race and racism and post-coloniality do not figure ostensibly in Foucault's work. But this has been challenged by the work of Stoler (1995) in a powerful re-engagment with Foucault.

Given the enormous interest in Foucault's work by historians and anthropologists, and in the exploration of the forms of governmentality and disciplinary modes in play in the imperial world and colonial forms of organisation, Stoler (1995) sets out to re-interpret one of the key texts, *The History of Sexuality* (Vol. 1), in relation to colonial studies, the interest in sexualities and the rise of Europe. Basically, her argument suggests that first, trying to reconstruct the histories of sexualities in Europe cannot be done without including the colonial. In other words, there is no binary, no 'West and the Rest' as Hall calls it. The two are bound one to another. Thus, Foucault's account 'misses key sites in the production of the discourse' (ibid.: 7) and these key sites are within Empire, which refracted the discourse of sexuality and the construction of the European bourgeois self. Second, 'bourgeois identities in both metropole and colony emerge tacitly and emphatically coded by race' (ibid.:7). Thus, 'Such a perspective figures race, racism and its representations as structured entailments of post-Enlightenment universals, as formative features of modernity, as deeply embedded in bourgeois liberalism, not as aberrant off shoots of them' (ibid.: 9). Stoler urges us to consider the colonies not simply as 'sites of exploitation' but as 'laboratories of modernity' (ibid.: 15) in which pre-figurative forms that defined modernity, like the factory or the panoptican, were extant or tried out. For example, the panoptican first appeared in Ottoman Turkey rather than northern Europe. Equally, the notion of culture may be a colonial invention, and the disciplinary modes outlined by Foucault as marking the rise of Western modernity and the bourgeois self may pre-date the seventeenth century. Foucault deals with racism in the *History of Sexuality*, especially the final section on degeneracy and the rise of Eugenics, but it has not been followed up, even by Goldberg (1993), who uses Foucault to construct his account of *Racist Culture*.

Stoler's (1995: 21) view elaborates this, 'Foucault conjoined the rise of racism and technologies of sex'. Only Balibar (1991) saw in Foucault's work the centrality of race, claiming that racism was the 'crucial phenomenon' that biopolitics set out to explain (ibid.). In interrogating *The History of Sexuality*, Stoler suggests that the attention to race and racism in Foucault's work was concerned with state rather then popular racism, especially during the period of the early nineteenth century, and that the earliest colonial distinctions were by race between black and Indian and white labour. Equally, the discourses around the body in the eighteenth century evince a concern with 'race', especially in relation to sexuality. However, as Stoler suggests (ibid.: 29) the concern is not with the plurality of racisms but with European racism and its origins in the upper classes as they were to become (cf. Anderson, 1991). These come together, if somewhat tentatively, in Foucault's notion of biopower and the ways in which these powers operate, not only at the individual level but also in relation to the regulation of populations and the 'health of the race', which was a series of discourses prevalent in the second half of the nineteenth century. Although concerned with the theme of degeneracy towards the end of his volume, Foucault never fully explores the issue that binds sexuality and race together in relation to state powers. Taking examples from the colonial Dutch East India Company as early as 1612, 'managed sex was on the state agenda' (ibid.: 40), and Stoler continues that by the mid-nineteenth century the issue of miscegenation was the source of considerable concern, and attempts were made to 'police the boundaries of the European community' through legal remedies and the development of racially coded categories of persons. It is this coming together of race, sexuality and class that is explored by McClintock (1995) in *Imperial Leather* which, consistent with Stoler's work, suggests that the colonial space was one in which the modes of regulation of sexualities and the categorisations that came to signal modernity were being worked out and deployed. Both writers, in this sense, emphasise the permeability of the European sphere and the rise of modernity as an articulation between the colonial power and the colonised. It is in precisely this space that discourses around race were generated as a means of legitimating colonial power, barbarity and the movement of labour from place to place within the increasing space of empire. These forms of colonial governmentality required a conception of 'the European' and it was classed, racialised and gendered.

Stoler suggests that the lectures provide a number of compelling insights that are anything but a genealogy of racisms. For Foucault, this was not their intention, nor did he pursue the project. Instead, he points first to the ways in which state racisms developed, albeit in the colonial period, not only externally but internal to the European nation-states as a tactic which generated internal divisions, 'the bifurcation within Europe's social fabric' (ibid.: 60). Further, and to paraphrase, racism is not unitary nor essential; it is deployed in different eras and by different powers within discourses, discursively constructed and contingent and allows for the constant recycling and re-appropriation of earlier modes for a current period.

To reconsider the work of Foucault in relation to 'race' confirms an account that is power-filled, and in which the importance of both power/knowledge and the body as a site for the deployment of powers are emphasised. The ways in which racisms are understood and the modalities for their expression, from the white supremacists of the internet to the patriot groups of the USA (Castells, 1997), provide further expressions of the forms of racial formation elaborated in the work of Winant (1995). A Foucauldian account of racism is consistent with Stuart Hall's notion of race as a floating signifier, given meaning through the discourses and practices within which it is embedded. Thus, race is constantly worked upon, changed, re-ordered and made intelligible within the social, and it provides a key point for understanding the ways in which the social is constructed and comes to deconstruct the binary between the natural/biological and the social. The categories of colour, notions of blood and breeding are naturalised within the power relations of the social. Equally, racial identifications are also constructed as markers of the line between the social and the natural–colonial discourse on 'the natives'. Jesuit accounts of the human and the soul sought to separate out populations and re-cast them within the natural/social binary.

Racialised identities

Winant (1995) adds a further dimension to the social constructions of racisms with his notion of a 'de-centred hegemony' in which both genealogies and contingent time contribute to the calling forth of racialised subjects. Winant is careful to consider the ways in which both whiteness and blackness are generated and sustained as 'a flexible set of context-specific repertoires' (ibid.: 274). Or, as Patricia Williams (1997) writes, 'Perhaps one reason conversations about race are so often doomed to frustration is that the notion of whiteness as "race" is almost never implicated' (ibid.: I.3). Thus, racial identities are malleable, and have come to be inscribed on the body through a series of narrations that often become part of the commonsense of Gramsci's hegemony. But, as the notion of hegemony makes clear, although racist attributions may become naturalised, nothing is fixed or immutable. Winant's account is also consistent with Hall's and the notion of the floating signifier of race. However, as they both suggest, it is the spatial and temporal relations that are crucial to the constitution of racial identities. In a Foucauldian sense, it is the sites in which identities are called forth, reproduced and ruptured that provides one way in which the articulation of the social and psyche can be understood. Patricia Williams, in the 1997 *Reith Lectures*, expressed this poetically when she suggested:

> It is helpful to remember that, for all its diffuseness, the power of race as dangerous and sensational has been perpetuated by very identifiable historical phenomena. Racism is not inevitable, however, entrenched. There have been better and worse moments in the history of race relations. Race as an invested feature of modern relations is scarcely older than the triangular trade.
>
> (Williams, 1997: 5.4)

She continues, 'I am certain that the solution to racism lies in our ability to see its ubiquity but not conceded its inevitability' (ibid.: 5.7).

As ubiquitous as racism is, it is also constructed within specific sites, and it is these sites, bringing together spatiality with time, class and gender that are the sites of struggle when racism and racialised power is contested. Such contestations are evidenced even within what appear to be the totalising powers of colonial rule, or apartheid, or the segregation of the South in the USA. Although these forms of racialised power are, as Winant suggests, seen to be timeless, to be naturalised, the histories of liberation struggles tell a different story: from the wars of liberation to the eventual freedom of South Africa. Wars and military power are one part of the struggle against coercion and the genocidal regimes of colonialism and latter-day wars in many parts of the world. But, there are also strategic encounters that are part of the lived, everyday world of life in the urban metropolitan world of Europe or South America in which struggles are racialised and in which the sites of struggle are localities and the contestations relate to the symbolic as much as to resource allocations. I want to consider two specific forms of struggle in relation to the diasporic politics of Britain at the end of the twentieth century. These struggles are not peculiar to Britain, but they illuminate the ways in which spaces are power-filled, knowledge and power are articulated and the relations between citizens and the state at the local and national level are constantly made and re-framed by the insistence upon a democracy, not of equal abstract individuals, but of ethnically, culturally, gendered and generationally distinctive and diverse subjects.

In adopting a Foucauldian-inspired account of 'race' and racism, the emphasis, in part, rests upon racism as a form of discipline which comes to rest upon the body, most importantly the visibly different body. Thus, black people, people of Asian descent and indigenous peoples are aware of the power of the gaze and the forms of governmentality within which they live, and with which they struggle, accommodate, contest and ignore on a daily basis. It was this understanding that was clearly enunciated in the work of DuBois and his account of 'double consciousness', as he writes, 'this sense of always looking at one's self through the eyes of others, of measuring one's soul by the tape of a world that looks on in contempt and pity...' (DuBois, 1989: 3). For DuBois, the social was constructed through difference; there was no universal, especially if it was constructed from the rational actor of 'the West' so central to Weber's understanding. Instead, these processes of difference, otherisation and racialisation are bound to specific sites in which racism operates through the forms of power which we are addressing here.

Encounters with the state from the moment of entry into the UK, the USA or Europe more generally bring the power of the state into face-to-face encounters between would-be entrants to a country and the officials who person the boundaries of the nation-state, and who check passports, motives, etc. This initial encounter may be repeated elsewhere in health services, housing, employment, and through these agencies the accounting procedures ensure that people are tracked, noted and defined as aliens and citizens, worthy and unworthy. These processes are not innocent but, as innumerable studies have shown, are racialised. How else do we account for the overrepresentation of black people in the prisons and psychiatric hospitals of Britain. As a counter to this, a number of political interventions have grown up around the criminal justice system and in relation to issues of racism and psychiatry.

Racism and mental illness

There is a long and inglorious history of the relationship between racism and psychiatry bound to earlier concerns in this chapter, the rise of 'scientific racisms' and colonialism in which the construction of a European, white identity was secured through the elaboration of the 'other', both within Europe and beyond its borders. Part of this elaboration related to the mind, psychic process and forms of mental health and illness (Fernando, 1988). Psychiatry, as it grew from a medical base, concentrated attention upon genetics and the life of the mind, ignoring the later plea from Freud to abandon an essentialist account of the psyche. Instead, genetic identifications of major illnesses, as they came to be classified, were developed and remain a powerful basis for diagnosis and treatment. But, there are debates within psychiatry and alternative accounts that emphasise the social and contextual factors of mental health and illness which seek to contest the biologism of much practice. What has become clear is that in Britain and the USA, black people are over-represented among patients diagnosed as mentally ill, and this has major implications for the relationship between black people and the state. It was these concerns and the deaths of black people in psychiatric institutions, coupled with a series of studies that showed the high incidence of schizophrenia among black people [similar statistics are produced and contested for populations of Irish descent (Harrison *et al.*, 1988)] that prompted a research project in which an attempt was made to give voice to the concerns of black people who had experienced mental illness (Westwood *et al.*, 1989).

The research process was part of an active engagement in the politics of mental health and its effects upon black people in Britain. People of African Caribbean and South Asian descent were interviewed, and encouraged to tell their stories producing a series of 'narratives of sickness' (Westwood, 1994). The people interviewed wanted to be heard, and research – later presented to the health services in a series of conferences – enabled them to be 'knowing subjects' not simply individuated through the power/knowledge complex of psychiatry. It was clear from the interviews with family members as well that their experiences were re-organised through the lenses of power relations. The doctors, the hospitals, the police and social workers were perceived and experienced as repressive and coercive, to return to our major themes. Power lay not with the black mentally ill or their families, but with the agents of the state who were encountered at points of exceptional vulnerability. Most families were bemused and in despair about the progress of an incomprehensible illness with its dramatic symptoms and strange, frightening behaviour, which turned people they knew well into strangers. Very often, despite their best efforts to involve local doctors and social workers, the only people who turned up were the police, which added to their sense of apprehension. Many of the people involved in the research had been 'sectioned', detained under a legal order in mental hospitals. They encountered the state as coercive, and were then processed in relation to their illness as patients inducted into disciplinary modes that left them feeling powerless. In another way, however, it was the power of indiscipline that families and authorities feared and which prompted the section and their transfer to hospitals where they were subjected to diagnosis and treatment with drug therapies and electric shock therapy. The fact that the police were involved added to the terror even though, by their own admission, the police felt ill-equipped to deal with the mentally ill, especially those displaying psychotic symptoms.

One of the clearest narratives that emerged from the stories people had to tell was of the loneliness of hospital and, for some, the shock of realising that despite mental illness, racism survived in the wards, between the patients and with the staff. As John, a young black man said, 'I couldn't believe it – even mad people hate us'.

Racism was a major theme in the lives of all the people with whom we spoke, from specific incidents in which they had been intimidated or denied, to the commonsense racism that suffuses life in Britain. Recalling these incidents produced pain and defiance in equal measure, and there was a strong sense that the constant processes of denial and being undermined had had a major negative impact on mental health. The impact of racism as a causal factor in the production of damaged and distressed psyches is a source of debate. Psychiatrists differ in the saliency afforded to the impact of institutional and everyday racisms. But, even at a commonsense level, it is possible to imagine the sense of hurt, the assault on the sense of self and the damage that this can do – more often expressed poetically in the work of Frantz Fanon, Toni Morrison or Richard Wright.

One form of resistance, especially for the mentally ill, was to reconstruct their lives around a sense of belonging which, in their accounts, also involved the pain of remembering the point of departure, the lost relatives and places which became part of a vision of home that was nurtured in Britain, and this goes some way to explaining the desire among people of Caribbean descent to return to the Caribbean. Under British law, it is possible for people to be repatriated as mentally ill patients and, although politically this appears racist and unacceptable for some black people, it is a choice that some wish to exercise. Consistent with this attempt to produce coherence amid a swathe of symptoms that often produced terror and disorientation, the narratives reconstruct life journeys in which dreams and visions of better things are very much alive and central. For some, this was understood in relation to the history of black struggles across the world, or to a conversion to Islam and the sense of belonging offered by religious conversion. For Christians, this was often a contradictory story because there still exists a discourse around demons and sin which are brought to bear upon questions of mental illness and psychosis.

The issue of mental illness demonstrates the myriad forms of power that come to bear upon the body, made visible through the power/knowledge complex that marks out the mentally ill and seeks to intervene, through the body, with forms of treatment that are chemically or electrically delivered: chillingly understood by one mother who said, 'they electrify my boy'. But even with this, the forms of resistance remain strong from passive forms of non-compliance to outright rebellion. In more subtle ways, too, the players in the drama re-write the story, and turn a hostile and overbearing world into one in which they insert their powers and which they can use as a landscape through which to travel. None of this is easy, or benign – resistance meets with increased force and coercion, whether physical or drug-based, liberty is deprived, but still the stories are re-made and the coherence for which people strive is sought in their personal biographies and in an attempt to see themselves as black people in a hostile and racist environment.

To reintroduce the notion of society returns the discussion to the notion of the social, and the boundaries of the social can be seen to be a distinction upheld through the practices of exclusion, of reason and unreason, mental health and illness despite the recent decarceration moves and community-based programmes. These programmes are an attempt to re-draw the boundaries of the social and to re-insert madness within the gamut of human hopes and dreams. This recalls the Shakespearean account of the power of madness as part of the human condition but this type of humanistic account, while laudable, is perhaps better served by a more malleable view of the human condition that cannot be frozen and can, therefore, incorporate the psychotic as a variant of human behaviour and perception. This is not the Deleuzian world of schizophrenia as the leitmotif of the modern age – the types of fragmentation to which this refers is no match for the hallucinogenic terrors of full-blown psychosis.

Also the debates about the causes, classification and treatment of mental illness bring into sharp relief the articulation between the psyche and the social, which is crucial to an understanding of the impact of racism on subjectivities. Fanon, a practising psychiatrist, understood well the deleterious effects of dehumanising racism, and this is reiterated by Fernando (1988) and Burke (1986), who place racisms in a causal position relative to both forms of depression and schizophrenia. Yet it is equally important to recognise that the majority of black, Asian, indigenous peoples throughout the world live within racist societies and do not become mentally ill, which leads to the suggestion that some psyches, for all manner of reasons, are more vulnerable than others. In some, the de-centring processes with which we all live and work to produce identities are tolerated as in flux and unfinished productions. The division created within Western modes of understanding of the social and the self as distinctive spheres, somehow interacting, does not necessarily help with the business of living. The more recent deconstructionist account of subjectivities as de-centred and unfinished, malleable and messy, as the stuff of the social is actually closer to the lived experience of biographies and histories, which are then re-constructed through narrations or 'life stories'. Thus, to speak or write of a reified social or the limits of the social is to constantly set up barriers to understanding, which the politics of mental health for black and white people deconstruct.

Diasporic politics

The politics of black mental health inserts an agenda that is not only concerned with resources but with both the symbolic and material powers that are organised within modern forms of the state and state agencies which define, classify and manage the population in racialised ways. In other ways too, black people have been 'up against the state', not least in relation to the politics of locale and the local state as part of a diasporic politics which is currently being made in cities across the world. I want to conclude this chapter with one story from this politics which demonstrates the importance of spaces as power filled, and the ways in which issues of belonging and citizenship are as important for community-based struggles as they proved to be for issues of racism and psychiatry.

Belonging and citizenship are part of the discourse of the nation and the national but they are ruptured by forms of racism and racial exclusion, which generate and sustain the inward-looking myths of national history and ethnic exclusivity around which national stories are built. For the diasporic populations of urban Britain, with their impact on local cultures and from which they draw to produce the growing number of hybrid identities that mark Britain, as they do North America, the island story is an old one that cannot be sustained. Initially, the Englishness of the national British identity, which excluded the Irish, Scottish and Welsh peoples, was counterposed to the politics of anti-racism in the privilege afforded a polemical and political Black identity, which was a crucial part of the anti-racist politics of the eighties in Britain. In one sense, it was always problematic because it sought a unitary identity for a very diverse population of people with African, Caribbean, Indian, Pakistani, Bangladeshi and Chinese origins who had been in British cities for decades or centuries, depending upon place and history. As a counter to the white world of Britain, before the understanding of Britain as diasporic had become part of the commonsense, and when the crudest forms of racist violence and racial exclusion were practices with National Front marches on the streets – a black identity was an assertion of self and was empowering. One group that sought to use this form of identification was a youth project in Leicester known as Red Star, which began initially to take on the local state in a politics of resources and later, I have argued, moved into a politics of space, consistent with a nationalism of the neighbourhood and then out of the neighbourhood to take on the nation and the political terrain through an engagement with the Labour party (Westwood, 1991).

Red Star was determinedly political from its inception, in part, because the leader, a Sikh, had been both a student and labour movement activist and was a member of one of the organised Left groups – the International Marxist Group (IMG). Red Star changed the political landscape of the city through their exuberant style of politics and the ability to engage with symbolic struggles as other social movements have done. The power of Red Star lay in the ability of the leader to call forth the members as political subjects, and this was not simply because there was a common enemy, racism and the local state, but because, within the diversity of the membership, it was possible through an appeal to gender and generation to forge a collective subject of politics. A collective identity as young black men was articulated with ethnic, religious and language identities that were very diverse, ranging from Muslim Gujaratis to African Caribbeans from many different islands. The young men lived both the diversity within the membership and the commonalities, 'we all come from different backgrounds but we all live here and we all know racism'.

Red Star claimed the space of the city where many of the members lived and the building which housed the project. The building was a powerful symbol of their emancipation and power because it had been the school where many had studied, had failed and been subjected to the humiliations of racist teachers and a system that gave them no credibility. They too, had been classified, disciplined and excluded and, at this time, they faced unemployment. Fighting this and claiming a space were central to the forms of resistance that the project used against the city council and in the Labour Party where Red Star fought a long battle at ward level. In shifting the struggle away from the building and the resources they needed and into the Labour Party, Red Star moved against their exclusion as part of the nation and used their rights as citizens to force open the Labour Party agenda. Equally, as citizens, they challenged the local council in the courts, and required that British justice be seen as a forum in which they could act. The issues raised were a crucial forerunner of many of those that are still debated nationally about the construction of a diasporic national identity and against the notion, 'there ain't no black in the Union Jack'.

In part, the political subjects that were called forth and the forging of commonality as Red Star members and 'black youth' was realised through the privilege afforded to masculinities and their expression in the football teams, which were a central part of the Red Star project. This was a cultural politics – the empire strikes back – exploiting sport, as C.L.R. James suggests for cricket in relation to the Caribbean in his celebrated volume *Beyond A Boundary*. It was through the football teams that the struggle against racism was carried beyond the inner city space, which the men claimed as their own, into the shires and the white working-class heartlands. The success of the teams and their difficulties, the way they were represented and penalised by the Football Association, helped to forge the sense of collectivity among the members who travelled and played together, shared the joy of winning and the pain of defeat and, through this, created their own history, a cultural politics alive with heroes, battles, gains and losses. The football teams were also a way of marking the distinctiveness of the politics of Red Star. Although there were Asian teams, Hindu, Muslim and Sikh, who played in Asian and Sikh tournaments, and teams with players of Caribbean descent, Red Star was consistent in the commitment to multi-ethnic teams that encompassed all of those involved in the Red Star project itself. Thus, Red Star teams came onto the field with players of South Asian and Caribbean descent, Muslim and Sikh, Hindu and Christian and, occasionally, a white player. This combination often led to difficulties with some of the Asian teams and, eventually the Red Star teams were barred from the Sikh tournaments unless they agreed to play only two 'black' players. The multi-ethnic composition of the soccer teams is part of the enduring legacy of Red Star, and it is stronger today than in the eighties.

The strength of the football teams is an ongoing legacy of the heady political days of the eighties. It is now harder to sustain a political identity and unity in relation to the building and to engage in community politics. The agendas of politics have changed and a new generation is more difficult to mobilise. But, in part, these difficulties relate to the success of Red Star in shifting the agenda, and in engaging in a symbolic politics which has now become part of the commonsense. However, it is still the case that despite the numbers of Asian councillors in the city, the area of the project has received more cuts in local provision, and battles over the use of the Red Star building continue in a protracted and unresolved way.

Racialised power

The concerns with which this chapter began, colonial discourse, and those with which it ends are both expressions of performative power. Difference and racialisation are embedded in the social, and construct the racialised, diasporic spaces of the current world. But, how are we to understand the relations between these spheres? As Werbner (1997: 229) notes:

> The issue is not…merely discursive, a linguistic paradox disclosing the limits of language. Policy decisions, state fund allocations, racial murders, ethnic cleansing, anti-racist struggles, nationalist conflicts or revivals, even genocide, follow an essentialist construction of unitary, organic cultural collectivities.

The point is that if we understand verbal, linguistic action and writing as performative, then we are faced with a multitude of ways in which racism as performative power is enacted. Equally, while we understand the malleability and situational constructions of ethnicities, we are equally able to distinguish between the processes which position ethnicities and the ways in which discourses represent and position ethnicities. The discourses may be generated by the state in relation to the mentally ill of Asian and African Caribbean descent or community-based youth projects, or discourses that challenge the essentialising constructions of what Hesse (1997) has called 'white governance' may be generated by political subjects engaged in struggles around space, resources and identities. Equally, this is related to the issue of ambivalence and the role of desire in the binary between self and other. Werbner argues strongly for an understanding that separates the banal, mundane world of ethnicities and ambivalence from the violence of racism. Werbner (1997: 234) notes, 'In a racist relationship desire and attraction are schismogenetically transformed into an impulse to violate, to rape and to molest. The key is to be found in the process itself, which is enunciatory, performative and dynamic, not static and logocentric'.

The current interest in diasporas has replaced a series of discourses on multi-culturalism and the multi-ethnic world of the late twentieth century. Instead, given both the successes and the failures of these projects, diaspora offers a mode of representation that can be reproduced through consumption, the world music and world food that stock the shelves. It is an important shift, and contributes to a way of knowing the world that resonates with the everyday reality of life in the large cities around the globe. Diaspora foregoes the difficulties of naming populations, of producing essentialised 'communities' of race, colour or ethnicity, and it allows for identities in process rather than as finished products which adds to the sense of the normality of difference, even a celebration of difference and diversity. Thus, diaspora has the 'feel-good-factor', but it should not seduce us into believing racialised violence has lessened (Runnymede Trust, 1994; Hesse, 1997, Werbner, 1997) or that the power of measurement, definition and forms of racial classification constituting violations have been disempowered through the discourse of diaspora. Neither should the discourse of diaspora divert attention from the costs and the pain of diasporic lives – the diasporic social is not simply a space of 'world music' and 'global foods'. Diaspora is embodied, lived and travelled as discontinuous, with huge psychic costs that relate very directly to racialised forms of power.

3 Class and power

The practical politics with which the last chapter concluded privileged the racialisation of power struggles and the ways in which racism is imbricated in all areas of life, especially in relation to struggles against both the national and local state. The subjects of power are not, however, encompassed by a single identity. As the discussion so far makes clear, identities are in process, and political action raises the class content of power and classed identities. The politics of Red Star and the black mentally ill raise class issues in relation to resources and the economic position of black and Asian people in Britain. Class is articulated with ethnicity, race, gender, sexuality, generation and locality, and although we currently understand and work with this, sociology has not always understood class in this way.

Class has, until recently, been a privileged category in sociology, and has organised a large body of empirical work focused on the lives of the working class. Theoretically, it is the debate between Marx and Weber, as it has been constructed in sociological discourses, that has provided the key understandings of class, while the empirical work has been organised around categories borrowed and constructed from official statistics. The huge corpus of work implied by the area cannot be reiterated here (see, for example, the discussions by Crompton, 1998 and Scott, 1996). Instead, I want to concentrate on the way in which class relations provide an account of power relations and the way in which class as a category did, at one time, come to stand in for the social in British sociology. It is also clear that although repression and coercion are part of the class story, strategic engagement is what has marked the modern era.

This chapter examines, initially, the impact of the work of Marx upon understandings of class and the ways in which the debate with Marx has been so important in sociology. But, sociology sought ways in which to delineate an understanding of social class, and from this developed a large number of studies of the social and cultural lives of class subjects, most especially working-class subjects. Understandings of class have been constantly refined and, more recently, there have been debates on the notion of an 'underclass' and the ways in which the state has sought to exert powers over sections of the population not integrated into society through employment relations. This raises a number of issues directly relevant to the consideration of power relations: most importantly, the ways in which citizens encounter the state and relate to the idea of the nation, as nationals. The chapter concludes with an account of life on the shopfloor and the encounter between ethnically diverse women workers and the employers, examining the play of powers in the factory space.

Marx and after

Early Marxist accounts of class focused attention upon the economic and political relations of class and, like earlier sociological accounts, sought to reify class and to divorce class from 'race' and gender. It is clear already from the previous chapter that for me, following other writers, race is constitutive of class in relation to the development of capitalism. 'The history of all hitherto existing society is the history of class struggles' (Marx and Engels, [1848] 1967: 79). What is important about this much-quoted account of history is that class is not treated as an inert, statistical or descriptive category. For Marx, as emphasised later by Poulantzas (1973), class is relational, and classes are formed ultimately in struggle. This means, of course, that class cannot be separated from power. Marx, despite the incomplete chapter on classes in *Capital*, had a more subtle and nuanced account of class than that with which he is usually credited. First of all, the objective relations of capitalism produced two major antagonistic classes, the bourgeoisie, who owned the means of production, and the proletariat, whose labour turned ownership into profit. This contradiction was the motor of social change within capitalism, and carried the seeds of a revolutionary struggle. These views in simplified form were advanced by Marx and Engels in *The Communist Manifesto*, and it is this simplified Marx that fuelled one account of Marxism, 'Manifesto Marxism', with which later Marxist intellectuals, such as Gramsci, took issue. This is not to deny the power of this pamphlet and the framework it offered for an understanding of capitalist development. However, Marx was quite clear in his letters to Engels that in the workshop of the world, England, the oldest and, at the time, most advanced capitalist formation, there would be no revolution because of the peculiar cultural and historical context of England. What Lenin later described as 'trade union consciousness', was born out of economic struggles, and produced a separation between economics and politics that did not happen in France, for example, where the union movement developed from the political, especially in relation to the role of the Communist Party. The two major classes did not exhaust class formation under capitalism. Marx was acutely aware that the bourgeoisie was fractured and that the land-owning aristocracy continued. Similarly, the role of the petty bourgeoisie was one part of a developing capitalist structure. Although the economic relations of capitalism defined positions in relation to the extraction of surplus value, the importance of these positions, of the class map, was political. But politically formed classes were generated from histories and within ideologies that had to be made, and that would generate the transformative discourses essential to political action. Thus, for Marx, it was possible to read of economic positions, but politics and power relations made people the subjects of history. It is this account of class as power that is elaborated by Nicos Poulantzas, who wrote 'By power we shall designate the capacity of a social class to realise its specific objective interests' (ibid.: 104) and he continues, 'This concept is related precisely to the field of "class" practices and of relations of class practices i.e. to the field of class struggle: its frame of reference is the class struggle of a society divided into classes' (ibid.: 105) Thus:

> The concept of power cannot be applied to 'inter-individual' relations or to relations whose constitution in given circumstances is presented as independent of their place in the process of production i.e. in societies divided into classes, as independent of the class struggle...
>
> (Poulantzas, 1973: 108)

Although Poulantzas clearly locates power/class, the one imbricated in the other, the complexities are manifest in the notion that 'power relations do not constitute a simple expressive totality': that is, it is not possible to simply locate power relations from positions, nor is it always clear that economic dominance coincides with ideological or political power, 'Political or ideological power is not the simple expression of economic power' (op. cit.: 114). The work of Poulantzas drew on the re-interpretation of Marx's work by Althusser (1969, 1972) who offered a structuralist reading of Marx, in part, to overcome the simplistic view taken from 'Manifesto Marxism'. But critics have accused the Althusserian view of being as deterministic as Marx's earlier work. In part, it was in response to this that Poulantzas insisted upon the dynamic and relational account of classes and power that moves power away from the simple zero-sum, football model in which one party has power and the other is powerless.

These accounts that gave such centrality to class/power could only incorporate race and gender as fractions of classes but not with a dynamic of their own. Instead, struggles around race and gender were constructed as part of the social movements that came to occupy the space of the political with the latter-day decline in class politics. In his theorising on class, it is clear that Marx looked to the economic and the political, and yet his writings are filled with accounts of working-class life in the factories, the lack of education that prompted him to call for shorter working hours, schooling for children, etc. In terms of the ethnography of working-class life, this was left to Engels who, with his privileged access through his housekeeper (and lover), wrote *The Condition of the Working Class* ([1845] 1987), which documents everyday life and, in part, the ways in which racisms constitute the working class, the fractions, ideological struggles and daily encounters. It was this materiality of everyday life and struggle that came to occupy such an important area of concern for sociologists.

While sociology was concerned to theorise class and classes, an important difference was in the emphasis upon social classes manifest in the classic studies of community life such as, *Family and Kinship in East London* (Young and Willmott, 1962) *Coal is Our Life* (Henriques and Slaughter, 1956) and *The People of Ship Street* (Kerr, 1958). This was the sociological soap opera and a reinvention of the working class through the lens of sociological discourses. At the time, these were blind to racism, sexism and homophobia and to the violence of working life. They often presented a saccharine view of family ties and networks, and recreated the working class in the public imagination, which are now expressed in the television soaps of *Coronation Street* or *East Enders*, which, in a different era, do not hide sexual violence, homophobia or racism.

Social class

It was the constitution of class as social class that preoccupied sociologists, and this is, in part, why the work of Weber, with its concern for status and lifestyle, came to occupy such a central role in class studies. Weber distinguished between class and status and a third category 'party' but, as John Scott (1996) suggests, 'command' might be a better interpretation. The notion of 'command' was central to Weber's work on authority and bureaucracy and the ways in which relations of authority are structured in modern states, in contrast to feudal and traditional social formations. More generally, the importance of Weber's work on stratification lay, in part, in his comparative focus, historically and culturally. Like Marx, he too wanted to understand the rise of the West and the peculiarities of the development of modern capitalism in Europe.

Weber, like Marx, tied class to economic relations, most importantly property, recognising that there were a variety of class positions and criticising Marx for over-simplifying class categories. Instead, a class was defined by 'life chances' and tied to the market; thus, market situation and class situation became synonymous. This, of course, generates a complex of differentiated positions within the marketplace, but does this produce classes? Even Weber recognised that class was more than this, and does refer to the generation of solidary ties. Weber's notion of 'life chances' has become part of the commonsense of sociology and latter-day culture. Although individualised, there are also groups who come to share common life-chances, and these are constructed in relation to employment opportunities. Weber's account is suggested by some writers to be an amendment to Marx, which does little justice to either writer. Most importantly, in relation to class theory, Weber is separated from Marx by the absence of a theory of exploitation, which was the key to Marx's elaboration of class. Instead, Weber's work has become the stock-in-trade of sociological studies because, as I have suggested earlier, he privileged social class and provided ways in which an empirically based discipline could measure, categorise and track class positions.

Class was not alone in defining positions within the social structure. Status was also important, and although it was inevitably tied to material wealth, status distinctions related to blood ties, to consumption patterns and notions of taste that could be viewed as having some independence from economics (for example, the status afforded religious functionaries, such as vicars, who have little money but considerable moral capital). As Craib (1997) notes, it was probably the case that the distinction between class and status had more saliency at the time when Weber was writing than can be acknowledged today. Historically, distinctions between clerical work and manual work, old and new money and the whole area of lifestyle, patterns of taste and consumption, which marked class and status identifications in public ways, generated a series of discourses that separated status from economic wealth – the genteel poor, for example, now recast within social policy – although not often far removed from the deserving and undeserving poor of the last century. This concern with status and lifestyle provided a notion of both power and the social, and enabled class to become social class when it was reorganised in this way. The work of Giddens (1973) was crucial to this reorganisation in which he elaborated an account of market situation which incorporated the different trajectories of waged work and salaried work, and which further incorporated an account of status as consumption. Thus, it was possible, using the theoretical work of Giddens and the earlier account from Polanyi (1957) of market situation and market groupings, to construct a complex map of social class. This, coupled with the importance of studies of social mobility, has given Weberian accounts a central role in the sociology of class. Large-scale empirical studies (Goldthorpe *et al.*, 1980) have tracked the degree of mobility between classes in the post-Second World War period. These exercises, which produce ever more technical measures of mobility, are at some distance from the account of class in Marx, which was constructed within the political and located with the economic.

The making of the working class

The importance of constructing an account of the social and class as social class generated a wealth of lifestyle and community studies that purported to represent the lives of the working class in Britain. These everyday worlds were constructed through studies of kinship, and focused attention upon 'community' and, in particular, the loss of community in late capitalism. Community studies became a whole sub-field in sociology, and produced a series of accounts of power that were focused on locale. The love affair with community was later translated into social policy, with community as a spray-can answer to the vagaries of capitalism, to poverty, poor relations with the police and so on. The discourse of community has latterly been revived in relation to communitarianism, notions of responsibilities and as a way of making the social intelligible and lived within. While the micro-studies of community provided a powerful data base from which the lives of the working classes were reconstructed, there was little attention given to middle- and upper-class communities, on the assumption that social mobility distracted these classes from locality and everyday worlds. Instead, patterns of consumption and lifestyle studies produced a more cultural account of class lives, and divorced these accounts from production relations. One crucial attempt to theorise both was found in the work of Bourdieu (1973) who, more than many other writers, still sought to theorise the relationship between economics and cultures.

Bourdieu's work suggested that in the reproduction of capitalism both economic and cultural capital were important and, although the two were very often expressed simultaneously, it was cultural capital that allowed access to economic rewards – that is, the networks and contacts that were part of the social lives of the privileged, and which for the majority were absent. The analysis was also concerned to discuss the ways in which class cultures operated to disadvantage or promote individuals, especially in the context of schooling, when children were invited to partake of certain cultural capitals that could only be accessed and unlocked if the child already possessed a degree of cultural competence. This set the lie to the notion of education for social mobility because schools basically rewarded what was extant. Induction into aristocratic culture was reserved for those who already possessed this. The great story of mobility and effort to 'better oneself' already marked off the bulk of the population against an ideology that promoted the effortless rise and rise of the upper classes. The student who goes to university and receives a degree can cash this in the labour market, but the aristocrat, with private wealth and family contacts, has no need to do this.

Bourdieu's work was important especially in relation to consumption and also in relation to the ways in which subjects are inducted into class cultures through the habitus into which they are born, including language patterns, aspects of taste, moral codes, etc. Despite the difficulties with some of Bourdieu's theorising, he is important to the concerns of this book because his attempts to theorise economic and cultural capital are attempts to theorise power, and to suggest that the economic does not stand alone nor can it be reified in this way. Instead, he posits what has now been recognised as important to late capitalism – the power of consumption and the types of differentiations that are produced within patterns of consumption and the symbolic power of goods, taste, culture, etc. Equally, he is concerned with elaborating the relationship between subjectivities and the social, in the notion of habitus and the ways in which class, gender, racialised identities are called forth and subjects are interpolated with the varieties of socials and cultures in complex societies. In this sense, the social is not separate and 'out there', it is simultaneously within and without, acted upon and acting upon, individuals. The social is constantly in the process of construction, myriad life-worlds made and remade through the practices of everyday life that are articulated with a powerful market, the vagaries of capitalism and the system of governance in play. The analytical framework used by Bourdieu contains the possibility of understanding difference, but the issue of race and racism, of gender and age as other markers of class relations is not discussed.

The underclass

It is interesting and predictable that race should re-emerge in debates around class in relation to the debates on the underclass. Faced with, on the one hand, the increased mobility of sections of the population and, on the other, increasing poverty in the USA (the wealthiest nation on earth), attempts were made to theorise how it could be that some people never managed to get into the game and came to be the dispossessed of capitalism in the USA or in the states across Europe. The language of the debates around the notion of 'the underclass' suggest that somehow a group of people is outside of, beyond, the class structure and, in so far as class is a defining feature of capitalist societies, this has placed sections of the population outside society. This was one way in which the underclass debate defined the social and definitely set limits to the social. Highly problematic, the debate was also bound to a racialised account of class in which the underclass was defined as black and consisted of the black ghettos of the major US cities. At one level, the idea is not new, for example, the lumpen proletariat of Marx's writing, the dispossessed and the 'residuum' of the Victorian era. But, there was no suggestion that these elements in Marx's analysis were not part of the structural processes of capitalism; the problem was the political fecklessness of the 'lumpen' element. This has been pointed out by writers like Dahrendorf (1987) and Field (1989) as a counter to the work of Charles Murray (1984, 1990), especially, who moves from the economic to the cultural, positing a ghetto mentality and suggesting, from within his work, a re-vamped version of the Victorian 'feckless poor'. The problem with the whole way in which the debate has been conducted is that it sees class structures as building blocks, as unitary slabs of population, and it fails to come to grips with the changing world of employment opportunities, which have been pioneered in many of the ghetto spaces of large urban formations throughout the world. This has led some writers to suggest that the precarious existences of many in the poorest sections of the population is part of the 'third worldisation' of the West – but caution is important in making these comparisons. The poor of America exist within wealth that can only be imagined by most members of so-called Third World social formations.

The initial categorisation had important implications for the ways in which power was implicitly constructed within the model of the underclass. This is a view of power on the zero-sum model in which some had power but the underclass had none, and this was linked to the empiricist account of social structure and social action which made a racialised population visible as victims. The reality is much more complex. It is clear that all manner of ways of living have been creatively devised, from the illegal to the legal. These combined with welfare benefits (not available in Third World versions of the poor) and work of all kinds show that an economic level of power does exist. Why else would property developers open up the largest shopping centre in Europe near the most heavily unemployed area of Britain (the north-east) in the eighties. This was a product of a marketing executive's understanding of what has come to be known as the 'black economy', racialised language which maintains the position of sections of the black population within the underclass thesis. The power that also comes from fear has both created the notion of the underclass and reproduced Galbraith's notion of the one-third/two-thirds society in which the complacency of the middle class is potentially threatened by the lower orders, a familiar story from the Victorian world.

More recently the discussion has shifted to the white working class and the growing numbers of male unemployed in a reversal of the racialisation of black people. It is now recognised that the poor and the dispossessed are also the large numbers of white people living in the 'parking lots' of post-war public housing on the periphery of cities and very often having 'only their race and their space' as Sivanandan (1990) wrote. In the USA, this has prompted a series of studies of whiteness and of 'white trash'. The concern expressed about this section of society in the UK was marked in the announcement (14 August 1997) by the Labour Government of a new task force on 'social exclusion': a term borrowed from the EEC fourth framework, to be headed by the Prime Minister. Social exclusion is a discourse in which there is a clear understanding that the excluded correspond to the Victorian 'dangerous classes' (Morris, 1994), and there have been a series of concerns expressed about the role of the poor and the excluded as citizens with rights and responsibilities. The main focus has been on the visibility (to the police and in law and order terms) of young men, black and white, many of whom may be excluded but may not be silent or ignored and who express this in public ways (for example, street fracas, stealing and burning cars, exercising powers that come to terrorise sections of working-class estates). The media representations of this section of the population are as the young, dangerous and disaffected element for whom 'the future has been cancelled' and who are not subject to the disciplines of work, trade union, church, family or party. Very often, forms of resistance to police and other citizens are antisocial, and a series of moral panics have been mounted around disaffected youth which completely reverses the notion of an underclass element as powerless victims. On the contrary, these people are presented as dangerous, out of control and empowered by their antisocial behaviour.

The young men who make the excluded visible have the power to disrupt the one-third/two-thirds society, and to burst through the marginalisation to which they are subjected, spatially and economically. It is not just that they have the power to expose the fears of other sections of society, they also have a strategic sense of their relationship with the state and state agencies. Many operate on the margins of the economy but with good results in terms of income and benefits. They use their initiative and their creativity to generate and sustain an income that is constantly under threat from state agencies and the police. These forms of informal economic activity, benefit scams, etc., are also of concern to government and sociologists. The informal sector is now a huge part of national income, and offers people power through consumption, which the capitalist firms, especially those concerned with youth and style, are very clearly able to exploit (Nike and Adidas advertisements – street life turned into expensive commodities). These forms of resistance through economic activities, which still produce the goods, are actually forms of inclusions in consumer society, and some will choose this option. Recent 'welfare to work' programmes in both the USA and the UK have generated considerable resistance from people who have their lives organised in relation to the absence of work and not the search for work, especially of the low-paid, menial variety. It makes no sense on a rational choice model to chose low-paid work over benefits and the cash economy, so no amount of moral exhortation is going to make any impact on this. This has been the subject of recent discussions on the role of the culture industries in Britain, and the ways in which young musicians, artists, photographers, etc., have learned their trade and developed their creativity with the material underpinning of welfare benefits. Equally, a recently founded group in Germany 'the Happy Unemployed' suggests that they are doing the state a favour, and that the real problem is 'the obligation to work'.

Although this is one section of the underclass and 'excluded' which is integrated through consumption, this is not the total picture. There are sections of impoverishment not assisted by the cash economy among women and children: the feminisation of poverty, which increases with age. The elderly, so many so desperately poor, are the real invisible and excluded – the dispossessed and the powerless. They cannot be constructed as 'dangerous' or potentially hazardous, so they receive little or no attention, no decent benefits and a pension on which to live – and their numbers are growing. Instead, the elderly are constructed as middle-class 'third agers' with money, free time and the opportunity to enjoy life.

Welfare to work

As I have suggested the invisibility of the elderly poor contrasts sharply with the visibility of the work shy in public discourses, the feckless, young deviants, single mothers and the growing list of those who come within the regulatory power of the state, state agencies and professionals. These sections of the working class are the ones most subject to forms of governmentality in which the power/knowledge complex comes to construct them in specific ways as the subjects/objects of state policies and part of the management of populations. Sections of the working class are now, more than ever before, subjected to the direct intervention of a moralising discourse which, sometimes, seems to resonate with the categories that constructed the 'work house'. Now that the loss of employment means that the disciplines of work and the responsible organisation of trade unionism is not in place, other mechanisms for producing responsible (docile) citizens must be found. Equally, workplaces and unions were spaces in which counter-hegemonic discourses and practices could be generated, and in which classed struggles over the social wage were fought. In part, these struggles helped to define the social in action, and the ways in which citizenship and notions of rights and responsibilities were addressed.

Throughout the history of citizenship rights, on the incremental model (Marshall, 1950), there has been a notion that elements of the working class needed induction into their roles as responsible citizens. The Adult School Movement, the Cooperative Movement and the Workers Educational Association all ran classes and courses in citizenship on a liberal democratic model. It was only the much maligned National Labour College that organised classes around a socialist vision of citizenship and the future (Westwood, 1992). If women are considered now to be 'bad' mothers this is not new, and the discourses from the Victorian era around feckless, morally degenerate mothers led to the Eugenicist calls for control on reproductive capacity, and also promoted the 'Schools for Mothers', which were a spectacular failure; basically, working women stayed away. These early attempts to regulate working-class lives have been followed by the rise of welfare professions, which form a network of surveillance with legal powers, growing numbers of registers and the power to intervene in family life on an unprecedented scale. These forms of governance generate the most resentment because they are in direct conflict with notions of individual freedom, adult responsibility and the idea of the home as a private space. So powerful are these ideas that they are part of the commonsense understandings of life in Britain and of what marks the boundaries of the private and the public. Despite the boundaries being constantly transgressed by the state in all its guises, there is a powerful cultural value given to the separation, and this has major implications for the ways in which the social is understood at a commonsense level.

The powerful impact of discourses around the family, the home and social responsibilities that are allied with welfare and employment contribute to the construction of an account of the social against the antisocial. But this is a classed rhetoric in which much attention is given to working-class youth, whether as football hooligans or car thieves, and in which the risks are turned into opportunities for technological surveillance. Eventually, the scam society promoted by the rampant individualism of the post-Thatcher era in Britain was voted out, but it took nearly 20 years and has had a profound impact on the social-scape. In part, it is summed up in the notion of the decline of the social. The New Labour pundits have given this a moral rhetoric bound to responsibilities, and their actions as government in promoting fees for almost everything, from education to eye tests, promotes the idea of social responsibility through the cash nexus and, thus, contributes towards the decline of the social and the promotion of a privatised world of which Mrs Thatcher would be proud. This has major implications for how sociology is able to reinscribe the social and in what ways it is now to be theorised because, at one level, more modern accounts have followed the development of post-war welfarist social formations. The response has, in fact, come from the theorising around post-modernism which has been timely and insightful in insisting upon the multiplicity of sites that constitute the social and the de-centring effects of this understanding. However, class, as it was understood, has not figured strongly in these accounts and, very often, they have been confined to a theoretical frame that has not generated substantive work.

The backdrop to much of the discussion of the underclass, social exclusion and the changes to welfare policies is the changing nature of work and the re-definition of 'jobs'. So much of the study of class was bound to occupational categories and work cultures that it also has major implications for sociological research. The suggestion from two recent studies (1998) from the Royal Society for the Encouragement of Arts, Manufactures and Commerce and the Industrial Society (1998) reinforce the notion that although the majority of the workforce is in long-term employment, new jobs and future jobs are likely to be casualised and uncertain. Indeed, this trend at the margins is beginning to have a major impact on the stability of work overall. Short-term, fixed-term and part-time work is growing and with it the service sector, compared with the reduction in the manufacturing and the skills base of industrial employment. There is also a tendency for work to be rewarded on an output rather than a task-based model. Thus, Valerie Bayliss author of the RSA (1988) report notes:

> The only certainty in the future of work is uncertainty. We are convinced that flexibility, in all the forms in which it appears – between sectors of activity, between paid and unpaid work, between different roles, between different

patterns of work and careers – will be a feature of working life as far ahead as we can see. The dominance of the traditional model of working life has been broken.

In this sense, consistent with a de-centring of the social, there is a de-centring of work, and this has profound implications for the social and subjectivities. In part, these changes are being played out and discussed in relation to the shifting understanding of class and the politics of welfare. But, as Rosemary Crompton (1998: 226–7) insists in the conclusion to her book, 'Classes may have changed but they still count' and she continues, 'Class structures may determine life chances, but increasingly societal fragmentation may render these facts more opaque'. The forces shaping this opacity relate to the individuation of society and the political marketisation of society in which the family and the market are privileged as organising forms and principles of the market. But, Crompton, like other writers, suggests this is no guarantee of social organisation or the conditions necessary to promote capitalist development. However, the ties of belonging, which were promoted through class alliances, politically and socially, have been weakened and no longer promote the same sense of belonging as in previous decades. Instead they promote state-sponsored calls to communitarianism, citizenship and the discourse of rights and responsibilities.

Class and nation

Harvey (1996) and Castells (1997) still maintain an important place for political economy despite their attention to spatiality and the power of new technologies and, in doing so, they raise some of the most important questions for class, power and the social. The most telling articulation of these comes in relation to the construction of the imaginary nation in which a class configuration brings together populist sentiment with territory and an account of a shared history. Nation-building and calls to nationalism attempt to neutralise class antagonisms and very often succeed in this. Social theorising has, until recently, also naturalised the nation, and has tended to equate societies with nation-states and national boundaries. This has had a major impact on the way in which the social is thought, and has contributed to the account of the social as the major institutions of a society when, in fact, these are a description of state structures. The nation conceived as the social also provides a clear differentiation between insiders and outsiders, aliens and citizens, producing a homogenising account of the nation rather than attention to the ways in which differentiation, especially on a spatial basis, is a constituent part of nations. Regional, linguistic, religious and ethnic diversities can become the sites of counter claims to nationhood, evidenced in Ireland, Spain, Kashmir, Punjab and Assam. In order to make sense of this, theorists have used insights from Gramsci's (1971) work, which offered an account of the economic and the cultural, woven together to form ideological hegemony, which is unstable. Gramsci was also clear that classes are fractionalised, and that a power bloc must be generated that maintains the power of sections of the ruling class. Gramsci's account provides the basis for de-centring a notion of power relations and the social while maintaining the importance of class relations and ideological struggles. Gramsci's conception of power relations, with its emphasis upon the cultural and ideological moments, has proved highly suggestive for the ways in which capitalist formations can be understood. Understanding the role of consumption and the generation of a series of commonsenses that provide crucial elements of popular cultures is useful, especially in relation to the coming together of the popular with the power of the ruling bloc. Crucial to the understanding of these ideologies as powerful, hegemonic forms has been the notion of the nation, and the ways in which sections of the ruling class come to stand in for the nation.

Gramsci emphasised the power of cultural forms and the way in which, to use Bauman's term, the seductions of capitalism have been erased from accounts of the power of capital and class rule. Despite the impoverishment of sections of the working class, in the longer term, working-class real incomes have risen, and lifestyles have been generated and sustained around a volume of consumption that is, of course, crucial to the success of capitalism. The present mood wants more responsible capitalism in terms of the environment rather than workers rights and, generally, the moralistic pressures towards lower levels of consumption are considered dull and at odds with the world, from Delhi to Cali. Instead, there is an acknowledgement that capitalism is fun, and consumer politics is given considerably more attention than class politics. The name of the game is not collective struggle as class actors, but as consumers who care about the environment, about food safety, etc. This shift is part of post-Fordist globalisation and the increasing power of trans-national corporations, but also of the wealth of the West and its impact upon the daily lives of subjects. Most recently, this power has been discussed in relation to the power of technologies, revisioned within the circuits of the information revolution, which puts television and other cultural products within the reach of so many people in the world. In his recent two-volume study Castells (1997) seeks to address the impact and production of cultural forms in late capitalism and he concludes, rather chillingly:

> Power still rules society, it shapes and dominates, us… The new power lies in the codes of information and in the images of representation around which societies organize their institutions, and people build their lives, and decide their behaviour. The sites of this power are people's minds.
>
> (1997: 359)

In Chapter 8, I will seek to address the issues raised by Castells in an exploration of the power of the visual and representational in relation to consumption and cultural reproduction within social formations.

Fordist production

Consumption is mediated by money and, although money itself has symbolic power and often seems to be invested with magical qualities, it is a medium of exchange. For most people, money is acquired through the exchange of labour power for wages or salaries; however, globally, work for many people is more and more insecure and casualised. However, many of the studies that have been generated from the class problematic have concentrated upon the world of work, wage-bargaining, struggles to form unions, and the cultures of work, forms of gender, racial inequality, etc. These studies are also a history of the different conceptions of power within sociological discourses and how they have changed over time.

This work of reconstruction is elaborated in Clegg's (1989) text *Frameworks of Power*, which traces notions of power historically and then relates these to organisational frameworks, including those concerned with employer/employee relations, seeking to provide a typology of forms of power in relation to what Clegg calls 'circuits of power' related to the rise of the nation-state and organisational forms. These concerns have been elaborated in the sub-discipline of industrial sociology in which early studies sought to elaborate the life of workers in factories. *Working for Ford*, for example, the classic study of the production line at the Ford Motor Company (Benyon, 1984), like the class theory on which it was premised, made gender and race invisible. Today, the study of Ford workers would seek to understand both working-class whiteness and masculinities and the culture produced, with its impact upon black workers. It was clear from this study, and others, that capitalists did not have things all their own way. Workers consistently sought to disrupt the production line, either directly or through forms of passive resistance. The capitalist labour process was shown to be anything but simply coercive and although it was certainly repressive in terms of the time, noise, conditions of labour, it also generated forms of negotiation that were played out through the shopfloor cultures of the workplace and through the union relations in the factory. Money was the key question for the unions, and action was related to wage demands, whereas the life of the shopfloor was one in which workers constantly sought to exercise greater degrees of control over their working lives and the production process. The studies of male workers and later of women workers (Pollert, 1981; Westwood, 1984; Cavendish, 1982, for example) were conceptually underpinned by Marxist accounts of work, labour process and authority relations, and these concerns produced a wealth of substantive work on the capitalist labour process in which power, although negotiated through shopfloor cultures, was understood in a strategic sense as a constant struggle between capital and labour over time, space and money. The studies incorporated notions of patriarchal relations as a variation on the forms of power in operation and developed a series of critiques of labourism and union power as rooted in patriarchal forms.

Similarly, studies of black and white workers emphasised racism and racist practices in the workplace, in hiring and firing as part of both an institutional and a commonsense form of racism, which divided workers and set up exclusionary practices often to the detriment of labour overall. These studies brought cultures, ideologies and economics together, but it was not until Foucault's work impressed itself into the field of industrial relations and the sociology of work that an alternative account was generated that could be related to both Marx and Weber, and in which forms of discipline and surveillance became crucial. Foucauldian interpretations have maintained the importance of strategic engagements and the constant processes of power as relational in which power does not reside with one party to the encounters but is a shifting, moving series of engagements. However, it is also clear that in terms of the power of the gaze, the visibility of workers through the design of factories, surveillance, clocking in, etc., employers start ahead of the game.

This is not, however, the end of the story. Working lives and relations are imbricated in identities and the way in which people position themselves in daily life. The struggles and forms of resistance do not begin and end at the factory gate but are an ongoing process, simultaneously subjective and social. Nowhere is this better examined than in the classic study by Sennett and Cobb (1972) *The Hidden Injuries of Class,* a deeply moving account of working-class masculinities in the USA which explores the emotional costs of alienated work and provides a poetic account of working-class life. The issues are ones of freedom and dignity and as the authors write:

> The puzzles of freedom and dignity described so far ought to drive people mad. Dignity is as compelling a human need as food or sex, and yet here is a society which casts the mass of its people into limbo, never satisfying their hunger for dignity, nor yet so explicitly depriving them that the task of proving dignity seems an unreasonable burden, and revolt against the society the only reasonable alternative. However, most of the people who appear in the pages of this book are not on the edge of nervous collapse, nor at the point of despair where revolt is kindled. On the contrary, they get by from day to day with a sense of balance, with a certain distance from the problems of class and class consciousness.
>
> (1972: 191)

On the shopfloor

In my own work, *All Day Every Day*, a study of life on the shopfloor in a hosiery factory, I sought ways in which to deconstruct, what was then, a current debate on the relationship between capitalism and patriarchy as forms of power. My own reading of this debate was that it was, and is, highly unsatisfactory. At best, the notion of patriarchy was a strategic intervention which focused attention upon gender relations, but the historical and universalising tendencies within the debate were untenable. I took issue with the notion that men were power-full and women were power-less, borrowed from the zero-sum view of power, which bore very little relationship to the lived reality of women's lives. The model gave patriarchal power to the world of the home and capitalist relations to the world of work. This was also untenable, and the study set out to show that gender relations suffused the world of work, and that femininities were as much constructed in the workplace as in the home, a pervasive theme in relation to masculinities and working lives. Equally, the homogenising unitary notion of woman was unsustainable in any context but, in particular, in the post-colonial, diasporic world of Britain in the eighties. The issue of racism had to be addressed and the politics of women united and women divided could not be ignored.

The debate into which I inserted myself was premised upon a series of binaries: men/women, power/powerless, home/work, workers/management and so on, but the crucial binary of black/white was not in the picture or was just emerging as a salient and political issue. I was also theoretically troubled by a feminist insistence on the use of 'experience' as somehow ready made and easily translated into action or mutual intelligibility. This was also deconstructed within the book, which provided a series of reconstructions of the lives of diasporic women on the shopfloor. The study was conducted over a 15-month period (and again my thanks to everyone concerned), and was then written up around a series of themes that brought together the theoretical background and the substantive data.

In terms of the central concern of this book, the story told of factory life was of an endless series of negotiations which, I suggested, were primarily played out through the power of shopfloor culture as a material expression of the attempt to wrest time, money, control of space from management, and that femininities were used as a strength in this ongoing war of attrition. The factory was, in fact, partly indulgent towards some of the shopfloor celebrations of weddings and babies as part of a paternalistic tradition into which management had also been inducted. These forms of resistance were, however, contradictory in so far as they also tied women into conventional modes of gender relations. However, given the exhausting nature of their working lives and the kind of pay that they received, which was among the highest in the city, it was not surprising that family relations, children and motherhood were more exciting, fulfilling and pleasurable for most of the women.

In terms of their working lives, despite the high levels of resistance to management, the women were paid less than the men, and were subjected to much higher levels of surveillance. These modes of authority contributed to the domestication of the workplace, while the routines of work travelled back into the home with money management and the organisation of domestic labour. Part of this surveillance was also concerned with racism as well as sexism. All women were subjected to the sexism of the shopfloor, especially from the mechanics who fixed the machines; however, the women had their own back in dramatic ways by ridiculing the mechanics. Asian and women of African Caribbean descent had to cope with the daily round of commonsense racism on the shopfloor and with the forms of institutional racism that divided the workers in particular ways, and promoted specific managerial discourses on Asian women, especially.

Re-reading this study today it is clear that while it sought to examine the commonalities and differences between women it had fewer tools with which to examine the politics of difference in an industrial setting. Equally, while racism was a central issue for the study, a better understanding of the modes of surveillance and forms of visibility that constitute the power of racisms and forms of racialisation are now available through a Foucauldian re-reading. It is possible to see that the collective subject that was generated through the cultures of the shopfloor was contingent and had constantly to be re-made in the light of the ongoing relations between the women. Equally, the ways in which Asian women did not associate with the political category of black is part of the refigured understanding of the politics of ethnicities and identities in Britain.

The factory constituted a social space, but it was highly differentiated by gender. The lives of the women in the making-up department generated and sustained a feminised social within capitalist production relations, and set the lie to the abstracted quality of labour power. Women enter the labour force as gendered and racialised labour, and are rewarded, managed and assigned to the division of labour within this context. The capitalist labour process is conceptualised and lived as more than the sum of economics, the division of labour and technical expertise. The lived relations of the factory constitute the social and the many socials that together form the factory as a site of production. This multicentric space is not a hermetically sealed world in which the relations of home are not present; the politics of gender and race are part of the constitution of the social. Sexualities are also everywhere within the industrial space, forming part of the ways in which femininities and masculinities are constituted and reconstituted, in part, as performance work but also in relation to the defining life-cycle events of gendered/ racialised identities.

Class and power

This, all too brief discussion, leads neatly into the considerations of Chapter 4 in which the issue of gender and engendered power is examined. But, before we move on, it is useful to reiterate some of the main themes of this chapter. Class has been and remains a central concern of sociologies, and it is clear from the discussion that class is more than the sum of official categories that divide people by their occupation. This is just the beginning, as Bourdieu and Sennett and Cobb have elaborated, class relations are constituted through the internalities of class actors' lives in which cultures, emotions and the psychic processes of class are made and remade in the working and family lives of people on a daily basis.

Sennett and Cobb (1972: 192) actually return to Nietzsche and to his 'extraordinary doctrine', 'join power and love', 'then you can never be hurt'. Sennett and Cobb's book is an exploration of the distance between power and love and the myriad of ways in which ordinary people, men in particular, are hurt by a system that is discursively constructed around the separation between the two which, they argue, promotes a form of splitting and a lack of ontological security. Forms of alienation are actively embraced as defence mechanisms, with the splitting of the psyche as an active response to capitalist conditions of labour. Or, as Sennett and Cobb (1972: 215) write: 'Fragmentation and divisions in the self are the arrangements consciousness makes in response to an environment where respect is not forthcoming as a matter of course.' The men interviewed disavowed any sense of intimacy and any sense of their own worth through a celebration of their talents and achievements. Instead, as one especially thoughtful man suggests, 'he isn't much, just part of the woodwork' (ibid.: 216).

For Sennett and Cobb, the world of capitalist labour is a 'destructive social order', and even when workers have higher degrees of autonomy they are still bound to the degradations of capitalist labour. The poetry of their account of 'degraded work' in the modern world is not simply an exposé or a hymn to the fortitude of male workers on the production line, the heroes of class analysis: their work tries to probe the relationship between the psychic and social processes that constitute the world of work and its effects. The issue of dignity is at the core of the confluence of capitalist labour with alienated lives and they conclude:

> The working people of Boston have been denied the *presumption*, rather than the *possibility*, of societal respect, denied some way of moving through daily life without being defensive and on guard, some way of being open with other people without being hurt. The humbling of toady is as oppressive as that of the *ancien regime*, but of a different kind: it is at once less brutal and more insidious.
>
> (ibid.: 248)

These words are bound to the study of class in the seventies, but they speak equally for the racialised and gendered indignities that also produce the splitting and defensive modes of being that mark the social. The issue of the separation of power and love, so crucial to the articulation of what Sennett and Cobb call a 'flawed humanity', is actually the starting point for so many of the feminist critiques of sexism, heterosexism and gender inequality. Centrally concerned with power relations, the next chapter brings the issue of engendered power into focus.

4 Engendered power

While class was the pre-eminent preoccupation of sociologists until the late seventies, the ways in which class was conceptualised was disrupted by the arrival of feminist debates and politics, which made a major impact on the social sciences and humanities disciplines. In so far as class was privileged in British sociology, a conception of the social tied to this preoccupation was sustained, which was gender-blind and which naturalised masculine accounts and practices as the social. The studies of class cultures that concentrated upon family and community (Young and Willmott, 1962, 1974) showed substantively the world of women as community, but this was glossed over in an account that basically concentrated attention upon the world of male workers, effecting a separation between the world of men/work and the world of the women/home. This binary was constantly transgressed in the studies of working-class community, which showed symbiotic relations between home, locality, family relations and networks as crucial to employment opportunities – the miners, the dockers and the printers, for example.

This chapter begins with an extended discussion of the relations between gender and power, and the ways in which this has translated into practical politics, invoking different forms of power and re-inserting the issue of violence. But, one issue that feminist politics has had to confront is the understanding and theorisation of the category 'woman', and this is examined in relation to the iconic status of the late Diana, Princess of Wales. This is an especially interesting example of the myriad twists and turns of power relations as the context for an engendered politics. One way in which this has been understood is through the debate with Foucault, which has been very important to feminist theoretical work. Recently, however, the concerns of gender studies have developed a whole series of accounts of men and masculinities in which the varieties of power are imbricated. Finally, the chapter returns to the politics of gender, using examples from Latin America on the ways in which mothers came to organise against the state and against repression and coercion.

Feminist politics: against coercion, constraint and violence

Feminist accounts took issue with the above but, in so doing, reproduced the binaries of home and work, male and female and, using earlier feminist writings (especially those from the USA), began a long debate on the notion of patriarchy and patriarchal power, constructing a world in which men were powerful and women were powerless. The debates and uses of the notion of patriarchy (Beechey, 1979) insisted that the issue of gender relations was one of power and that feminist politics was fighting for a reversal of the status quo in which men were seen to be dominant. It was a crude account of power that produced a politics from which many women were alienated. Women were cast as subordinates, oppressed by patriarchal power. The reasons for male domination were discussed in a number of ways, from biological oppression through the child-bearing role to the subordination of women in the workplace. Early studies developed the notion from class studies of a secondary labour market or, on a Marxist model, that women were the reserve army of labour (Breughal, 1989). Equally powerful were the debates on women's role in the reproduction of capitalism, through domestic labour and the campaign 'wages for housework'. In relation to these economic issues the debates raised the invisibility of women's labour in relation to economic development and the success of capitalist production, and women trade unionists forced the issues onto the union agenda. It was clear, and is still the case, that most women earn less than men, and that this represented a pattern that had developed historically in relation to the trade union movement and the definition of skilled and unskilled work.

The debates around skill also prompted an examination of the ways in which women were inserted into official discourse, whether via the state or in the trade union movement, where skill was defined as a masculine attribute and the male wage as a family wage. Equally, within the language of benefits, women were consistently treated as dependents of men and located in families. The power of familial discourses to construct commonsense accounts of women and men, femininities and masculinities, was construed by some to be part of the patriarchal power of the state, with its emphasis upon law and order, the military and discriminatory practices in relation to immigration and citizenship.

The debates on patriarchal relations and power were re-organised in the contribution by Sylvia Walby (1990) who suggested that earlier forms of patriarchy were located in the realm of the home, and that this privatised patriarchy had, with the development of modern forms of the state, become part of the public patriarchy of welfare societies in the West. Her work suggested a series of areas in which patriarchal relations were sustained – work, family, the state, forms of cultures. This provided an important way of trying to bring together sociological concerns with feminist analysis, but it also left the problem of power unresolved and under-theorised.

Where the discussion addressed forms of power directly, writers produced an account of power as masculinist, in terms of the use of force and coercion and a series of discourses developed, some still extant, on women as nurturers and on the side of peace. There was an important political issue here that actually used the binary woman/man, nature/culture as part of a political rhetoric against war, weapons and violence in the world, but even as a description it was untenable. Similar accounts of forms of power suggest that specific modes of power are feminised, especially those concerned with manipulations, and this was built into the colonial account, especially of India. Within British colonial discourses, the power of Indian men was celebrated among those who were designated the 'martial races' of Northern India, which included the Punjabis and Sikhs whom the British brought into the army and sent around the world as police people in the outposts of the Empire. But, there was also another vision of Indian masculinity expressed in the notion of the 'wily oriental', very often Hindu, who was viewed as feminised through an association with manipulative skills and behaviour that made him untrustworthy in the eyes of the colonists (Westwood, 1990). What is interesting about this is the way that power was gendered in these accounts and the different values that were placed on them – the noble men, 'real men', of Northern India who impressed the British with their prowess and their ability to ride horses and the ignoble, 'feminised men' of the Hindu world who being less intelligible to the colonial British were simultaneously otherised and feminised. These engenderings of power are not, however, simply of historical interest, but are part of the ways in which powers are understood today. It is expressed crudely in the 'recipes for control' that adorn women's magazines such as *Cosmopolitan*, which are aids for keeping ahead in the games of sexual politics. The advice on offer constitutes a series of tactics that can be applied in relation to personal relationships and, more recently, relationships at work and how to compete more effectively in the workplace using femininity as one of the tools. The importance of this feminised account of wily ways is clearly that women are not seen as powerless. Their power may be underdeveloped and need the kind of advice on offer, but women are not the victims of the earlier patriarchal story.

The work of feminists concentrated upon the lives of women, and sought first to make women visible as part of the process of empowerment. A considerable body of historical work was developed around this theme (Rowbotham, 1973, 1983, for example). Similarly, in sociology, women were inserted into studies of factories (Pollert, 1981; Westwood, 1984; Cavendish, 1982) and into debates around trade unions and political forms (Beale, 1982). But the confines of this approach, with its emphasis on visibility and the important chronicles of women's lives, did not advance the theorisation of power relations because the articulations between forms of power were not discussed, and men were mostly absent conceptually, a taken-for-granted norm against which feminist work struggled. It was only later in the eighties that the debates shifted and the discussion of men and masculinities came into view.

In part, the neat patriarchal assumptions of much earlier work were disrupted by racism and black, Asian, Chilean, Palestinian and many more women demanding a voice, and demanding that the issue of racism be addressed. Whether it was on the editorial board of *Feminist Review* or in the women's refuges, racism blew apart the world of women and the unitary subject 'woman'. In fact, it had never existed. Class divisions had already caused deep divisions in both theoretical and practical work, and racism, once again, privileged issues of power, not between women and men but between women. Thus, many of the platforms and rhetoric of a white women's movement made no sense in the context of racism. For example, the call for abortion on demand did not take account of the politics of reproduction in which black women and poor white women had been subjected to enforced sterilisations. Of major importance too was the rethink that had to be done around home and family, which was constructed as a space of oppression by some of the early feminists, whereas black women, and also many white women, saw the home as a site of power in which they exercised legitimate control. This was especially evident in relation to a series of racist discourses that constructed Asian women, in particular, as victims of a cultural nexus, which many of those who were providing comments upon did not understand and did not know. The interventions by black and Asian women were seminal, a turning point in the understandings of engendered power, because they re-focus issues of power in the home and the household and demand that racism be addressed; these concerns also invoked state power and how it comes to bear upon the lives of minorities, women and men. The power of the state to define citizens and aliens, and the arbitrary way in which black people were treated as entrants to Britain, for example, became key issues in the campaigns that brought together issues of gender, race and power.

The issues of gender and power in relation to the state were addressed in a pioneering analysis by Sonia Alvarez (1990) in which, in relation to Brazil, Alvarez analysed not only the practices of the state in relation to women and men but produced an analysis of 'genderic' discourses. These showed that the way the state positioned sections of the population was imbued with a gendered perspective. These themes are further explored in Anne Phillips' (1991) work on citizenship and the ways in which, over time, citizenship has been constructed in relation to men and, in Western democracies, as Pateman (1998) suggests, the notion that there is a voluntary contract between citizens and the state which is undermined by the position of women within marriage and the law. Pateman suggests that the issue of rape is the signal moment – women could not be raped within marriage (although recent cases have led to a change in the law). As Phillips points out, what is crucial to Pateman's argument is that citizens are not abstracted individuals, they are embodied and thus gendered. Equally, I would want to emphasise the racialised body as a key factor in the development of democracy – especially in the USA (as dramatised in the film *Amistad*, which narrates, through a court case, the struggles of ship owners to claim the human cargo of a slave-ship, and in which the key moment of birth for American democracy is bound to contestations over the black male body) where the struggles for equal rights under the law are ongoing. My own concern is that the abstracted individual was tied, in fact, to property and, initially, this was fixed property held by men because women could not hold property and were therefore not able to claim full citizenship in relation to voting rights. The extension of voting rights to working-class men related to their property in labour as labour power and although women were also labourers, they were not recognised as such within either state or popular discourses. Thus, it was not until much later that women received voting rights. In Britain this was in 1928 but in Mexico, even with the revolution, it was not until 1957, and the arguments for the disenfranchisement of women were similar throughout the world.

Radical feminists insisted upon the embodiment not only of female and male citizens but that embodiment was tied to male power. The physicality of men was debated and denounced in relation to a radical feminist politics, which forced the issue of male violence towards women centre stage in a series of effective campaigns and produced the refuge movement as places of safety for women who had been subjected to male violence in the home. These are women-only spaces with women workers, and attempt to maintain a secret location. The issues occupied the space in the public imagination and debate that is currently occupied by the issue of child sexual abuse.

The importance afforded to male violence within radical feminist discourses and practices culminated in books like *Femicide: The Politics of Woman Killing,* using material from North America and India. It is a deeply depressing book, and one which incorporates many of the basic tenets of the radical feminist approach to male violence as it developed. This is naked power, aggressive and coercive, expressed in physical violence. Power is embodied in the physicality of men. However, one of the problems of this approach was the way in which it encompassed all men rather than some men; that is, men who are violent – although some radical feminists did, and do, believe that all men benefit from the male violence of a few because they pose a threat to women. Equally, although all men were culpable on this violent coercive version of power, all women were deemed powerless, reproducing the earlier discourses on patriarchal power and their attendant problems. The second problem was the lack of attention to context or spatiality in which acts of violence take place. It was not long before the home became the major area of concern, and the radical feminist insistence on bringing what was deemed to be the private world of the home into the public sphere was of major significance.

The issue of domestic violence came into the public sphere in ways not previously experienced. Campaigns have continued and have secured changes in the law to make rape in marriage subject to the law. Resources were secured for refuges up and down the country and a debate on the relationship between domestic violence and the state, especially in relation to racism, was initiated (Mama, 1989). Police forces made provision for domestic violence units, and feminist groups, especially the Southall Black Sisters, promoted public debates, with an impact in parliament and on the criminal justice system, which eventually secured the release of several women convicted of manslaughter against persistently violent men – Mrs Aluwhalla was the first. More recently, in a development of the principle, the Crown accepted a plea of guilty to manslaughter in the case of Diane Clark who stabbed her husband after 24 years of marriage to a violent man. She was put on probation for 3 years. A spokeswoman for Women's Aid said, 'A woman who has suffered continuous abuse and violence has finally broken down and killed her partner. It is good to see that the judge has shown mercy and understanding for Diane Clark' (*The Guardian*, 11 November 1998). However, it is still the case that we know far too little about these forms of violence, and the ways in which forms of masculinities are implicated in the power relations that promote male violence towards women. Initially, there was no discussion of masculinities, power relations and the place of violence within specific cultural tropes, but this has changed with a growing number of studies of men and masculinities and the forms of knowledge, practices and cultural values attached to aggression and violence among groups of men.

Disrupting woman

The theoretical disruption of the unitary woman of so many feminist discourses was further contested through the politics of the eighties and nineties, when women like Mrs Gandhi and Mrs Thatcher eschewed any notion of powerless women or of sisterhood, demonstrating how bellicose and authoritarian women leaders can be. The emphasis, instead, was on the gains made by women in many societies in terms of employment and earning power and a general shift, especially among younger women, away from feminist discourses. Mrs Thatcher produced a right radicalism, located with the market and the individual, while strengthening state intervention and rupturing the consensus within the British Conservative Party and the notion of the 'one-nation' Tory.

There have been a series of attempts to codify the new mood, from accounts of 'post-feminism' to a recent intervention by Harriet Rubin (1998) in her book *The Princessa*. Rubin turns to Machiavelli and uses her reading of Machiavelli in the cause of women's power. In part, the book is in the traditions of self-help guides to take control over one's life. But, it is interesting because it marks a shift in understanding and presents, in effect, a Foucauldian technology of the self based in Machiavellian accounts of war. Having announced the war, Rubin is clear that the terrain for this war is the field of intimacy and interpersonal relations, from kinship to the corporation. What is required to win the war is a series of strategies and tactics, overwritten with memorable phrases like 'The art of the princessa is to balance the terror of being a woman with the wonder of being a woman'! The strategist plays by her own rules and is 'brilliantly disruptive' while understanding the micro-processes of power. Rubin (1998: 37) notes:

> Power used to mean control over many people, enormous holdings, empires, nations, corporations. The wider your span of control, the greater your power. Today the only power worth having is micropower, the power to act in small, tight, dangerous spaces. Strategy is the art of maneuvering by using nothing more than a gesture or by acting on the merest perception. Armies are often a detriment, full-scale battle plans a nuisance. A princessa realizes that her life is dependent on how her own moves orchestrate others' moves. Strategy is her cure against idiocy.

The second part of this manual for power invokes Gandhi, among others, in relation to tactics that are the producers of results. These range from the use of the body to convey a sense of power to the development of networks and, ultimately, to knowing when to quit. As the author suggests, these tactics are, indeed, a recipe which can be routinised and used in all encounters with colleagues and superiors and in personal relationships. Finally, the subtle weapons that are available involve the body and playing with the fear that all men have of women. Armed with this modern, and somewhat idiosyncratic version of Machiavelli, women can be powerful, not on an adversarial basis or a masculinist basis but in an authentic mode that secures best outcomes for the self and the position of a woman in the world. The book is interesting in the ways that it seeks to offer an alternative to the notion of control through the combination of accounts of power polarised within a therapeutic discourse. It draws upon the Machiavellian notion of the virtuous prince who gains moral superiority but who is willing to be ruthless. This is affirmed within a language of interpersonal relations and tactics, some of which are, indeed, seductions. At its base is the notion that while power is struggle, there is no position of powerlessness, and women are not the victims of the patriarchal story. Rather, the micro-processes of power suggest a much more Foucauldian account of the intrinsic relationship between power and the social. This is somewhat different from the ways in which Machiavelli is being reinvented within management manuals, such as the recent book by McAlpine (1998), which does, nevertheless, emphasise the point that self-interest is not the best source of successful management or thriving capitalism, and that altruism and a concern for the whole, rather than individual trajectories, is crucial to success. The virtuous prince/princessa definitely has a role in corporate culture.

The attention to the micro-processes of power is reproduced in the story of another Princessa, this time the story of Diana, Princess of Wales, the 'Queen of Hearts' whose death unleashed Latin American style mourning in London and elsewhere, with flowers, tears and public emotions that surprised the world. Two recent books, one by Julie Burchill (1999) and another by Beatrix Campbell (1998) have reached similar conclusions, although they followed somewhat different routes in tracking Diana the disruptive.

The life story of Diana, Princess of Wales, demonstrates the ways in which the micro-processes of power can be amplified through the media. Diana was ingénue, victim and superstar during the course of her life, and the turning point was her television interview in which she played the victim of a loveless marriage and the monarchy machine. In all her supposed powerlessness she was more powerful than she had been as the wife of the future monarch, demonstrating the importance of visibility and the confessional mode. 'Diana as victim' actually displayed her powers and, through the medium of television, managed to seduce vast numbers of people. She recreated herself and became an icon against the institutional power of the monarchy and the legitimation of the hereditary principle in Britain, declaring herself the 'Queen of Hearts' which folksy, populist style appealed directly to the televiewing public.

Beatrix Campbell (1998), in part, uses the life of Diana to launch an attack on the monarchy and the hereditary principle in British social life. It is clear that Diana has disrupted the monarchy and fuelled both republican sentiments and their opposite, in so far as her life also fuelled the fairy princess story and generated popular support for a royal. Diana went about her good causes in much the same way that all royals and other sections of the aristocracy do, but her actions were celebrated as populist, in part because she used the media and was credited with the popular touch. Suzanne Moore (*The Guardian*, 22 November 1995) noted:

> She is the new model and she knows in her heart that they cannot be like her…she is a greater threat to republicanism than a hundred debates on the immorality of hereditary privilege would be to the monarchy because the great majority of people have let her into their hearts …romance has let her down so now she wants power, to be not the wife of the king but the mother of the king.

And Suzanne Moore encourages this, 'Go for it Di. Go down screaming'.

For Campbell, the legitimation crisis amplified by the Diana interview, media attention and her death has it roots as much in the patriarchal underpinnings of the monarchy as in the power of the media. Thus, she notes:

> The economic and political power of the monarchy, albeit limited by its form as a constitutional monarchy, cast an authoritarian shadow over society. But it was only the inflammatory sexual politics ignited by Diana's life and death that created the conditions for a great debate about royalism and republicanism.
> (Campbell, 1998: 7)

Diana was disruptive because the monarchy 'changed nothing but its clothes' and could not accommodate a sexualised princess who, given iconic status, actually initially restored the popularity of the monarchy. For Campbell, Diana lived a dialectic '…she was both empowered and endangered' (ibid.: 121). Much of Diana's life was a sexual tragedy in which she sought love and did not find it. Rather, as Campbell suggests, 'Imprisoned in an inhospitable milieu, her body became the bearer of her crisis in which her distress surfaced not as a coherent story but as symptoms which accelerated dangerously when the reality of her marriage was unveiled'. Charles, it transpired, had never loved Diana, and had continued to love Camilla Parker-Bowles. The great romance was a sham and, in part, this was why so many people were sympathetic towards her; they too felt duped, having shared in the fairy story. The public felt her betrayal as their own. This, coupled with the power of the media to present her life and its intimacy to the public, succeeded in making her someone that people felt they knew. The weeping crowds on her death claimed her as kin, and were shocked and moved by her death in ways that did shake the monarchy and has produced a slow mood of reform. But, in other ways, the death of Diana has strengthened the monarchy and the aristocratic heritage of the Spencer family from which she came.

Beatrix Campbell's book is deeply sympathetic to Diana and presents her as victim/heroine of a royal tale, replicating an earlier account of her before her wedding as 'the national dish' served up to save the monarchy. Despite the overt displays of emotions, commentators have suggested alternative ways in which the out-pouring of affection and loss at her death may be interpreted. A dominant view sees the displays as part of the 'sentimentalisation of society' in which a rootless population clutches at the vestiges of connection through a public figure. Diana was an empty signifier into which diverse sections of the population could invest a variety of meanings, aided by the constant media exposure. As a woman, and latterly a divorced woman, she came to signify the times and the place of women within the changing social relations of later twentieth-century Britain. The coming together of the personal and the political in her life and the way she tried to live it evidenced the changing nature of the social and the importance of gender politics and feminisation. Few questioned her wealth or her aristocratic background, making of her a populist princess without ever seeing or exploring the contradictions of this. Neither has there been any discussion of her as a celebration of white, upper class femininity. In death, she was reclaimed as a daughter by the house of Spencer, who have since organised a museum that contains clothes and artefacts from her childhood. Her life and times were public and presented the micro-processes of power in her relationships in relation to the constitutional power of the House of Windsor and, as Campbell suggests, this was a sexual politics that the monarchy could not ignore. But, it was not Diana *per se* but her visibility through the media, used by the Murdoch group in a serious campaign to discredit the monarchy, which proved so compelling. The Diana story raises many of the concerns of a Foucauldian reading of power relations: the relational constitution of power; the importance of discipline and the production of a woman who became a disobedient subject of the state and the monarchy; and the ways in which Diana, as victim and vulnerable woman, was powerful through her visibility. Equally, in terms of an account of performative power, Diana was working precisely in the transgressive modes suggested by Butler's (1990) analysis in which cross-dressing is a subversion. For Diana the cross-dressing was played out in terms of royal and popular and in relation to class.

Foucault and feminism

The impact of Michel Foucault's work reproduced many of the hostile concerns initially expressed by some radical feminists towards the use of Freud's analysis in feminist theory. Many feminists have used the work of both Freud and Lacan, who developed Freud's account of the ways in which gendered identities are formed. This work has been used in relation to literary theory, and endures because, despite the difficulties, there is still no more adequate theorisation of the development of gendered identities located with the social rather than the biological. One of the problems for some critics was the misunderstanding of Freud's work as biologically based. It was simply read too literally, and later feminists have been at pains to dispel this 'innocent' account.

As early as the work of Juliet Mitchell (1974), it was clear that Freud offered a way of engendering social life which still had major relevance, and which was determinedly anti-Eugenicist in the language of his own times. However, the rather blunt criticisms persisted in the dislike of 'male' theorists and in the mistaken idea that Freud presented women as deficient and white males as the norm. This is a highly problematic reading of Freud and one that does not do justice to the impact his analytical insights have had on the development of feminist and later post-modernist theorising of gendered identities. There is plenty of room for critique, discussion and debate, but a wholesale condemnation seems misplaced.

Foucault has met a similar fate – derided as another DWEM (dead white European male) while sympathetically used and developed by some current feminists (Lois McNay, 1992, for example). I fall with the latter theorists in stressing the importance of Foucault's work to the development of both feminist and sociological analysis, but not simply because his work can be endlessly reproduced – it cannot on the whole – but because he shifted our vision of the social, the actor, etc., in ways that other writers had also nudged us towards. Foucault's project, like Marx or Weber, was to understand the rise of the West, and although Marx emphasised the synonymity between capitalism and Western development, Foucault sought other ways in which to understand this, although his earlier work was deeply influenced by the Althusserian reading of Marx. Like Weber, he was interested in the ways in which the scientific project and modes of rationality had become pre-eminent. This is not the point at which to present a précis of Foucault's work but to underline the ways in which Foucault's analysis of power and the body have had a major influence on the way that gender and gender relations are currently understood and debated. Like feminism more generally, Foucault was categorical about the importance of the body as the site for plays of power, from the state to interpersonal relations. Equally, his work on sexualities had major resonances with the importance attached to sexuality by radical feminists, in particular. It is clear from a wide range of work that Foucauldian analysis is enormously useful for understanding the development and reproduction of generic discourses that have a major impact on the lives of women and men. One example of this is the way that Bartky (1988) uses a Foucauldian analysis to discuss anorexia and eating disorders, claiming that forms of femininity are subjected to normalising trends and discourses that celebrate thinness, and locate beauty with the fragile frame and almost androgynous shapes of highly paid models. This aesthetic exercises a powerful discipline on women's bodies, which have constantly to be policed, watched, weighed, creamed, made over – and this is the stuff of women's magazines. It is hardly surprising, therefore, that anorexia should be so much in evidence among young women faced with 'the beauty myth'.

Critics (Ramazanoglu, 1993, for example) have raised a series of very valid questions about Foucault's account of power, and the ways in which it can be useful for the practice of politics. It is not only that Foucault's bodies are neither gendered nor racialised, but that there is no locus of power. Thus, as Ramazanoglu writes: 'While feminists define men's power as repressive and illegitimate, Foucault moved towards a position which defined all power as productive – that is, as producing knowledge rather than repression' (ibid.: 21). This is a very particular reading of Foucault, and some would suggest that in his institutional studies it is clear that forms of governmentality are considered repressive – the whole point of Foucault's critique of the accepted version of incarceration. However, in the same book, another author points to a problem raised in previous accounts (Dews, 1986, for example) in which if the suggestion that power is constitutive of all human relationships 'then power cannot itself be seen as a bad thing' – exactly. This comment returns us to the football model of power from which Foucault was trying to escape. However, there are issues related to the exercise of, and struggle for, power in Foucault's work, which are important to raise, and one of these was raised by Nancy Fraser (1989) and is re-iterated by Grimshaw (1993). The issue is that, for all his analysis of power and societal forms, Foucault does not offer a vision of the future or the means to a vision. This is an interesting criticism because it suggests that all deconstructive work must have an outcome, an alternative vision, rather than it allowing us to a see an infinite range of possibilities, or just better able to assess the modes of surveillance and forms of governmentality with which we currently live. Walzer (1989) in his critique of Foucault's work raises similar problems, and suggests that the writer moved between being a functionalist, imprisoned in a web of surveillance and, on the other hand, being an anarchist – all part of, Walzer suggests (to use the title of his essay) 'the lonely politics of Michel Foucault'.

Thus, it would seem that some feminists are keen to use a mode of analysis that borrows heavily from Foucault, and which helps us to understand better the technologies of the self in play in late modernity in relation to gendered bodies. Other feminists, more inclined to maintain a binary world view, are working with the creative tensions generated by Foucault's work in relation to feminist politics. The account of power sustained by Foucault is subjected to critique by a wide variety of writers, and one common thread to these is the lack of an account of agency within a world of discourses. Although Foucault is famous for having acknowledged that 'where there is power there is resistance', there is little attention in his work to the forms of resistance and their expression in prisons, schools, welfare, etc. However, this does not mean that his analysis does not contain ways in which these forms can be made visible and analysed (see Westwood, 1990, 1991). The problems posed are real problems, but they do come from a series of discourses and political practices that require an object of struggle, and to suggest, as Foucault does, that there is no absolute power or powerlessness creates huge problems for feminist politics. It is also the case that we do want a theoretical and political defence for our abhorrence of male violence and the lack of safety for women. However, this does not preclude an analysis that can give important insights into the ways in which femininities and masculinities are constructed as disciplinary modes in which embodied women have a crucial role in maintaining what radical feminists would call repressive modes. In this sense, then, Foucault's understanding of power as constitutive of the social is crucial for sociological analyses, and provides a point from which embodied and engendered accounts can be written. One of the ways in which this type of analysis has been used is in the growing work around masculinities.

Men and masculinities

Although feminism initially made men problematic, it was a while before attention was turned to the construction of masculinities and the ways in which the plurality of masculinities could be understood. The shift from the privileged category of women to that of gender necessitated the developing theorisation of masculinities and the contributions of Brod (1987), Connell (1987) and Hearn (1987) were seminal in developing a body of work that influenced the growth of studies of men and masculinities. The work of Tolson (1977) was an early and very important attempt to relate masculinity to class and capitalism through the attention to the body as the basis for the generation of wages and through this sources of self-esteem and status. Cockburn's (1983) work looked at this again in relation to skill and issues of equal opportunities. Subsequently, work by Brod (1988) and others also sought ways in which to deconstruct masculinities, and to relate this to the development of a new gender politics. These accounts were influenced deeply by the feminist critiques, and sought ways in which to develop links between the political and the personal. Embodied masculinities were crucial to all these accounts and to the development of an understanding of ethnicised and racialised masculinities. My own attempt to contribute to this work again raised the issue of racism, and sought ways in which to explore diasporic masculinities through an ethnographic study conducted with black and South Asian men in Britain. It took as its starting point the notion of sites; thus, spatiality was crucial to the understanding of masculinities and used the deconstructionist account of de-centred subjects to undermine the stereotypes of black working-class men (Westwood, 1990). Masculinity was understood to be plural and unstable, and the men involved were conceived as having complex and shifting identities that related to cultural repertoires drawn from specific South Asian and African Caribbean backgrounds, which generated difference via kinship, language, cultural norms and practices. But, they also shared the similarities of being working-class black men in diasporic Britain. These are urban men, and the story that was told was of the ways in which masculinities were constructed in urban diasporic spaces, which included the power of the police and modes of surveillance set against the forms of knowledge shared by the men to generate a streetwise identity, which was crucially about being masculine and 'handling yourself'. This re-cast an understanding of being streetwise as an intellectual project rather than located simply in physicality. These aspects of urban diasporic life came together in encounters with the police and also in football, where the display of masculinity and power is bound to notions of honour, pride and romance. Equally, crucial to the theorisation of black masculinities was an understanding of the sites in which masculinities are constructed: the world of the streets and its dangers and the world of the home and its safety. Football in black men's lives was construed as a political space in which racial antagonisms were played out; as a dramatic space in which men could excel; and as a romance in which histories and dreams are part of the game. Theoretically, the paper explored the notion of sites as a way of understanding the relationship between the social and the spatial within the context of the multiplicity of the social and identities. Woven through these descriptions is the issue of power as competition between men and as control over resources, space and time.

In a more recent account, Linda McDowell (1997) discusses City Culture in which the forms of masculinity among predominantly white men from the upper and middle classes, but which also includes working-class men, exercise a powerful hegemony over the culture of the City in to which women have come latterly as employees of major merchant banks. The streets of the City are the trading halls in which masculinist discourses combine in the pursuit of profit in a demonstration of 'street cred' with a great deal more money attached. The performative gender work necessary to negotiate working lives in the City is demonstrable, and it is an issue for both women and men within the specific sites of the City institutions and the bars and gyms as well. The workplace is also sexualised in the language and practices of everyday encounters and financial transactions. The focus of McDowell's study is the way in which women negotiate the sexualised spaces of work – the forms of play, masquerade and parody that are invoked to negotiate a career. This is not, however, simply strategies in relation to women and the work of femininities; it is also important to men and, within the heterosexual world of the City, especially to gay men. For black and Asian men, there is the commonsense racism that casts them, like women, as the others of the male club, with its bonding mechanisms that are structured by the classed, gendered and racialised educational institutions from which recruits to the City emanate. It is not that women, like some Asian and black men, do not have private schooling, but that the rituals and practices are deeply imbued with a white masculinity of a specific class from the colonial era. Women constitute the feminised other of the City front men, imbued with their mission as risk takers and financial wizards, whereas this actually only applies to the minority; it is part of the romance of the City.

The shift in attention towards the deconstruction of masculinities also shows the ways in which the social is gendered, and how gender relations are played out in the variety of sites that constitute the social. As an account, this is at some distance from the early models of patriarchal relations and even the revamped notion of public and private patriarchal forms. However, the work of Connell (1995) has done more than most to attempt to theorise not only a set of institutional relations but the relationship between the social and the psyche, bringing these together in an account which seeks to relate discourses to practices. These are then related to what Connell chooses to call 'hegemonic masculinity', but this remains a highly problematic notion because trying to think about the varieties of masculinities in relation to a consensus around one form invokes ethnicities and class relations to produce, in the British context, a form of working-class masculinity as hegemonic. But, although culturally hegemonic, this masculinity is not invested with the power of upper class white masculinities in relation to the social structure more generally. In fact, the problems may relate to a mis-reading of Gramsci in the attempt to provide an account of a dominant masculinity because at one level, hegemony is always de-centred and not about a once-and-for-all account of culture, masculinity or femininity. There are clearly competing accounts of masculinities from the 'new man', so beloved of the media in the eighties, to the current 'lads and ladism' and the 'street cred' of the Budweiser advertisements for which there seems to be much substantive evidence, probably because lads have never gone away.

In part, these representations of masculinities are organised through media forms and youth cultures that have a high profile in Britain and the USA. The new lads of the nineties are now said to be yesterday's men and an advanced version of the new man is being presented in the media, while magazines that promoted ladism, such as *Loaded*, are still in print and Tony Blair, the current Prime Minister, is accused of ladism. What is especially interesting about the revival of ladism is that it is gendered but can be appropriated, so there are also ladettes who can out-drink and out-swear the boys. This macho/a version of masculinist popular culture is in part a late nineties–millennium hedonism, which is being lived at a time when yet another crisis of masculinity is being organised through the media and the reports of school failure among boys. Coupled with continuing joblessness for men and the rise of women into middle management and through the professions, these phenomena are presented as a crisis of masculinity that requires urgent action by government, schools and employers. It is a very interesting conjuncture, and it returns us, in part, to issues of class and the body, which were discussed 20 years ago by Tolson. What is seen to be unacceptable are the numbers of young men, black and white, who have never worked, and who have a lifestyle sustained by state benefits. A more creative commentary has suggested that it is this lifestyle which has produced Brit pop, artists, writers and designers who are currently sold as 'Hip Britain', and what has occurred is a subsidy for the arts through welfare benefits, which has generated and nurtured a culture without work in the conventional sense. The moral panic being generated, however, sees this not as a creative response but links unemployment among young men to delinquency–crime, drugs and antisocial behaviour.

The current moral panic organised around the delinquency of young males is an old story, but it does demonstrate the ways in which governmentality and the discourses that generate and sustain areas of state intervention are gendered. Sonia Alvarez's pioneering work in relation to the politics of Brazil and the ways in which women enter the discourses of the state and are equally constructed by state powers is one way in which these issues are explored. In part, this returns us to the notion of citizens and Pateman (1998) and Phillips (1991), both of whom explored the gendering of citizenship in Western political theory and practice and in the construction of the citizen who, very often, tied to the wage and wage labour, was seen to be male. The situation shifted dramatically in the early nineties with rising male unemployment and equally rising female employment. Women were often in low pay, casualised work, but not exclusively as a new generation of women graduates have found their place in managerial jobs, as members of parliament and, in increasing numbers, in the professions, such as law, accountancy, psychology and medicine.

The state, aware of these shifts, now plans major restructuring of welfare benefits, and has begun with single parents – the majority of whom are women, while it has re-ordered notions of good parenting and parental responsibilities. The site for much of the remedial work that the Labour Administration intends to initiate is the school–schooling, and disciplinary modes figure strongly in political rhetoric, which has a strong moral agenda – very Foucauldian. The government wants inadequate parents to go back to school, and delinquent youngsters and the unemployed to go on its welfare to work schemes, borrowed from the USA. And, the government does have the means to propel people towards these programmes through its control over benefits and its ability to intervene in family life through the courts.

One major recent example of this in Britain was the introduction of the Child Support Agency (CSA), designed to track errant fathers and move lone mothers off welfare. Since its inception it has been hotly debated, criticised and productive of one of the major encounters between men and the state in the last decade. The work of the CSA was to settle claims for maintenance, and to enforce the payment of sums of money set by the Agency. For the most part, the only fathers it managed to track were those who had already settled economic relations with former wives. Many women refused to cooperate and still do. What it produced was a discourse on the 'feckless father' who would be disciplined and made to provide for his children. This produced from white middle-class men an uproar and a well orchestrated campaign against the Agency and most especially against the designation 'feckless father' (Westwood, 1996). The campaign showed forms of resistance to state intervention by an articulate well organised middle-class lobby who were being, as they saw it, 'trashed' and parted from their salaries. The campaign was very successful, and the CSA has been modified and mollified because most of its attempts to encourage women to cooperate have been unsuccessful, and the number of outstanding claims and backlog of paper work simply grows. The Labour government has revised the procedures, and instituted categories of payment as a way forward but, somehow, everyone seems to agree that it is a failed project. The forms of resistance included street demonstrations, but demonstrations that invoked the emotive but mythical distinction between the public and the private, and the limits of the state in its interventionist mode.

These forms of discipline have been glimpsed before, from the 'schools for mothers' in the twenties, which were actually boycotted by working-class women for whom they were intended as a remedial measure when working-class women stopped going into service and went to the corruptions of the factories. Their resistance will be repeated in all kinds of ways in the coming years of government policies and practices on family and economy. These social policy concerns are matched by the interventions in the health sphere, which bring together conceptions of the natural and the social with powerful generic accounts of these spheres. One sphere exemplifies these concerns and the power relations of the field, and that is the area of new reproductive technologies: the heroic medicine organised around infertility, which involves government policy and private sector medicine.

The personal is political

New reproductive technologies raise issues of power: from the power/knowledge complex of medicine to the disciplinary modes in which moral judgements construct those who will be treated and those who will not to the issue of the power of money and the spatial relations of health services. Articulated with this complex of power relations is the way in which techniques to overcome infertility deconstruct the binary between the natural as the biological and the social – the modes by which intervention in infertility is researched, addressed and administered. The personal becomes the political within the complex of practices and discourses that constitute the field of fertility treatment programmes. A personal desire for a child encounters the public debates and resources of medicine. For some, this is yet another example of the medicalisation of social life and the imperialism of medicine, and its ability to intervene in every area and, ultimately, in the creation of life itself.

Early on in the debates, the treatment was criticised and abhorred by specific religious groups who regarded the intervention of medicine as 'unnatural' and ungodly on the basis that life is god-given. Radical feminists, like Corea, regarded new reproductive technologies as part of the extension of male power over women, to the point of conception in which women's bodies were used for the advance of male science and the careers of male doctors. It is the case that the most eminent among the early practitioners were, and are, men and, that the whole area became a form of heroic medicine, celebrated within discourses that wrote women out of the whole process. The idea, now part of the commonsense, that what were being produced were 'test-tube' babies suggested an abstract process devoid of embodied men and women. *In vitro* fertilisation was simply a process that produced a fertilised egg outside the body, in a Petri dish, and then reinserted the egg into the womb or the fallopian tube. Babies still needed a nurturing womb in which to grow and women to give birth.

Stanworth (1987) presents the techniques as a double-edged sword, offering the hope of parenthood to many, while effectively producing live births in only a small percentage of those taking part in the programmes. Nevertheless, for those who are successful, it is of huge benefit and importance. The treatment is not, however, available to all because very few opportunities exist for treatment on the National Health Service. Rather, it is the world of private medicine that has developed the programmes and is the mainstay of infertility treatment in Britain. More importantly, Stanworth suggests that it is not the treatment, the hormone regimes or the surgery that women undergo, but the way in which the treatment has re-cast infertility, and encouraged the elision of woman with mother as female destiny, which can now be aided by science. On the other hand, however, by deconstructing the divide between biology and the social, it has also reconstructed the notion of motherhood. The state has intervened here in a number of Royal Commissions, which have sought ways in which to define the moral grounds for the use of embryos that can be stored, but only for a prescribed period, and, in line with welfarist discourses, those who can receive treatment – basically, heterosexual couples in long-term stable relationships, preferably married. This has not, however, stopped lesbian women and single women making full use of the services if they have the resources, and most of the clinics regard their philosophy and practice as being non-judgemental. The clinics use the umbrella of medicine as a basis for this. They are interested in the health of the bodies with which they work and not their legal relationship. Thus, new reproductive technologies have provided, for some women, increased options within reproductive politics, which may or may not be realised through the competence and skill of both male and female medical practitioners. Practitioners and clinicians exercise their skills within the power/knowledge complex of medicine and the law, with implications for the ways in which motherhood, fatherhood and ties of kin are understood within the social.

But, there are other ways in which the politics of reproduction and understandings of motherhood as political have been constituted (Westwood and Radcliffe, 1993). The most well known of these come from Latin America, as the Mothers of the Disappeared. In Argentina and other states, women in the seventies, faced with the brutality of the coercive power of the military and the arrest, imprisonment and death of numbers of citizens, turned the rhetoric of the state upon the state. The state claimed to be protecting the citizens and working for the national good to secure family life, while it systematically destroyed civil society and many families. The mothers of those who had disappeared protested as mothers, in full view of the military and the world via the global media, asking for a voice, and claiming their disappeared sons and daughters. They became 'disobedient subjects of the state' turning their powerlessness on the state. Jennifer Schirmer (1993) calls these groups 'motherist', and they formed a powerful new mode of politics. Although there were many groups throughout the Latin American states, the most well known were the Madres of Argentina who secured a cross-class alliance and who mounted a silent protest on a weekly basis in the main square of Buenos Aires. But, despite their protest, the matter of the disappeared, those erased from the national story, remains unresolved, in part, because an amnesty was instituted in 1986, which all but absolved the military.

Women throughout Latin America have sought ways in which to engage in political action, which, during the most repressive periods of military rule and authoritarian populism, has secured the conditions of civil society and maintained the basis for the return to democracy in the eighties. Whether this was in the motherist groups organised by the Roman Catholic Church (Corcoran-Nantes, 1993; Vieira Machado, 1993), which offered a safe space in which to explore issues of daily life, or through their work in trade unions, women fashioned a series of discourses on power relations and their impact on their lives. Women protested in relation to the daily round of reproduction, and fought with the state in order to secure basic material goods for their lives, in terms of clean water, health care and safety.

In El Salvador and Guatemala, women organised to insist on the visibility of the repression, and to overcome the erasure from memory of the many who disappeared and the horrific experiences of the eighties. Schirmer (1993) suggests that this is a form of political motherhood in which the concern for a future generation is translated into political action.

As Schirmer suggests, there is no simple way to understand this form of politics, and Western feminisms do not offer an analytical frame in which to constitute the power relations and 'gendering of consciousness' that is central to the organisation of women in Central America. Instead, there are different questions that are premised on the contestations around mothering and politics, which women in El Salvador and Guatemala have exploited in their attempts to promote human rights and protect women from abuse.

Engendered power

It is clear from this chapter that the subject of engendered power could fill a whole book. Instead, this chapter has sought ways in which to consider the modalities of power, from coercion, repression and constraint and the issue of violence, to strategies and seduction, in relation to the ways in which femininities and masculinities are constructed and analysed within sociological discourses. The feminisation of power has become increasingly visible through the entry of women into the professions and the political realm, but it is important not to read this visibility in innocent ways. Power is relational and constitutes the social in a multiplicity of ways that are often invisible, like the strategies of 'the princessa'. Part of the work of feminist sociology has been to make the forms of power more visible, and to show that these forms are genderic, from state discourses which construct women and men in specific ways through the power/knowledge complex to the forms of coercive power in operation. However, as women's groups in Latin America demonstrated, it is possible to generate and sustain a counter-hegemony by using state rhetoric against the state. In part, these protests were against physical abuse in which sexuality played a key role. The use of rape as a political tool within repressive regimes was countered by a collective voice.

This was the violent combination of military power and sexuality, but sexualised power exists in a variety of forms, and it is to this discussion that I now turn.

5   Sexualised power

In this chapter the discussion moves to the allied but distinctive site of sexualities and the ways in which different modalities of power are allied with and define sexualities. As Foucauldian analysis has shown, sexualities have been constructed and re-constructed within repressive and coercive powers and redeployed within a multiplicity of bio-medical, racialised discourses from the Eugenicists of the turn of the century to, more recently, the socio-biologists. The debates and practices surrounding new reproductive technologies, for example, make explicit the ways in which sexualities are everywhere confined by the powers of moral regimes, codified through the state in legal regulations and subject to medical surveillance. Simultaneously, sexualities are central to a discourse on individuality, freedom, the soul and the mainstay of capitalist seductions to consume. Given all of this, it is hardly surprising that the politics of sexualities and sexualised powers should now be so central to modern states and sociologists alike.

This chapter begins with a discussion of Marxist inspired accounts of sexualities and power, foregrounding forms of seduction. But this discussion also invokes the state and the ways in which, as citizens as well as consumers, sexualities are an important source of political struggle. Both of these concerns offer a view of the social, and the discussion examines the ways in which sexualities and the social have been analysed in sociology, especially in relation to the regulation of sexualities. Consistent with the discussion of power and violence from earlier chapters, the discussion of sexualised power includes an account of violence and of sexual harassment as part of the politics of sexualities and an elaboration of the forms of power in process in relation to sexualities.

Marx, capitalism and seduction

While Marx's analysis of capitalism focused attention upon production relations, his analysis begins with the commodity and the way in which, with the arrival of the commodity and the exchange relations of the market, the relationship between people and things changed. This process had far reaching consequences in that so little opportunity was given to self-expression under capitalist labour relations that people displaced their sense of self on to commodities. Marx used the term 'commodity fetishism' for this process, drawing upon the notion of the fetish that has magical properties or is imbued with spirits. People within capitalism imbue the market and market relations with a sense of reality that masks the unequal conditions of capitalism. Thus, commodities become an expression of self and commodification, as a process, comes to embrace more and more aspects of social life, for example, tourism turns places into commodities, the body becomes commodified and also sexuality. Thus, Marx was acutely aware of the power of consumption but it was Bauman (1992) who elaborated the view that the real power of consumption lies not so much in the fetishisation of commodities but in the ways in which consumption seduces. Despite the inequalities of capitalism, it offers people objects of desire that they believe to be freely chosen. Thus, consumers are not just duped by capitalism, they have an active role in the seduction.

Seen historically to be part of feminine wiles, but elaborated within the folk heroes of Don Juan and Casanova, seduction plays on and with desire and is, as both Marcuse (1968) and Bauman (1992) have made clear, an essential component of capitalism. As Laquer (1992: 185) notes, 'Factories, cities, shops, markets, novels and medical tracts were all themselves engines of desire and not just sites for indulging or writing about it.' Laquer develops this account in an articulated reading of sexualities and the industrial revolution. Capitalism does not have to coerce subjects, it seduces through things and the fetishisation of commodities and objects that are represented as signifiers of innumerable dreams which, via the cash nexus, we can purchase. This was, for Marcuse (1968), characterised as part of a system of 'repressive tolerance' in which the real forms of liberation and freedom, like sexuality, were subjugated under capitalism. Bauman's (1987) work, especially, has emphasised the ways in which consumption has been so crucial to the post-war world and how resistance is re-framed into lifestyles and cultures which can be bought. The problem for capitalism, as the economist Galbraith suggests, is that consumption is not available to all and this creates deep fissures within capitalist societies – the one-third/two-thirds society of the USA or, for Bauman (1998), the one-third/two-thirds worlds which comprise tourists and vagabonds. Bauman provides an ongoing critique in ways that try to puncture the seductions of capitalism. Our desires are constantly recycled, reinvented and even invented in relation to new products, the endless pursuit of the new, which fuses the thrill of invention with the status afforded innovations and newness in most of the world.

Seductions are powerful and suggest the sexualised construction of capitalism – the eros of the market, which is itself a construction around which production and consumption are organised. There is no social without sexualities and power relations. But, romance tries to tell a different story in which the world of the emotions is pre-eminent. Consumption is filled with emotions, from the food choices in the supermarket to the new clothes for a weekend away. Most of these stories are heterosexist in their boy meets girl formula, blighted love, enduring passion and pain, two people thrown together in destiny from different communities or at the opposite ends of the hierarchy. It is a very familiar script and one that seems never to lose its allure, thus its commercial success in films like *Titanic*.

All cultures have romances, they are not a monopoly of the West; the script is a global one.

Latterly, romance is one part of the myriad of ways in which 'sex' became sexuality and part of the modern period as Foucault suggests. Just as sex can never be liberated from power it is an enactment of power and is constituted via discursively constructed sexuality (Butler, 1993). To reiterate my earlier point, such views suggest that bodies are bearers of the inscriptions of sexualities but not the authors. Seductions are thereby the classic enactments of sex/power although the context may be very varied. The seductions of politics and politicians, or workers within organisations, feeding desire and individual power plays, massaging egos and, generally, generating a sense of well being, worth and the feel-good-factor. The feel-good-factor, so beloved of politicians, is a seduction, and a vast industry of advertising, public relations, spin doctors, etc., knowledgeable in the manipulation of signs and symbols are in play, invoking behaviour of a specific kind from large sections of the population who inhabit a world which Baudrillard (1988) called a 'signifying culture', one in which we are assailed by signs and messages. This form of culture has finally destabilised the relationship between the use-value of a commodity and its meanings as developed by advertising and marketing companies. Selling dreams, especially those concerned with sexuality, is the stuff of advertising, expressed graphically in the recent advertisement for the Citroen Xsara Coupé in which Claudia Schiffer, amid Hollywood style grandeur, sheds her clothes because 'the only thing to be seen in is a Citroen Xsara Coupé'. It is a powerful set of images in tune with the history of the confluence of cars and sex, from the Pirelli calendar to the current television advertising campaigns for cars, which all use signs of sexuality, desire and sexual gratification. It is all possible and perfect in the dream scenarios of the advertisers addressed to the male gaze and at a distance from road rage, gridlocks, accidents and breakdowns. The advertisements are slick, stylish and offer men an image of themselves that is expressed through the car that they drive. Market research suggests that the advertisements work well with audiences who can decode them but, nevertheless, enjoy the seduction. Featherstone (1987, 1992), for example, emphasises the ways in which we are educated in the ways of consumer culture and use our reflexivity to negotiate the world of advertising and the hard sell. This, he suggests, is a counter to the notion that we are simply cultural dopes and spend our lives duped by capitalism. Instead, it is through consumption that we express and augment our identities and develop social scripts.

No longer part of the intimate spaces of personal lives, seductions are everywhere the public face of power in which the materiality of seduction is made possible through the spatial and temporal relations of the social. The importance of the visual in the power of seduction is understood by advertising and marketing agencies, shop-owners and shop interior designers. We are hooked on visual signs and the images which are presented as part of the aestheticisation of everyday life in commodity culture, from packaging and branding to the bags that encircle our purchases. But, before we explore more fully the issue of visual power, pursued in Chapter 7, there has been a recent amendment to the attention to the surface and signs of shopping. In a recent book, Daniel Miller, an anthropologist, suggests that shopping is 'an act of love' in which the binds of family and affective ties are secured through the purchase of commodities which are chosen with care and tenderness for loved ones. There is an interesting point here. Miller (1998) suggests that women (and it is mostly women) shop for others and, in so doing, are trying to imagine and act upon the desires of family members, lovers and friends. Thus, shopping becomes a ritual of gift and repair in relation to the constant reconstitution of social lives and the social. It is the crucial emotional work of social reproduction which falls largely to women who in shopping are constituting social worlds rather than just engaging in something trivial or bound to the cash nexus. Instead, shopping engages consumers with a larger world, a transcendental world invoked through the emotional labour of women. Again, this is not lost on advertisers and marketing strategists who make appeals in relation to products directly to women as emotional labourers, and they use a system of signs that can be read in relation to love, care, trust and the reconstitution of social life. Such a view is allied with the notion of the shopping mall as the cathedral of post-modern lives, a space in which, like the airport lounge, the whole drama of life is enacted.

Sexual citizenship

Evans' (1993) construction of sexual citizenship is one attempt to bring scripts, signs and discourses together with a materialist account of the social, drawing on Marxist analysis in which the notion of the citizen is re-visioned beyond formal/ legal criteria and embraced as a discourse of rights which includes sexual minorities. 'However, the sexualisation of modern societies cannot be fully comprehended without attention being given to the material dynamics of late capitalism and their repercussions on the state and the material relations through which populations relate to both' (Evans, 1993: 35).

Thus, Evans is keen to point out that citizens became consumers, and the discourse of rights became bound up with consumer rights, and he quotes from the 1991 Citizen's Charter:

> The modern citizens' prime rights are to have the freedom to make a well-informed choice of high quality commodities and services in public and private sectors, and to be treated with due regard for their 'privacy, dignity, religious and cultural beliefs.
>
> (Evans, 1993: 10)

Citizens are consumers but they are also culturally and religiously distinctive. However, sexual minorities are not part of the matrix of citizenship despite the long political battles that have been fought over sexual freedoms. Thus, despite the politics of gay liberation, the age of consent in Britain was 16 years for heterosexuals and 18 years for homosexuals until December 2000, when the Labour government, using the Special Powers Act, finally overrode the House of Lords, where the change had been consistently blocked. At the same time, the attempt to construct the 'gay consumer' has continued to develop. One of the most recent versions of the commodification of gay identities is the selling of London as the gay capital of Europe in the hope of attracting the 'pink pound'. The emphasis upon consumption which, in particular, makes gay men visible has not had an impact on the inequities of their legal position.

Evans' thesis also ties the development of sexual freedoms for women to the rise of consumerism, which opened up spaces for the intervention by the women's movement and feminist politics. It is in one sense a very crude reiteration of the relationship between the economic level as base in Marxist theory and ideological struggles as superstructures that can be read from this base. Thus, he suggests that while cross-dressing has a long history and now has specific shops, catalogues and clubs which cater for transvestites, transsexuals have considerable difficulties associated with both the legal position and the medical facilities and treatments that are required. Most of the treatment will not be available through the public health system and, for many, more importantly, transsexuals cannot legally re-order their gender identities. Only in Malaysia, after a campaign in which a prominent soap opera star was involved, is it now possible to change a birth certificate. Recently, one transsexual has been very much in the news. This is Dana, an Israeli male to female transsexual singer who has won the Eurovision song contest. She is reviled by many of the orthodox communities in Israel but has been very vocal in her commitment to minority rights, the need for peace with Palestinians and against the racism of Israeli society. Transsexuals are part of the world of entertainment and are commodified in this sphere, but some also work in the sex industry and suffer the same harassment from the legal authorities as other sex workers. In some Latin American states homosexuality is still illegal (Ecuador, for example), and transvestite prostitutes have been shot and physically abused. Just recently, Brazil has passed laws outlawing the presence of sex workers on the streets and in public spaces close to schools, housing areas, etc. These are also issues related to racism whereby a racialised minority is further marginalised through their sexual identities and forms of labour. Less so in Thailand and parts of South East Asia where the 'lady-boys' are part of the culture of pleasure and also, more generally, available sex/gender scripts. Commonsense accounts of gender identities in Thailand stress the existence of a third way against the binary man/woman.

Also in India, the existence of the hijra, with a specific ritual function at births and marriages, points to the recognition of an identity beyond the binary. In northern India the hijra dress in women's clothes and are traditionally performance artists, said from local accounts to be biologically hermaphrodite. However, one of the few studies, by Serena Nanda (1990), discounts this view, and among those she interviewed most had voluntarily joined hijra communities as adolescents. The plight of the hijra was explored, in part as a way of exploring sexual politics in India, in the film *The Square Circle*. In the film, a hijra is thrown out of work after the arrival of female singers, dancers and actresses in the then Bombay film industry and has to seek out a living in the villages of India amid derision and physical abuse. S/he is assisted by a young woman who has been abducted and raped and who assumes the role of a man and seeks to protect the hijra and, through men's work, secure their survival. The film seeks ways in which to explore masculinities and femininities and their malleability.

The power attributed to the hijra relates to their supernatural connections through their renunciation of sexual relations and male sexuality. This, as Nanda comments, is confounded by those who act as prostitutes for homosexual men. The layers of meanings and confusions are born out in the portraits of hijras explored in Nanda's study. As young men, some had been practising homosexuals and had sought sanctuary with the hijra community, whereas others had been gradually absorbed into the community. Those who had husbands also retained their ties with the community, while acknowledging that their relationships with their husbands were the most important.

Although the hijra may be ridiculed and stigmatised, their legal position as citizens is not compromised and, as Nanda suggests, they have managed to secure an economic niche that protects them from the worst vagaries of the market. This is assisted by the social relations between hijras, within a hierarchy which handles disputes and seeks ways in which to maintain the traditional roles of hijras, especially in north Indian villages. The threat of expulsion acts as a compelling form of discipline against antisocial behaviour and the possibility of destitution. The ritual performance of dance and song at weddings and the birth of a child have less saliency than previously, and their attempts to maintain their position as essential is increasingly difficult. However, few who encounter the hijra wish to engage in confrontations with them and would rather offer money to ensure that they move on quickly. Nanda (1990: 51) notes, '…the hijras have used their position as sexually ambiguous persons outside the normal framework of society to manipulate and exploit the cultural norms of proper behaviour to their own advantage.' Thus, in my own experience of the hijra, rather than being shamed by the looks and comments of people around them, they find ways in which to embarrass and shame which are powerful inducements to offer money and receive their blessings. The outsider status of the hijras in their avowedly sexualised identity is one very specific example of sexualised power. People around them fear the hijra because no one knows what they may do and with what consequences. Their potential power lies in the contradiction of their status as a stigmatised group.

Sexual politics

The hijra are one moment in a complex and infinitely variable sexual politics, which has found expression in metropolitan areas through the politics of gay liberation, gay pride and more recent nomenclature such as Queer politics. Located with social movement politics and identity politics, issues of minority rights have been invoked and struggled over in order to secure protection from harassment at work and in the community. In Britain, recent challenges have been mounted to the blatantly discriminatory age of consent at 16 years for heterosexuals and 18 years for homosexuals. This was overturned in a free vote in 1998, but was still opposed by the House of Lords and has now, as I reported, been overturned by the

Labour Government. Equally, gay activists, both lesbian and homosexual, have challenged their position in the British Armed Forces through the European Court of Human Rights. They did not win this time around because of the principle of subsidiarity, which allows member states to invoke specificities, but it is an unfinished story.

The transgressive and performative power of the Gay Pride marches or the Sydney Mardi Gras are, in part, bound to the insistence on the visibility of gay sexual identities and their claims to public space. This visibility is also a key factor in the 'outing' campaigns, which insist upon the public acknowledgment of gay identities. However, these forms of politics have been founded upon a homogenous, unitary 'gay subject', which might be strategic in terms of the politics of social movements but which has been subjected to the same processes of deconstruction as the unitary black subject in the politics of race. Seidman (1995) suggests that part of this shift is explored in the work of Queer theory, which makes the binary heterosexual/homosexual problematic and engages in a different but important form of outing at the cultural and theoretical level. As Seidman (1995: 128) notes:

> Queer theory is less a matter of explaining the repression or expression of a homosexual minority than an analysis of the hetero/homosexual figure as a power/knowledge regime that shapes the reordering of desires, behaviors, and social institutions, and social relations – in a word, the constitution of self and society.

And Seidman (1995: 137) continues, following Butler (1990 and 1993), 'This power/knowledge regime needs to be exposed as social and political; drag or performative disruptions are practical counterparts, as it were, of deconstructive critique. They do not replace the politics of interest but supplement it.'

In an ideal world of differences, sexualities, like identities, are not constrained by the binary of male/female, heterosexual/homosexual but exist in the fluid spaces of the social. However, as Seidman suggests, identities are more than just constraining and regulatory mechanisms. However, Queer theory does expose the heterosexism and bi-polarity of the ways in which the social is thought and theorised and around which gay politics, it is suggested, has been organised. However, the emphasis upon the cultural and the textual raises important issues in relation to how the social will be constituted and the historical understood. Hennessy (1995: 149), commenting on Butler, sees Butler's account of the social as collapsed into the cultural with no account of the specificities of the different sites of the social in which the regime of heterosexuality, as a regime of power, is constituted and reconstituted. As one way in which to sustain the materiality of cultural and social forms, Hennessy addresses the question of visibility in relation to commodification. In an attempt to re-inscribe the material within post-structuralist theorising and political action, she comments:

> ...changing the Bart Simpson logo on a T-shirt to 'Queer Bart' may disrupt

normative conceptions of sexuality that infuse the circulation of commodities in consumer culture, but it offers a very limited view of the social relations commodities rely on and, to this extent, it reinforces their fetishisation.

(Hennessy, 1995: 162)

Hennessy writes against the notion that with the aestheticisation of everyday life, style is all, and, through lifestyle, identities are produced and presented and with this, in Butler's phrase, gender identity becomes a 'style of the flesh', which can be endlessly disrupted through cross-dressing, drag, etc. While acknowledging the importance of style, Hennessy wants, unfashionably, to maintain a place for political economy and the analysis of the structures of capital below the surface of visible signs and performative selves.

The importance of the visual and the politics of visibility are discussed in more detail in Chapter 7. Here, I want to explore one example of the complexity of the visual in relation to gay and lesbian identities, analysed in a recent contribution by Lewis and Rolley (1998).

Lewis and Rolley consider the ways in which women's fashion magazines present forms of visual pleasure enjoyed by both heterosexual and lesbian women, in part, because lesbian themes are represented through the modality of fashion. The authors suggest that rather than, as commonsense suggests, fashion magazines reinforcing the regime of heterosexist desire, they can operate in more subversive ways in relation to female sexuality. This is crucially bound to the images of women presented and the viewing positions of the women readers who can frame the women on view as part of heterosexist desire or who can re-frame the women as the objects of female desire. Thus, women's magazines are more inclusivist than initially appears to be the case. Fashion magazines regularly use cross-dressing alongside images of women that resonate with those in soft porn magazines. The authors conclude (ibid.: 307): 'Lesbian chic and post-modern theory have only highlighted what was already going on: that buying, reading and sharing fashion magazines is for many an indispensable part of being a girl'.

Sexing the social

Within sociology, after the work of Gagnon and Simon (1974), and later Foucault (1980), sexualities have been understood as constructed culturally, historically and socially. As Connell (1995: 386) notes:

Social constructionism has displaced scientific nativism, not as an alternative explanation of exactly the same object, but because it has brought into view a wider object of knowledge...Social constructionism insists that sexuality is historical, and this idea has been scandalous to people who correctly take sexuality to be about bodies, but wrongly assume bodies to be outside history.

However, as Connell goes on to argue 'social constructionism' does not solve the problems of understanding sexualities because it tends to fall back on biology and end up in accounts of discourses. I sympathise with Connell's critique and his insistence upon the importance of representations within the power-filled world of sexualities. Sexualities understood as part of the social are constructed somewhere between the field of representations and the unconscious. For many people, however, sex and sexuality abide in the realm of the natural and of nature, and this construction of sexualities, for that is what it is, has powerful generic resonances. This raises, of course, just the issues with which this book is concerned: the nature of the social and the ways in which sociology has attempted to constitute the social against nature. Sexualities constantly reinvent the binary nature/culture in an attempt to explain and police sexualities. My starting point is Foucault's ironic statement that in the modern era sexualities are constantly invoked in the public sphere while being exploited as a secret. This seems to be the crux of what we are trying to understand in relation to power and the social as lived and invented through sexualities. It is clear that the world of advertising and pop imagery understands this well.

Sociological discourses, however, seek, whether by default or design, to domesticate sexualities and denude power and danger from this sphere of the human imagination, in part, because there has been little attention to fantasy within sociological analysis. How are sexualities to be understood? Theoretically, power relations are important and articulated with the theorisation of sex, gender and embodiment. But, as Stevi Jackson (1996: 15) notes, '...we have yet to find satisfactory ways of conceptualising sexuality as fully social'. In discussing the construction and reproduction of heterosexuality, Jackson brings into focus the difficulties of constructing an account of sexualities that brings discourses and individual desires and practices together. But, her emphasis is upon the power of patriarchal relations as they are expressed in heterosexuality. While recognising the power of heterosexuality as discourse and practice, the reiteration of patriarchal powers does little to advance our understanding because it fixes a form of power and sexuality in ways that are no longer tenable, as evidenced by the discussion in the previous chapter.

More interestingly, Giddens (1991) offers us an account of a 'plastic sexuality' in which the game of sexualities is understood as linked to the realm of consumption as a post-modern freedom and a source of experiment. Desire is crucial to this understanding and one development is to view sexualities within two realms: one sex/erotic and the other sex/gender, which involve both embodiments and forms of fantasy and imagination. Although, as Ken Plummer (1996) reminds us, these are often scripted in particular ways and form part of the 'sexual stories' that are circulated and reinvented. Plummer's work seems to offer a way forward in attempting to relate the world of the imagination to the regulatory world of sexualities as part of a politics of sexualities. What is of interest to Plummer is the issue emphasised by Foucault that the places, spaces and forms in which sexualities are articulated have multiplied and continue to do so. The question for Plummer, which reiterates that of Weeks (1989) and Seidman (1995), is how can a terrain be constructed in which the variety and diversity of sexual stories can be told and lived without one account becoming pre-eminent and reducing other accounts to the margins. This is part of the issue of a radical democratic response and a lived politics which have been so crucial to sexual politics as part of the social movements for radical democracy. However, sexualities are up against the state and forms of governmentality in which the sexual lives of citizens, from reproductive issues to the institutionalisation of heterosexuality, have a long history.

Thus, sexualities, their definitions, regulations and the debates within specific areas become crucial for illuminating both the nature of powers in social formations and the construction of the social. For example, entry into the social as the body politic and as adults is regulated through the notion of the age of consent, which separates childhood from adulthood, and legitimate from illicit sexualities. Similarly, the debates on prostitution and its regulation and the anxieties over the de-regulated internet, with its myriad of sites related to sexualities, speak of the ways in which sexuality is a crucial site for the management of populations and the generation of disciplined subjects. Equally, it is also important to understand the ways in which, in societies of the metropolitan core especially, but not exclusively, privileged categories of heterosexuality and the regulation of reproduction are racialised. The sexualities with which sociology has been concerned have most usually been 'white' in an unexamined naturalised way. In fact, I would argue more forcefully that while the social constructionist accounts of sexualities in sociology displaced the nativist, commonsense, naturalistic accounts, the new commonsense erased the issue of racialised sexualities so crucial to the history of the West, and normalised the white world, displacing difference to mean only hetero- versus homosexualities. I see this, in part, as the outcome of the importance of feminist discourses for the study of sexualities and especially those of the earlier radical feminist accounts.

Regulating sexualities

Foucault's thesis on sexuality demolished the commonsense account that there had been a period in which sexualities had not been repressed before the development of Victorian repressions. Instead, he suggested that sexuality had been constantly reinvented through the ways in which it was framed. Thus, the notion that Freud had liberated sexuality from repression through the confessional mode was disputed by Foucault who saw Freud more as the analyst who had reorganised and codified previous accounts of sexuality. However, Foucault borrowed from Freud the notion that sexualities are multiple, and that the counter to the power relations within which sexualities are thought of and described is the reassertion of the power of bodies and pleasure within an economy of desires.

Foucault emphasised the ways in which, over time, sexualities have been drawn into the increasing regulatory powers of the state. As we have already discussed in the section on 'sexual citizenship', this process also generates a variety of political struggles between citizens and the state. While this is most clearly demonstrated in relation to the construction of homosexual identities, it also relates to the debates on the age of consent and the ways in which juridico-medical discourses formed a potent part of welfarist accounts of the citizen. The state invoked its powers in relation to reproduction, and this was often related to conceptions of the nation and the health of the nation because biology, blood and legitimacy were crucial components of the national culture. These elements are explored in Stepan's (1991) account *The Hour of Eugenics* in relation to Argentina, Mexico and Brazil, where Eugenicist practices were racially specific in countries trying to generate nationhood from hybridity. Like the Eugenicists in Europe and the USA, the appeal of Lamarckian ideas related to the appeal of science and the rationalisation of reproduction. In the UK, with its powerful class discourses and at the height of Empire, this was another way of ordering the world racially and in terms of class against a religious account of the miracle of birth and the rising pressure of democratic politics. For the moralists, Eugenicist notions allied sexuality exclusively with reproduction and dangerous desire could be domesticated. This was part of a backdrop in which legislation sought ways to order the sexual selves of subjects in tandem with the power of medicine. Laws against homosexuality, which still exist in countries like Ecuador, emphasise procreative, heterosexual sex as normal, thereby disenfranchising the variety of sexual preferences. Laws against homosexuality, as gay rights campaigners in Latin America make clear, contravene the notion of the free citizen and, more generally, human rights.

The forms of power invoked in relation to state regulation are part of a wider governmentality within a legal, rational framework that constructs normal sexuality and defines the realm of the sexual. It is one of the many attempts to demarcate the sexual and thereby domesticate and confine sexual behaviour. This is mirrored in the laws relating to prostitution in many countries, whereby the space of prostitution is confined and sex workers are not protected by the law but harassed, penalised and fined or imprisoned. The forms of power invoked here are coercive and repressive. Individuals are 'up against the state' as citizens either for their sexual behaviour or because they sell sexual services. Despite the panoply of laws and police powers in relation to these forms of sexual behaviour, sexualities still elude the law. Neither homosexuality nor prostitution has been annihilated by the legal process and what has become clear is that the law and criminalisation are very blunt instruments in relation to the regulation of sexualities.

The law has also proved deeply contradictory in relation to constructions of male and female sexualities. Although the laws surrounding rape emphasise penetration and construct the perpetrator as male and the victim as female, until recently, little attention was given to men and boys as victims of male rape. This relates to the account of male sexuality as active and ever-present in relation to heterosexual desire, while it is denied in relation to homosexual desire. The invocation of legal means to curb sexualities and set up the binary licit/illicit suggests that the fiction of sexuality as private and personal is constantly exposed. In so far as sexualities have been policed, proscribed, defined and fought over, sexuality has been, since its naming, part of the social. What is clear is that we cannot think of sexualities outside the social and, like so many other facets of modern life, sexualities deconstruct the binary private and public – although in the politics of sexualities this fiction may be invoked.

Similarly, sexualities cannot be thought of or analysed outside power relations. The very language in which the governance of sexualities is expressed seeks ways in which to separate coercion and consent. The notion of consenting adults appropriates the Foucauldian 'knowing subject' but it is then tied to context and to age as biology, which would appear to push sexuality back to nature. Consensual sex signals adult status in opposition to childhood in which sexuality is erased. Clearly, these conceptions are related to the modern development of childhood which sexually ceases at 16 years of age for heterosexuals and for homosexuals. Lesbians do not enter the public discourses of sexuality. Sexual relations with young adults below these ages is a criminal offence and has most recently been the focus of considerable anxiety and public debate.

Denuding children of sexuality contra Freud has generated a current moral panic around paedophilia, which is unprecedented. Not surprisingly, what has shocked the public imagination is its practice within schools and children's homes and by carers, teachers and priests. It would seem very naive to suppose that those sexually attracted to children would not seek jobs that offered maximum opportunities for the abuse of power relations between children and adults and the rupture of trust in settings organised around trust relations. While these have been very public events promoting campaigns like 'Megan's Law' in the USA, these should not detract from the home as the major setting for sexual abuse. Both boys and girls have been abused by both women and men, although men figure more prominently. The concern expressed has led to a flurry of accounting practices concerned with child sexual abuse – registers in hospitals and in social work for children at risk, and the call for convicted sex offenders to be registered and local communities to be informed if such a person moves into the area: one of the demands of Megan's Law and now policy in some US states. These measures are intended to curtail, constrain and, in part, shame the offender into normalisation. But, the theory, such as there is any theory, seems to be woefully lacking, and it brings us back to the problems associated with theorising sexualities and the theorisation of violence. There are very few facilities that provide 'treatment regimes' for sex offenders. The complexities associated with the punishment and treatment of sex offenders revolve around the very issues that are too often ignored in discourses on sexuality and which relate to fantasy, the space between representations and the unconscious that are part of the social. In fact, this is discussed in relation to the arguments concerning pornography, which suggest not only that the objectification of women's (it is usually women's) bodies is unacceptable, but that pornographic images contribute to the processes of otherisation in which women, and/or children, are reduced to things and can, therefore, be the objects of aggression and violence, usually perpetrated by men. The debates here fill volumes, and the suggestion that there is a direct causal relationship seems weak but the larger issue, which involves male fantasies about women, often specific women, does form part of the picture of male violence towards women.

Sex and violence

Sex and violence form a powerful couplet (as so many movies attest), but this couplet is not free-floating and the forms of power involved relate to the context. Interpersonal forms of sexually related violence can move from rape to consensual forms of sadomasochism and the levels of confusion around the latter seem to be constantly hitting the headlines. The idea that pain and pleasure can be experienced simultaneously is certainly understood within the pornographic film industry and has been expressed in literature, most famously in the work of de Sade. The notion from the legal framework surrounding sexual acts turns on consent and adulthood, but this has been overridden in the celebrated case of the Cambridge professionals prosecuted for sadomasochistic sexual acts. The counter to these acts being a matter for the law was the issue of privacy and of consensual sex in which the state had no role in policing such events. Much of public opinion concurred with this view, whereas the gay community was outraged by the infringement of personal liberties. The background to these cases suggests that what was invoked here were power plays, games for adults in which there were clearly expressed rules – a discursive space that was constructed within a rule-bounded frame. Just like any other game, infringe the rules and the yellow card comes up, followed by the red card and you are out of the game. Or, as Bauman (1996: 32) writes, 'To make sure that no game leaves lasting consequences, the player must remember...that this is but a game'.

Sex and violence, however, are not confined to the world of artifice in which power is negotiated through the rules of the game, and domination and submission are played out in very stereotypical forms. Instead, sex and violence come together in the crudest forms of coercion, terror and torture – often through the act of rape in times of war and communal strife. The violence involved invariably has both generic and racialised elements, although the modality for the articulation of both may be religious or cultural. What is said to be at issue are nations and identities located with mythical blood and land ties. Women, it is suggested, symbolise the honour of the opposition and defiling women is one part of war. Similar encounters occur within nation-states, between the colonisers and the colonised, and with the brutal collapse of a hegemonic account of the nation as occurred with the break up of Yugoslavia and the descent into a series of murderous wars. Similarly, at the time of partition in 1947 between India and Pakistan, the Indian state intervened to recover women and children abducted or defiled and restore them to their 'homelands'. The women were treated as a question of national honour and as daughters of the nation – evidenced by the lack of interest in their children (Das, 1996; Menon and Bhasin, 1996).

Women have not been alone in suffering physical violence and coercion in relation to national honour or community pride. The most public and infamous cases of lynching in the Southern states of the USA and across the colonial world were reserved for black men who were used as a symbol of the distance between black and white and constructed as a threat to the symbolic universe of the white order, while white male colonialists raped black women. This was a politics not of desire but of conquest. It is reproduced in the encounters between the poor and the police in states around the world where the threat of rape, castration and humiliation is part of the armoury of military and police torture, and its threat hangs over all encounters. It is correctly understood to be an abuse of power. Abusive, coercive and terrifying, these acts and their perpetrators could be seen as aberrant moments but, sadly, these are not beyond the social but form part of the intricate web of power relations that constitute the social. Are these acts the limits of the social? In so far as consensus is constantly invoked in relation to sexual acts, then maybe. But, the problem is that the script is available and readily seized with each new conflict whether within nation-states or at the borders of these 'homelands'.

The emphasis upon war and inter-ethnic 'communal' strife should not, however, divert us from the ways in which sex and violence are racialised in more routine ways and with the assistance of public discourses emanating from the state. One example of this, in which legal–rational powers were articulated with the commonsense racism of the time, can be seen in Guy's (1991) study of Jews in Argentina at the turn of the century. Anti-Semitism (which was later fuelled by Peron and the safe haven given to Nazi war criminals) was used to place Jews and prostitution in the same discourse, and to produce a threat to the nation, morally and socially, via the alien presence and its racketeering. The discourses mirror many of those surrounding black men and prostitution in Britain today, and place otherness and sexuality side by side as Jewishness or blackness. This constitutes a violence fuelled by racism, which seeks to police the other via shaming and reinforcing the outsider quality of the Jewish man or the black man (Gilman, 1991).

Thus far, it would appear that sexualised power is marked by violence, coercion and constraint, organised through a rational–legal framework around the notion of consent (Jamieson, 1996) in which heterosexuality is privileged. I have also suggested that many of the forms of sexualised violence are also racialised and generated through the processes of otherisation. Racialisation also forms a part of the eroticisation of power, often associated with charismatic forms of power and the political realm, the symbols of which can be seen in the military style presence of leaders more often related to masculinity than femininity. However, Mrs Thatcher managed to elicit this response with a handbag! The idea that Mrs Thatcher could be an object of eroticised power suggests the sexualised nature of power itself. But, it is never power without context or framing which, rather than circulating as part of the play of powers, comes to rest in a specific site. The office of the president is distinguished from its embodiment in which power is seen to reside and is thereby eroticised. The erotic signals desire, and it is desire that the regulatory mechanisms associated with sexuality seeks to police. Laws regarding sexual relations, with whom they are appropriate etc., seek ways in which to demarcate and contain the sexual, and separate the sexual from other forms of social life. The problem for all social formations is, that despite the panoply of laws, sexuality is everywhere, like power, it is part of the air we breathe and the texture of everyday life. But the law and politics seek ways in which to name and constrain and to provide norms of behaviour appropriate to the workplace or the college.

Sexual harassment

Lovers in lifts, trysts in the car park and office romances are the essence of soap operas and Mills and Boon novels and latterly of legal actions, usually (although not exclusively as the movie *Indecent Exposure* demonstrated) between men in positions of power and women. Recently, the eroticisation of power and the issue of sexual harassment have become entwined in the person of the US President and the comically named 'Zippergate' scandal. The President survived, battered but unbowed.

Sexual harassment, once named, has turned the routine banter of office culture into a legal battlefield. One of the most recent cases has been within the law itself – a recorder found guilty of sexually harassing a pupil by the Bar Council. Mr Sutton-Mattocks has since voluntarily resigned from the bench and has suspended legal work (*The Guardian*, 25 February 1998, 3 March 1998). Routine banter 'with the girls' was considered by men to be part of the fun of office life. For women, it is distressing and disruptive, ignoring their professional competence, reducing them to an embodied and objectified sexually available woman. Age is also often a factor in these encounters with older men in positions of authority and power who direct unwanted attentions to younger women (as in the case cited above). But, this is not simply a story of women as victims of their vulnerability in relation to men. Rather, the organisational framework, the hierarchies of our working lives place women in positions of vulnerability.

Hearn's (1987) work on sex/gender relations in organisations was underpinned by an account of patriarchal relations, whereas accounts from Cockburn (1983, 1991) explored masculinities in relation to an account of embodied masculinities, both among the printers and later within hierarchical organisations. These accounts concentrated on gender relations, whereas recent work has sought ways in which to understand sexualised workplaces and the market in labour (Adkins and Lury, 1996; McDowell, 1997; Witz *et al.,* 1996). As Witz *et al.* (1996: 175) comment:

> Once we see bureaucracies as embodied systems of social relations the articulation of gender and sexuality becomes clearer. Both gender and sexuality are inscribed on, marked by and lived through the body. Indeed, it is because real jobs and real workers are embodied that workplace interactions are infused by both gender and sexuality.

This is one way in which sexualities in the workplace may be understood, but it is a reductionist account in which the body and biology provide the ultimate explanation, and that is problematic. The body as signifier, the role of fantasy in social relations and the modes of representation are equally important in relation to the sexualised encounters of the workplace. The embodied account suggests instead that sexualities are carried, imported into workplaces, but it is not quite like that. Expectations, narratives around sexuality and work form part of the social that is infused with sexualities. Only if we begin to understand the power of signification can we begin to unpack workplace encounters. Adkins and Lury (1996) suggest that it is women who have to work on their gendered and sexual identities in relation to the labour market and the workplace in very self-conscious ways as part of the ways in which gendered identities are forged. But, I would argue that this account makes the binary between men and women too simple, and does not take account of the fact that gendered identities are constituted in difference. According to Adkins and Lury, women are doing all the work and men are out of the picture – far from it. It is precisely because work is gendered and sexualised and men are in the frame that it is possible for gendered identities to be produced, reproduced and articulated.

Trying to theorise sexualities, whether in the workplace or the home, and produce an account of the 'sexualised social' taxes sociological discourses, in part, because of the refusal to move beyond the structure–action dichotomy. The dichotomy is displaced to the organisation and the body, thereby reproducing the same problems with a different set of names. The plasticity of sex, to which Giddens (1991) refers, and his theorisation of structuration is one part of an attempt to overcome this. Butler's (1990, 1993) emphasis on performativity and subversion is another. The Foucauldian accounts of governance and an understanding of racism and sexism as regimes of power are more helpful in fine-tuning our analyses of the sexualised organisational forms that are the modern world. The idea that it is the arrival of male and female bodies is an empiricist account that sustains only a very partial understanding of the social milieu within which we live and work.

Sexualised power

In our attempt to elaborate the forms of sexualised power, we need to make use of conceptions of masquerade and transgressions as modes of resistance and refusal within a sexualised, gendered fabric of social life, which is organised around 'compulsory heterosexuality'. The performance of sexed and gendered selves is, however, bound to specific contexts and contingencies as part of the plasticity of sex.

Seductions name the processes of power and link the unconscious to the world of representations and of goods as part of the subtleties of modern societies. It is a mode of address that is linked to the rise of individualism and technologies of the self to the point of narcissism. The diffuse quality of the myriad of seductions with which we are involved on a daily basis suggest that it is the form in which the sexualised social is normalised against the coercive and violent powers of rape, harassment and sexual abuse. The emphasis upon the latter has forced sex and sexuality into the public sphere in unprecedented ways in which the moralisms of the nineteenth century are reproduced and anxieties concerning children, adults and their relationships are expressed. Thus Dyrberg (1997: 116) notes, '...Foucault's power analytics is better suited to deal with the growing contextualisation of power, and the widening of the field of the political, than the agency models of power and politics, such as behaviourism/pluralism'. This has been explored in this chapter in relation to sexual citizenship and sexual politics as one moment in the 'widening of the field of the political'. But, I have also suggested that sexualities are as much a part of the world of consumption and the seductions of capitalism as they are social movement politics. This brings us to the next site, the spatial, and the final chapter, the visual, both of which are important to our understandings of sexualised powers.

6 Spatial power

The theorisation of spatiality and its importance in social theory has become a major preoccupation within sociology and the new geography of late, often producing tautological accounts of the social, the spatial and power-filled imaginaries (Lefebvre, 1974, 1991; Soja, 1989, 1996; Massey, 1994, 1995: *passim*). In this chapter, I want to examine the forms of power most relevant to the spatial ordering of the world. These include the importance of nation-states and control of territory, which leads to a discussion of the politics of space and the ways in which people both produce and defend their own localities. Thus, spatial powers are not external to our lives but part of our everyday worlds and the ways in which we imagine them, in the home, at work and in the neighbourhood.

Giddens recognised early the importance of time/space in sociological theory and the absence of discussions, commenting:

> The fact that the concept of social structure ordinarily applied in the social sciences – as like the anatomy of a body or the girders of a building – has been so pervaded by spatial imagery, may be another reason, together with the fear of lapsing into geographical determinism, why the importance of space itself has rarely been sufficiently emphasised in social theory.
>
> (Giddens, 1979: 102)

Latterly, the obverse appears to be the case and sociology, taking off from Foucault and the geographers, has buried urban sociology in favour of a spatially aware account of the social and the cityscape.

As Harvey (1996: 210–12) suggests, space and time are certainly social constructs with different societies and communities living within different space/time frames which, for example, order the world of the convent or the farm. But, this is the beginning of the story rather than the end. Harvey attempts a clarification of simplistic accounts of space/time suggesting that as social constructs time/space has a materiality born of human endeavour. But, time/space also relies upon metaphor and imagination for its construction and also that these cultural constructions work as 'facts', taken-for-granted knowledge around which and within which lives are ordered. Finally, following Bourdieu (1977), he suggests that these 'taken-for-granted' ways of understanding time/space 'are implicated in processes of social reproduction' (ibid.: 212). The suggestion from Harvey's account is of embodied spaces in which there is a constant interaction between people and spaces, creating and reproducing social space. However, Pile and Thrift (1995: 7) note: 'What is clear is that the body, understood as a biological unity, has undergone significant spatial augmentation', and they cite the use of new technologies as an extension of the body, and the use of surgical skills to manipulate and change the body. The emphasis for Pile and Thrift, and their contributors, is on the individual, the self, the subject in spatial/social discourses, but we are often more impressed by the power of new technologies to shrink both time and space and to sustain and create social relations in novel ways. The internet and mobile phones have become part of the everyday lives of many people throughout the world, and both have an impact on our spatial understanding. In this chapter I want to suggest some of the ways in which an elaboration of spatial powers can be understood.

Nations, territories and borders: landscapes of power

In terms of the development of the modern world and the globalisation of capital, there is one form that exemplifies the coincidence of the geographical imaginary with spatial power and that is the rise of nations and nation-states. This is not the point at which to rehearse a long and growing literature on nations and nation-states. However, one writer, Benedict Anderson has had a major impact on the ways in which we have come to understand the rise of nations and nationalism. Anderson (1991) located the rise of nation-states with the development of capitalism and the modern world in Europe. He emphasised both the importance of print medium and the rise of the intellectual as mechanisms for the imagination and diffusion of the idea of the nation. Anderson's work has been very important because he shifted the emphasis from the institutional mechanisms of the state that underpinned the idea of the nation to the ways in which nations are imagined as a community of people with common bonds. The development of the imaginary of the nation is bound crucially to the idea of land and a shared history and, although Anderson's work concentrated on the development of nations in Europe, it is clearly the case that peoples throughout the world have fought for their own space in the world, referring to this place as a homeland. The Palestinians and the Kurds are still involved in struggles to secure a homeland and define themselves as a nation. Thus, one criticism of Anderson's work is that the emphasis upon the literary and its relevance for Europe ignores the histories and aspirations of peoples throughout the world (Radcliffe and Westwood, 1996). Anderson, too, has revised his notion of the imagined community of the nation because his initial account has now been updated by a chapter on mapping and maps, and the ways in which maps become potent symbols of nations and are turned into logos that stand in and represent the nation (Anderson, 1991: 175). This brings together spatiality as territory with the complex class and power relations of nation-states because it is states rather than nations that mark out territory and seek to guard against incursions with the organised assistance of the military. Throughout the world, this has given the military a privileged position to might and the threat of violence.

Geography, territory and issues of borders have preoccupied geographers, most especially one of the founders of modern geography, Ratzel. His work has been subject to considerable scrutiny, for example Giddens (1985) and more recently Hepple (1992). Both Giddens and Hepple are concerned with territory and the notions of borders and frontiers in relation to the rise and sustenance of states. Ratzel, while adhering to an organic notion of the state, was interesting because he suggested that it was borders that were crucial to the integrity of states. But, as Giddens (1985: 51) suggests, 'Borders are nothing other than lines drawn to demarcate states' sovereignty', rather than those which coincide with topographical features like rivers or mountains, which are often viewed as natural borders. Demarcated borders and territory are not natural but political and therefore generated and sustained by power relations. Thus, Hepple (1992: 136) notes, 'Geopolitical discourse, and the organic metaphor, have been very influential in the military academies and in military thought about the state'. Hepple's concern is with the military and the states of Latin America and the ways in which 'organicism' and geography have produced an account of the state and the nation in which territory and mapping come to represent the nation. Even with the liberalisation of the eighties, 'Territorial issues, both of economic development and international tensions, are politically important in the South American states, as are legitimate questions of military security' (Hepple, 1992: 153). However, these issues may have taken a more internal turn within the newly democratised states as part of the general 'management of populations'. I want to use the case of the nation-state of Ecuador as a way of exploring the ongoing articulation between internal questions of security and the externalities of border claims and disputes. Ecuador is a small nation with a population of over 10 million and a territory which is smaller than neighbouring Peru or Colombia.

The power of mapping and cartography in relation to the military is spatially expressed in Ecuador in the historical role of the military and the development of the *Instituto Geográfica Militar*, perched high on a hill overlooking the capital city, Quito, with a panoptic view of the region. Within the Institute every *casa* and field is mapped; some maps are secret and the issue of security is paramount. The military interest in geography is expressed in the school curriculum and basic text books, which give a vital role to the geographical understanding of Ecuador as a nation (Radcliffe and Westwood, 1996). This cartographical power is central to the nation-ness of Ecuador and is called up in the ongoing border disputes and minor wars that are fought between Ecuador and Peru over the 'protocol line'. This was drawn in 1942 and gave to Peru a part of Amazonia that Ecuador has never accepted. This is clear in the maps of Ecuador, which still include this land and show the protocol line through it. Peru provides the 'other' of Ecuadorian nationhood and is constantly invoked as the threat on the border, requiring constant vigilance, a military presence and defence against incursions, which seem to happen with almost routine frequency. Coupled with the military concern for borders is the internal relations of the state, the need for order and integration, articulated through a populism emphasising shared values and aspirations. This produces a military in which there is an expressed concern for the integration of all sections of the population. The military in Ecuador was also one of the first to engage in human rights training and has promoted development projects especially in the Amazonian region. The vision of itself that the military promotes is of a modernising force, incorruptible and at the service of the nation. This was forcefully expressed in the deposition of President Bucaram in 1997 and again in 1998 when the military stood back from direct intervention, or in relation to indigenous rights when the military negotiated between landowners and the leaders of the indigenous organisation CONAIE (Confederation of Indigenous Nationalities of Ecuador). In an alliance with CONAIE the military was involved in the most recent overthrow of President Mahuad in January 2000, which also involved the USA and the designation of Ecuador as a dollar economy.

The military in Ecuador is also a key player in economic development with its own bank and factories for the supply of boots and kit and farms for the supply of food. The military and the nation are one and the same, shown in the naming of the military football team – *Nacional*. While the Ecuadorian military look to the territorial integrity of the state against the external aggression of Peru, neighbouring Colombia spends a third (if not more) of the national budget on counter-insurgency, trying to centre the nation against the guerilla struggles that have been for so long a part of Colombia's history. In both cases, mapping and geographical imaginations allied with military might are central to the spatial relations of the nation-state, and it is through the constant surveillance of space that forms of geographic governance are secured. For example, the border between Ecuador and Peru is heavily militarised, and tracts of land have been annexed by the military in the name of security within a region that is also of crucial economic importance because of oil. Local people resent the annexation of land and the levels of surveillance that the military bring despite the army's attempts to engage in development work in local villages and thereby integrate the Amazonian populations into the modern nation. There are important reasons for these attempts. The Shuar, an Amazonian people, started the first federation of indigenous peoples, which was a forerunner to CONAIE, and they have a major role in mobilising Amazonian peoples against the state in relation to oil explorations and counter-claims for land.

More recently, territorial claims and the spatial relations of the nation-state have to vie with global capital and trans-national corporations. This has prompted a contradictory account of the national interest in which, in Ecuador, the attempt by politicians to privatise the basic infrastructure of electricity, water, etc. met with fierce opposition from unions in these industries but also from the military, who opposed privatisation on the basis of strategic concerns and invoked the national interest in relation to basic resources that were located with the geography of the country (Westwood, 2000). Similar attempts have been made in relation to the rise of global media networks and their impact across territory and within nation-states.

The power of the global economy, especially finance capital and media flows, is no respecter of territorial claims and borders. These capital flows, futures markets and media products are not bound to the terrestrial and therefore have powerful impacts upon conceptions of nations and states as bound to geography. As Appadurai (1996) suggests, it is no longer the externalities of nations but the internal struggles that tend to implosion, in part, through the processes that are central to modern states. 'In its preoccupation with the control, classification and surveillance of its subjects, the nation-state has often created, revitalised or fractured ethnic identities that were previously fluid, negotiable or nascent' (ibid.: 162). However, it is also important to recognise that the power of nation-states may be changing, but claims that the era of nations is now over have only to consider the plight of refugees or asylum seekers who are facing borders and claims to territorial integrity in more and more forceful ways.

Refugees and migrants are part of the growing numbers of people on the move, generating diasporic populations with complex identifications and loyalties. This is, in part, the consequence of earlier global phenomena, such as colonial domination, which organised the flow of goods and workers in a previous era. What is now apparent is that there is no less mobility of labour between rich and poor countries, but that the metropolitan core has become de-centred in ways that generate a global world that is 'multicentric'.

A multicentric world requires a new geographical vision away from the old binaries East/West, North/South, First/Third. It is now clear that these designations, which organised an imaginary geopolitical map of the world, have become imbricated one with another. Consequently, wherever we look and travel there is a so-called First and Third World, wealth and poverty, within and across the territorial borders of nation-states and mega-cities. Equally, in relation to ethnicities and national identities, it is clear that the myriad of diasporas have fractured the imaginary of a homogeneous, stable national identity allowing, instead, for multiplicity, hyphenated identities and more. It is out of these myriad of identities that the current politics of nations is generated, and this often invokes counter-claims against the geography of governance that organises the nation-state.

Consequently within the nation-state of India there are counter-claims to territory linked to a discourse of self-determination from Kashmir, Punjab, Assam and the South, matched by the nationist claims within Sri Lanka from the Tamils. Throughout the world, the territorial claims allied with nation-building ideologies that forge national and geographical identities are contested. Tracing the histories of these contestations, it is possible to see why this should be so in relation to Palestine and Israel, for example; here land deemed to belong to one group was annexed to another; or in the case of Kashmir, where a population shares historical, cultural, linguistic and religious ties with Pakistan but was allocated to India by the local prince on the basis of his relations with the British.

Land is constituted as territory historically within specific political moments, through plunder as with colonialism and empire and then through the liberation struggles that succeed through force in securing a counter-claim. This is the basis of many of the new states and the history of earlier struggles, especially in Latin America. While Ecuador continues to fight wars on its border with Peru and make international claims to land, there is another power struggle ongoing in Ecuador in which land rather than territory is the key, but in which territorialisations form part of a complex politics of identities in which place is crucial.

Following the repression and military regimes of the seventies, Latin American states were in the process of transformation through the return to democracy in the eighties and into the nineties. In tandem, this has generated new forms of organisation and the politics of liberalisation in relation to the economy. Consequent upon the restoration of democratic regimes, there has opened up a new space of politics that was previously kept alive in subterranean ways. The return of civil society, which in some countries is still fragile, has opened up contestations around national identities and forms of democracy itself, in an era in which the play of politics between the military, politicians and the trade unions has taken new turns. One example of the new actors of politics and the formation of collective subjects in the political arena is the work of the CONAIE.

CONAIE developed from the Amazonian Shuar federation and grew in strength throughout the eighties, stepping into the limelight in 1990 and 1992 with nationwide marches on the capital, Quito, and the politicians in 'The Uprising' that signalled a new and very strong voice in Ecuadorian politics. The demonstrations brought the capital to a standstill and insisted on talks over land, status, bi-lingual education and the constitution, calling up Ecuador's claims to be a *Pais Amazonica*, symbolically represented by an indigenous person. CONAIE, as I have noted, has intervened in national politics throughout the nineties and into the new century as a major force in Ecuadorian politics (Westwood, 2000). It is noteworthy that CONAIE sought to generate a collective political subject from the diversity of indigenous groups in Ecuador and to have trans-national links with indigenous groups, especially in the Andean region. The diversity in terms of histories, cultures, linguistic groupings is enormous, but the terrain on which CONAIE sought to fight was both material and symbolic. Despite the differences, especially between Amazonian and Andean indigenous groups who found themselves sharing a nation-state rather than a language or customs, the issues that brought diversity together were twofold: one was, and is, land and land rights and claims, whether in the Andes or Amazonia, against the powerful haciendas of the highlands or the multi-national oil companies and the incursions of the army in Amazonia. The second issue was citizenship and how indigenous peoples were represented in the constitution, in the assembly, how people were to be schooled and in which language. CONAIE demanded and secured bi-lingualism in education, but the language was Quechua, which is an Andean language familiar across the Andean region despite the varieties of dialects and state borders. The incursion into multi-culturalism did not last long, and did not survive the Borja government and the arrival of President Bucaram who, like some of his predecessors, had little sympathy for a self-conscious, state-sponsored multi-culturalism.

The issue of land, however, could not simply be withdrawn and, using the military as the major broker, CONAIE secured land rights for indigenous peoples. At this time, there was a class action by groups in Amazonia, supported by a group of New York lawyers, against the oil company Texaco. The Ecuadorian government certainly wished to defuse the situation, but the military settlements in Amazonia were essential for security reasons, especially close to the Peruvian border. Indigenous peoples in Amazonia had set up a series of projects related to the mapping of the land in order to secure their land rights. This populist form of cartography very often involved local people walking their way around the terrain and mapping it, tree by tree or stream by stream. This exercise in populist geography brought together the material and the symbolic in defence of local interests (Radcliffe and Westwood: 1996). Indigenous peoples claim ancestral rights to land that they have fished, farmed and nurtured for generations. Land is imbricated in the claims to indigenous identities, and these rights cannot be separated from the politics of identities. It is, in part, a claim for authenticity that the organisation re-framed within the legalistic language of the modern state. In this sense, it demonstrates a geography of resistance in which space, place and spatiality are not simply the terrain of struggle but its very heart. Well organised and politically conscious, these groups allied their land claims to an account of the nation and its revisioning within a pluralism that would give credibility to all ethnic groups in Ecuador and sustain a pluralistic identity for all citizens. Thus, this was no single issue social movement but one in which radical democracy (Laclau and Mouffe, 1985) and a polyvalent agenda are much more akin to what we understand as post-modern politics (Westwood, 1998). This brings together a clear trans-national concern with a refocused nationalism in which the nation-state and its nation-building story is both deconstructed and reconstructed to bring all sections of the population into the story but not in terms of hybridity, which is the official ideology of *mestizaje*. Rather, it is the opposite, with an emphasis upon difference in which commonalities are not taken for granted or assumed on the basis of a shared territory, but are seen to be constructed, envisioned and fought over within democratic forms.

The politics of space

Geographies of resistance and the politics of space at the national level, as exemplified in the case of CONAIE, is also a crucial part of the relationship between citizens and locality. Recently, in England, the politics of place has been forced on to the national agenda through the work of the Countryside Lobby: a loose confederation of rural groups, orchestrated by the National Union of Farmers, who have brought the rural to London in huge demonstrations involving farmers, rural dwellers and sympathisers in an effort to secure rural livelihoods and more resources for rural areas. The demonstrators sought ways in which to make city dwellers aware of rural poverty and the exploitative relations between city and countryside by riding tractors and threatening a rural revolt.

Recent ethnographic work on urban spaces has concentrated on the ways in which locale has become a primary identifier in worlds that appear more shifting than ever, giving rise to the couplet global/local or 'glocal'. The geographies of resistance, generated at the local level, are very often a response to geographies of exclusion that prompt the sense of territory associated particularly with young men and masculinities organised in the defence of space against other groups of young men. In the cities of Britain, the USA and elsewhere, these encounters are more often racialised and a response to racism in its broader sense. The politics of space then becomes bound to the encounter between groups of young men, white, Black, Hispanic and Asian, in ways that can be violent. Recent work by Barnor Hesse (1997) uses the notion of territorialisations to theorise racial harassment in urban Britain, and earlier work by Phil Cohen (1988) emphasised the ways in which racial tensions produce a 'nationalism of the neighbourhood' that is organised around territory.

The account of a black youth project in a provincial city in England, which was introduced in Chapter 2 and which will form part of the discussion in subsequent sections of this chapter, demonstrates the politics of the space and the territorialisations of inner city black youth. What is especially interesting about the *Red Star Story* (Westwood, 1991) is the ways in which a political struggle between the local state and a black youth group moved from resource politics, when the project was threatened with closure, to a symbolic politics conducted through the Labour party, a terrain in which the demands of young black men were articulated with the sense of citizenship that they felt was denied. The complexities of the political twists and turns suggest that the forms of exclusion and invisibility of young black men were crucial to the forms of organising against the closure of the project and through the local Labour Party. This was a politics of the streets in which a collective subject of politics was called forth from an ethnically diverse population but who, nevertheless, could be called forth through an appeal to 'youth' and to masculinity, which was organised around a series of successful football teams in which the struggle against racism was a key factor. The inner city area in which these struggles took place is heavily policed, and one of the important contradictions of young black men's lives is the ways in which, for the police, young black men are highly visible, made visible through the policing and technologies of surveillance, which technologically define the social space of the inner city and those within it, very often, as dangerous. Yet, in terms of the politics of exclusion, it is this very group who see themselves as invisible and excluded from job opportunities and having a voice and their concerns articulated within political agendas. It is not surprising, therefore, that the local, 'our turf, our yard', assumes maximum importance and becomes a territory that must be defended against the incursions of the police or outsiders, including rival groups and gangs. These encounters are racialised through and through, from the agendas of political parties as an absence to the violence of street encounters. The recognition of racialised urban spaces is part of the governmentality of the city in which state powers attempt to discipline these spaces against the subversions of the locals. The spatial and the social are one and the same for both the subversives and those who seek to discipline the ungovernable of the inner city. Instead, policing and ever more sophisticated modes of surveillance, from the helicopters overhead to the cctv in the local housing blocks, encounter disobedient subjects of the state in a constant battle to be recognised as citizens.

This suggests the ways in which spatial powers are imbricated in the domain of the social and this has been explored, often graphically, in recent work on cities. Mike Davis's (1990, 1998) accounts of Los Angeles with its 'aggressive grass', high-tech surveillance and sense of doom are the most well known of these accounts. What is also important is the ways in which the technology is both generated and sustained by a series of discourses on risk and safety in modern societies. As Bauman (1987) makes clear, the old risks to life and limb have been largely eradicated, but instead of this generating a sense of well being the opposite has occurred. Instead, sections of the population demonise other sections, fear of crime and violence has risen and spaces of the urban landscape come to represent and symbolise these fears, especially the inner city. It would seem that economic developments have brought an unprecedented sense of insecurity whether in the streets or the shopping malls, the car parks or social security offices. The response has been more modes of surveillance in which cameras at strategic points present a kind of de-centred panoptican for the new century. This, coupled with the growth in bureaucratic forms of surveillance, suggests an attempt to mirror the disciplined spaces of institutional forms like the prison, the school and the workplace, generating Foucauldian networks of surveillance that are not neutral, technologically filled spaces and places, but part of the diffusion of powers as constituting the social.

Spatiality

The insistence upon the indivisibility of the spatial and the social is one of the primary tasks in Lefebvre's classic work *La Production de l'espace* (1974) and is reiterated by Soja (1996: 71) in what he terms a 'trialectic' Spatiality, Historicality, Sociality as being always, already present. Soja wishes to counter the notion of spatiality as a context or an environment, a container in which history and social life occur. On the contrary, spatiality is central to any ontological sense of living in the world and to a complex array of identities that have too often been understood in relation to a spatial metaphor of centre/periphery. This binary collapses in relation to the level of de-centring in the global economy and globalised societies. Nevertheless, as the previous argument has suggested, there is a sense of place that relates to inclusion and exclusion, and that is represented in ways that 'otherise' places and spaces of resistance – like the inner city, which comes to represent disobedient subjects and an outsiders world, although the language in which it is framed is 'inner'. One consequence of the growing levels of technological surveillance in modern societies is the visibility of social life through the spatial ordering of the world. Soja (1996) invokes the philosopher Heidegger (1977) and his notion of *Dasein* (literal translation 'to be there') and Sartre's notion *être-la* ('to be there'), both understood as 'being-in-the-world', as ways in which the spatial, historical and social come together as one. There are also alternative ways in which this might be understood once we place visibility more centrally. The point about visibility, whether in relation to racism or alternative forms of exclusion, is that social/spatial is made one and the same through visibility. This, however, creates a conundrum for our central concern with power, the social and the spatial, because it might begin to look as though the trialectics of spatiality/sociality/power can only be understood through empiricist eyes, that is, as phenomena that can be seen. The difficulty is, of course, that in trying to understand power and its exercise, it is only in specific moments that we can see the exercise of power. An immigration official refuses entry to a visitor; a young man beats another young man; a teacher says no to a student and so on; these are all examples of the very transparent power relations of social life, but this is not the totality of power relations and the modalities of power as constituting the social. It has, however, become part of the commonsense in which surveillance and the rise of security technologies are seen to stand in for the social/spatial relations that these forms represent. What is missing from this understanding is power, and yet it is these technologies, as part of the power relations of social formations, that allows them to be seen as standing for the social. Visibility is not a function of cctv cameras but exists with greater power within the bureaucratic procedures of administration within the state. At the same time a Foucauldian analysis of racism, for example, emphasises the visibility of 'the other' and the ways in which processes of racialisation and otherisation use cultural and embodied signifiers to stand in for the diversity and complexities of peoples. The resonances with accounts of social life based on what we can see are clear. These accounts can produce 'social facts' related to observation, but this is a very partial understanding of the processes of the social and at odds with an analysis that emphasises fluidity and the complex articulations between subjects and social life.

It is these subjects and their subjectivities that have become the focus of debate in relation to identities and place, producing much of the new geography with its emphasis upon 'mapping the subject' to take the title of the collection edited by Pile and Thrift (1995). Both the recent volumes by Castells (1997) (*The Power of Identity*) and Harvey (1996) (*Justice, Nature and the Geography of Difference*) try to develop the debates concerning the relationship between subjectivities and place identities. Such debates face the same difficulties as those within cultural studies and sociology in so far as they address the key question for social sciences – the relationship between subjectivities and the social. In our book, *Remaking the Nation,* Sarah Radcliffe and I tried to address this though the use of two terms, 'geographies of identities', '…defined as the senses of belonging and subjectivities which are constituted in and which in turn act to constitute different spaces and social sites', and 'correlative imaginaries', which '…generate and sustain an ideational horizontal integration with a shared space, through a form of interpellation which correlates subjectivities and social spaces' (Radcliffe and Westwood, 1996: 27–28). In short hand, the first of these definitions emphasises the emotional links between self and place, and the second emphasises the imaginative ways in which individuals are able to place themselves in a frame, very often alongside people with whom they are sharing a common experience, such as a sense of the nation in a sporting event or through a televisual community watching a new broadcast. In their own ways, both these definitions emphasise the confluence of space and the social and the role of the imagined in the construction of identities.

However, these are not just labels giving saliency to place or the imaginary; they are part of the processes of placing and naming referred to by Harvey (1996: 264) in the following manner: 'The power to individuate within a given spatiotemporal frame is associated with the power to name; and naming is a form of power over people and things'. Examples of this have been discussed previously in this book but, in terms of place, the issue can be restated. The renaming of places within the post-colonial world has been a key symbolic indicator of the end of colonial ties and the celebration of national figures. The colonial era ignored indigenous languages and cultures and proceeded to name the world and places within the world in the image of the home country, embellishing this by the style of architecture and the gardens and parks that were built. The 'geographies of exclusion' that marked apartheid and the colonial era, with spaces designated for whites and which displayed signs such as 'whites only', demonstrated the power of naming and the importance of boundary maintenance. As Sibley (1995: 43) notes, 'Moral panics bring boundaries into focus by accentuating the differences between the agitated guardians of mainstream values and excluded others.' For example, those of the 'purified' suburbs, as Sennett (1970) calls them, who feel the threat of the outsider who, more often than not, is a racialised other. Designations like inner city, upmarket and gentrification re-position areas in relation to the economic concerns of estate agents, the policing concerns of the state and the administrative regimes.

There is no doubt that the places in which people live have a very deep impact upon their identities, but they are also placed by the locality in which they live. Council estate tenants complain that they are marked by the reputation of an area and they are not wrong. Finance companies and insurance firms use postcodes and zip codes to designate risk in relation to debt or insurance claims. The materiality of place in terms of resources and access to resources is well known – middle-class people move in order to secure good schooling in a different catchment area. However, one has to be careful in claiming too much for place identifications and constructing a romance in relation to geographies about which people are very strategic. It is hard to feel a sense of belonging on an estate where you do not even feel safe, and where the street life is dominated by groups of aggressive young men. However, people may come to the defence of locality in ongoing struggles for resources, to protect extant resources or secure greater resources. This happens throughout the world on a daily basis. For example, women in the poor areas of Quito, Ecuador, organising to secure a medical centre, protecting the water supply, trying, in effect, to create an environment in which they want to live rather than exist. These power struggles do build a coalescence between place and identity because it has been a process, one in which locality has been produced through social action.

The politics of belonging

The Red Star story demonstrates just such a strategic engagement with place, in a period when struggles against the local state and struggles against racism were allied, and produced specific identities re-formed within post-colonial Britain. The emphasis was locality and the resources that were available to young black and Asian men in the area. These young men are a diasporic generation who have grown up in the cities of Britain and who had to struggle through poor schooling, racial violence and finding a space for themselves. Their relationship with white Britain is ambivalent, and they sought to assert their right to be in the city, to be citizens and to have resources. But more so, it was a symbolic struggle about the sense of belonging that they claimed within Britain, and it was focused on their knowledge of the local area and their struggles against the incursions of gangs from outside. They won many of these battles and a younger generation, born and brought up in urban Britain, do not have to ask the same questions about belonging. This has also produced a different response to the struggles of Red Star in which a younger generation impressed by education and money and anxious for social mobility out of the inner city identify much less with an inner city project and a collective sense of belonging. The attempt to generate a collective subject for political action is much more fraught, and marks the shift in political culture that Britain has experienced in the last 20 years. This seems to suggest the saliency of a comment from Appadurai (1996: 179), 'But locality is an inherently fragile social achievement. Even in the most intimate, spatially confined, geographically isolated situations, locality must be maintained carefully against various odds.' In his essay, Appadurai addresses the sometimes glib accounts of the local and the global and the suggestion that with the globalisation of consumption, media forms and forms of labour there is a flattening out of local diversity. Instead, he suggests:

> The many displaced, deterritorialized, and transient populations that constitute today's ethnoscapes are engaged in the construction of locality, as a structure of feeling, often in the face of erosion, dispersal and implosion of neighbourhoods as coherent social formations. This disjuncture between neighbourhoods as social formations and locality as a property of social life is not without historical precedent, given that long-distance trade, forced migrations and political exits are very widespread in the historical record.
>
> (Appadurai, 1996: 199)

The disjunctures as Stuart Hall commented have 'made migrants of us all' but this does not mean we exist outside cultures and histories although we are often in transit between them and in the process of the production of locality, as Appadurai suggests. What this means for the importance of place is that it too, is in production. Bauman (1998) provides a critical account of the unfolding global order in which he characterises the world as divided between 'tourists', those who travel between places but always within the same hotel and airport ambience, and 'vagabonds', the poor and displaced. It would appear from much of the cultural studies' literature on our now global identities and shifting lives that this is mobility without any costs, whereas everything that film, literature and those who are part of the diasporas seek to tell us is that the psychic costs of being global, mobile and metropolitan are high. Perhaps this is also why the romance of belonging to place, or person, or both, has such high saliency and generates the huge investments that it does. These investments are part of the production of 'communities' and localities through which subjects sustain a sense of belonging. Importantly, these very productions are part of the politics of belonging which stake claims by specific populations within the public sphere – for land, schools, space for temples and mosques, which change the landscape forever and help to sustain the ethnoscapes of modern urban areas. In these, the trialectic of spatiality/sociality/historicity, to return to Soja (1996), is merged and conjoined through the power relations that play such a central part in the ways in which people stake claims to belonging.

One important example of these claims to belonging is the expression of a sense of place through architecture and its subversion by local people. This can be seen in the cities of the USA where the increasing presence of Latino/a peoples has produced bi-lingual cities such as Miami and Los Angeles. Corona Park in Queens, New York, is transformed into the site for the celebration of Colombia Independence Day. This does not go uncontested, but the cities are changing in response to the Latin presence. Sciorra (1996) suggests that the Puerto Rican population of New York have reclaimed parts of the South Bronx and have built, on derelict land, the kind of small houses, *casita,* reminiscent of the island of Puerto Rico. When a fire destroyed this area, people in the locality came together to rebuild the houses. The remaking of housing, just like the dance halls and Friday night celebrations, is part of a remembering that is active, not simply a nostalgic response but an attempt to make a home in a new landscape. Similarly, Flores (1997) explores the ways in which Puerto Rican and African American young people share rap and graffiti, dance forms and social space in New York, which promotes a 'growing together' out of which comes a sense of 'AmeRican' and, in relation to New York, 'Nuyoricans' as new trans-national identities. The account of New York does suggest the fluidity and malleability of ethnic/national identities in the city and the importance of the spatial in producing cultural identities.

In south central Los Angeles, there have been a number of violent encounters between young men from black and Latino gangs fighting for control of the locality. However, the gangs succeeded in calling a truce in relation to a common enemy, the Los Angeles Police Department, the LAPD, and the graffiti announced: 'Crips, Bloods, Mexicans. Together. Forever. Tonite' with LAPD crossed out and '187' written underneath. Ambivalence marks many of these encounters and coalitions are often fragile.

In a very different space in Texas, migrants have sought ways in which to forge a sense of belonging in the unpromising borderlands of the Rio Grande through the formation of *colonias.* These are a form of self-help housing known throughout Latin America, often the consequence of land invasions, which are then recognised and services developed. In Texas alone, some 400,000 people are living in these settlements without services, although they have legal titles to the land unless they default on the mortgage. These are areas way beyond the city boundaries that provide an answer to the housing needs of migrant workers. However, the state of Texas is not impressed by this form of self-help, and has pathologised the inhabitants and learned to use the term 'colonias' in a derogatory manner. But, Ward (1999) suggests that other poor sections in Texas are also looking at these developments, seeing an improvement on trailer parks and a possible way forward. Ward and his colleagues have been involved in a state-sponsored study encouraging Texas to learn from Mexico. This is another example of the ongoing mirror dance between the two Americas and the co-extensiveness of two spatially distinctive nations moving beyond the boundaries to create a new social space.

Spatial power

As Massey (1995: 284) has written, 'One of the most powerful ways in which social space can be conceptualised is as constituted out of social relations, social interactions, and for that reason, always and everywhere an expression and a medium of power.' This expresses the concerns of this chapter and uses the insights from earlier writers on the productive quality of social life in relation to spatiality. The structures of feeling, so crucial to Raymond Williams (1921–1988) and latter-day theorists of the cityscape, are also evident in what Williams calls 'militant particularism', which generates a commitment to locale and marks, Williams (1983) suggests, the socialist agenda, especially in the UK where regionalisms gave a specific turn to the forms of socialist discourses that developed.

Williams used the term 'structures of feeling' as a way of addressing the emotional commitment that people have to ideas and to places, but he wanted to suggest that such emotions could also be organised in specific ways. This is most evident in relation to national sentiments in which citizens are offered an account of the nation, such as Englishness and what it means to be English, which is mythical and invented but nevertheless can be used to produce an emotional investment. Similarly, Williams was ever mindful of the regional cultures that fractured the working class and gave rise to specifically nuanced versions of class cultures, whereas socialism made an appeal to a simpler version of a unitary working class. The notion is a useful counter to the cosmopolitan concerns of many social theorists who, perhaps, understand too little about the ways in which the dreams of belonging are bound to forms of 'militant particularism'. However, this is not to endorse, as Williams would certainly not have done, a negative version of 'militant particularism', which can generate a xenophobic, inward looking and static worldview opposed to change and the democratisation of social and political life.

Massey's assertion that place/space equals the social/power also relies upon the complexities of all these forms. In my understanding of the social as de-centred and fractured, there can be no simple equation between social/power/space, but a more textured account of the different spaces of power in which the forms of power are variable. Thus, the panoptican gaze of the prison is also backed by coercion, the threat of violence and the institutionalisation of routine in which both space and time are ordered for subjects defined as 'inmates'. Although the coercive power of the police and the military may be very visible in some states and on the streets of cities, the task of policing and maintaining public order is more diffuse, and also relies upon the moral codes and the modes of discipline within citizens. However, as I have suggested, urban spaces are contested terrain in which the administrative power of the local state meets the collective aspirations of citizens for resources, change and ways in which to name localities as their own. Many of these contestations are racialised within diasporic cities around the world, as we have seen in the examples discussed in this chapter. Equally, the ways in which religious identities play a role has often been underestimated. More conventionally, it is possible to see the power of diasporic spaces as areas of consumption for the middle classes, especially in Britain, as another twist to the tale in which the middle classes have fled from the inner cities to the suburbs, only to return at weekends for curry and shopping! There is, perhaps, more to this than just consumption. It is now official that curry is the national dish in Britain and that some of the old forms of racism and ethnocentrism which set up the binary 'them' and 'us' have been eroded in favour of multi-ethnic accounts of the urban world, which is enjoyed in its diversity rather than feared. This may be part of the specific form of power discussed in the last chapter – seduction which coexists with the ongoing forms of exclusion which are resisted. It is out of these varieties of powers that identities are formed, especially in relation to the urban world as coalescence and collision. This reinforces the view I have expressed elsewhere (Westwood, 1997: 6), '...the city is many cities and that place–positionality has an important impact on the ways in which subjects understand, negotiate and live in cities.'

The seductions of place are high on the agenda of marketing organisations that 'place-market' cities and countries around the world. Much of this relates to the world of the tourist whether it is London as the gay capital of the world or Ibiza as the clubbers' capital of Europe. Cities, countries, areas of the world are re-packaged in relation to dreams of escape, rurality, pleasure, etc., and the power of these seductions is evidenced in the growing profits from tourism. Sold through brochures, brand creation, image management, at the core of these activities are the slogans and visual imagery that recreate countries and peoples within the tourist gaze. It is to the power of the visual that we now turn in a discussion that seeks to understand the myriad of ways in which the visual is a site of power.

7   Visual power

The culture of vision is a central element in the development of modernity and the 'rise of the West', debated and analysed by philosophers before and after Plato. Thus, Foucault was by no means the first thinker to ponder the relationship between vision and power, vision and knowledge. Discourses on vision and thought, reason and seeing are the basic ingredients of a history of Western philosophy and the subject of crucial debates on the nature of knowledge and truth. It is not surprising, therefore, that a book on power should close with a chapter on visual power. Visual power can be totalitarian, coercive and authorial, maintaining a hegemony through cultural forms of the visual alongside modes of surveillance. The crucial link between vision and power/knowledge constitutes science and technology and the ways in which these modes of understanding and exploring the world organise our lives. Equally, visual power uses seduction, the pleasures of seeing as part of the world of consumption, and the visual and the visionary are used as counter-hegemonic forms of resistance. So much of the work of social movement politics is about gaining visibility for an issue, for protest, being visible in relation to the national and international agenda.

The visual and the spatial are often interwoven, and this can be seen in the main exercise of power through the processes of mapping. Cartography provides a visual representation of land mass and topographical features, overlain by the political boundaries that were the subject of the previous chapter, to the point that the map of a nation-state becomes a logo for the political terrain it represents. The issue of representation is taken up by Soja (1996: 66–8) in his re-reading of Lefebvre's work in which he suggests that there is a distinction to be drawn between 'representations of space' and 'spaces of representation'. The first of these is used by planners and administrators as part of the panoply of powers within capitalist states that demarcate a socio-economic spatiality, a tool in relation to the management of populations. However, the power of 'representations of space' is, in Lefebvre's view, subordinate to the 'spaces of representation' which incorporate the imagined and the symbolic, 'sometimes coded, sometimes not'. This is the world of art and of signs, of the interpretative power of subjects to read their spatial worlds in metaphors and visual imagery and to displace this on to practices of everyday life, global politics and the world of economics. Soja suggests that it is this radically open space that corresponds to his understanding of Third Space.

It is this world of signs and symbols, which constitutes the visual power discussed in this chapter, that I want to suggest presents a 'semiotics of power' that is so diffused through social formations that it forms part of the commonsense of our everyday lives. I begin the discussion by returning to the nation, which formed an important part of the discussion on spatial power in the previous chapter. This is followed by a discussion of religious imagery and the role of miracles as a powerful element in the visual economy of religions. But, the most commonplace forms of visual power are to be found in the world of consumption and television. These forms are not, however, the only visual images available to us. There is a world of art that has an important contribution to make to our understanding of visual power. The chapter closes with a discussion of the visual and the social. Initially, however, we return to the world of the nation, which sustains a multitude of visual symbols as part of the ways in which we imagine the nation.

Visible nations

The previous chapter alerted us to the spatial power of the nation, and this is articulated with the nation as the purveyor of visual images and signs essential to the production of an imagined community of the nation. Visual images can invoke the power of the military and the importance of a shared history and are part of the way in which the centring project of the nation and the national gaze is offered to all subjects/citizens through flags, ceremonies and football teams. In Britain, for example, royalty have figured strongly in the ceremonial aspects of the nation, whereas in the USA and Latin American countries, presidential ceremonies and the daily practice of saluting the flag in schools are visual reminders of the community of the nation. All these visual moments appear to 'stand in' for the nation and have the power to effect an identification and emotional bonds that Anderson (1991) has called 'political love'. National moments, like national monuments, are also critical points in the definition of the social as synonymous with the national and against 'the other'. This normalised social, which coalesces with the nation, is racialised and organised around the fictive ethnicities that are the basis of national identities. However, these are often contradictory phenomena, especially in the nation-states of Latin America where the attempt to normalise hybridity and *mestizaje* has coexisted with the reinvention of indigenous histories.

This is clear in the case of Ecuador, discussed in the previous chapter, with its contested borders and multi-ethnic population, some part of which has been politically active in changing the account of nationhood through an assault on land tenure and the constitution. During research on national identities in Ecuador, (Radcliffe and Westwood, 1996), one of the ways in which the idea of the nation was explored was through the use of symbols such as the flag and the map. These were shown to people, and it was clear that all the interviewees across the country could identify these easily. But the use of the visual to construct the imaginary of the nation and provide points of recognition did not end with the flag and the map. People were also asked to name an image, place or thing that represented the nation and this elicited a far wider range of responses, suggesting the variety of relations with the nation. Indeed, the same would be true if we had asked people in England or different parts of the USA. Texans, for example, would offer a very different response from those living in New York. In Ecuador, peoples at the coast might suggest bananas (a national export) or the famous Galapagos islands, whereas people in the Andes suggested Cotopaxi, a snow-capped volcano, and those near the Equator line outside Quito, the Equator. Geographical features were the most common with a commentary on the beauty of the country and its location at the Equatorial line. Similarly, people were also asked about the most beautiful and least beautiful place in Ecuador and while the mountains figured strongly in accounts of the most beautiful, rural peoples and those in Amazonia chose their own locations as the most beautiful, again demonstrating the importance of locale discussed in the last chapter. The answers to these questions are one way that locale is represented and becomes a space of representation. More interesting still was the way in which the elite populations considered Esmeraldas, the town with the largest concentration of black people in Ecuador, to be the worst place in Ecuador.

This racialised response was consistent with the racism against the black population who were simultaneously made visible and invisible within the imaginary of the nation. Some sections of the middle classes in the cities, especially in Quito, when asked to produce an ethnic map of Ecuador over-estimated the indigenous population and often excluded the black population from their account. This erasure is a measure of the importance of visual power. When the black population did re-emerge in the account of the nation and the social of Ecuador it was as people living in the worst place in the country, according to the urban middle-class women and men of Quito, the capital city. The ethnic mapping exercise was an important part of the attempt to understand how the nation is constructed and visualised by nationals in a nation-state in which ethnic statistics are not collected in the census, a deliberate policy in line with the official account of the nation as hybrid/*mestizo/a*. It is an injunction reproduced throughout Latin America. Instead, the military, the most redolent symbol of the nation throughout Latin America, and Ecuador is no exception, is organised around the importance of inclusion and has special programmes for indigenous and African descent Ecuadorians. As a way of reinforcing this, the military football team takes the name *Nacional* and black players dominate the team. It was, in part, some of the black footballers who figured in black people's accounts of who represents the nation. Their responses to this question were a counter to the racial amnesia of sections of the middle class when asked about the ethnic map of Ecuador. While these twists and turns within the national fabric foreground the importance of positionality and racialised identities as a counter to the fictive ethnicity of the national story, the reinvention of the indigenous past was part of the claims to autonomy and cultural authenticity.

It would interesting to produce a similar exercise on ethnic mapping and how the nation is visualised in Britain and the USA, where ethnic statistics are collected and make visible the ethnic diversity of both countries.

Ecuador underscores the flag and the anthem with the words *Pais Amazonica* and the nation is often visually represented through the image of an indigenous woman – this too is repeated throughout the Andean region. However, the contradiction between words and pictures is underlined because the indigenous woman is most likely to be a woman of the Highlands, not a woman from Amazonia and, at one level, not substantively from either, but an image constructed from an account of a past that may or may not have existed. The figure is one part of the myth-making of the nation which, during the research, was being reinvented with the assistance of television in relation to a revisionist history of glorious relics and civilisations to match Mexico or Peru and which would constitute a specifically Ecuadorian history. This, of course, is to read the modern national project back in time but to represent it visually.

The power of the visual in relation to the constitution of the nation is explored by Deborah Poole (1997) in relation to Peru. Here, there was an attempt by key intellectuals of the nineteenth century and early twentieth century to constitute Peru, and especially the capital city Lima, as the height of sophistication. As Poole's work suggests, the ways in which different sections of the population were incorporated into the visual representation of the nation is instructive. At the time, one key figure, Fuentes, produced an account of Lima as the centre of the nation and, in his attempt to present the population as sophisticates, he marginalised the indigenous and black populations, suggesting that somehow these were pre-modern elements or geographically irrelevant. More importantly, however, the taste and decorum of Lima is represented through a series of photographs of bourgeois white women. Fuentes draws attention to their whiteness as a counter to other sections of the population. Fuentes was writing for a European audience using a discourse that was familiar and which drew upon biological and scientific accounts, bringing these together with the new powers of photography, much as criminology or anthropology were also doing at the time. Thus, Poole (1997: 166) notes:

> For Fuentes, however, race was not a quantitative discourse of heredity and blood but, rather, a qualitative calculus of taste and distinction. By mapping Peru's races onto the statistician's bell curve, Fuentes drew on contemporary aesthetic discourse in which 'beauty' was defined as a state of harmony or balance – a middle range of values, tones and angles in which extremes did not exist.

The burgeoning bourgeois world of Europe would certainly have recognised these sensibilities, and the point for Fuentes was that they should do so and thereby stop characterising Peru or Latin American states as wild, exotic, fanciful places. This could not be done without the power of the visual to re-frame an understanding and to suggest the mirror of Europe.

The importance of the visual in the construction of racial imaginary cannot be underestimated because it works within subjectivities, returning us to some of the concerns in Chapter 2 where the discussion examined the discourses in which race was placed and constructed. The visual power of images of 'the other' in

Western society initially and the export of these images around the globe was clearly allied with the biologism and accounts of 'scientific racism' as it developed. This has had major implications for the politics of race across Latin America. Many of these visual images became fixed in relation to a lexicon of black/white with all the hierarchical connotations of colour. Latin America, with its ideologies of racial mixing and hybridity, has the same histories of enslavement, indentured labour and the genocide of indigenous peoples (Taussig, 1987) with which the visual economy works to produce a series of racialised discourses on the diversity of the Latin American states.

Miracles: seeing is believing

There is, however, one other central aspect to the power of the visual economy of race in Latin America and that is the role of religion, more specifically, the role of the Roman Catholic church and its indigenisation through the Latin American states. The earliest missionaries and the Jesuit priests set about classifying the peoples among whom they worked, and there were long debates on whether the indigenous peoples could be said to have souls. Clearly, the hierarchy decided this was the case and the catholicisation of Latin America began and has continued since. The imagery of Catholicism has reinforced the aesthetics of whiteness with both Jesus and Mary images cast in whiteness, blonde hair, blue eyes, and the figure of the great white father – the Pope. This has not been without contestations and the ways in which the teachings and practices of Roman Catholicism have been indigenised are countless, from the festival days still celebrated, to the saints and spectacular miracles, which invariably involve the indigenous poor, while Cuba has a black Madonna.

Latin America has a powerful popular Catholicism which is, in part, generated by local practices but also allied with the 'option for the poor', which was announced in Medellin in 1968 and which turned the work of some members of the church to the poor and the oppressed, creating a radical politics that was crucial to the struggles of the seventies and eighties against the repressive military regimes. Part of the success of popular Catholicism relates to the powerful imagery of ordinary people in miracles and as local saints and the use of songs, fists in the air, and the celebration of solidarity across the globe. The power of the vision remains a central element in Christian religions, and sightings of the virgin are numerous and celebrated and then represented through statues, high above every major city and town, and in huge processions as in the famous virgin of Guadalupe in Mexico. Statues that suddenly have tears, hearts that bleed, relics of Christ and the saints are all visual reminders of the power of Christ, Christianity and the Church.

Roman Catholicism is not alone in presenting believers with this form of material reassurance. Miracles are common to religions and the common denominator for all is visibility, the sign of the power of extra-terrestrial forces as described in biblical sources like the burning bush and in the Hindu epics. Recently, within Hinduism there has been 'the miracle of the milk' in which small statues of sacred cows have been offered milk and have been seen to drink the milk in temples across the world. These events provide an empirical proof for the power of the god, or gods, and rely on their visual effects. Equally, these events graphically represent the fragile coalescence between the community of believers and the deities presenting forms of hegemonic power. Visual signs are everywhere in religions, from the sign of the cross to the sign of the fire, from the symbolism of the star to the elaborate and powerful spatial imagery of religious buildings, reaching to the sky, facing the East, decorated and organised as elaborations of sacred spaces.

However, although religious practices are seen to invoke the power of the visual, this does not suggest an absolute separation between the religious, or the scared, and the profane. Religious practices are not separated from the market, or the vagaries of capitalism as the shrines make clear, or the cash nexus in relation to priests and sadhus. Forms of divination, shrines and deities with a responsibility for material success are invoked as one part of a strategic engagement with the market. In Ghana, the Ga priestesses of the capital city, Accra, provide answers to the vagaries of the market, invoke assistance for business ventures and protections for workers, projects and families. These forms of explanation are related to the contact with gods and spirits for whom the priestess is a medium, and it is through her that they speak. The gods need gifts and have to be contacted through divining mechanisms, throwing cowrie shells and eggs or sacrificing chickens, which will provide answers to questions via the priestess who has the requisite knowledge and can 'read' the answers. Similarly, protections are offered by healing baths that use herbs and spells and through small cuts on the skin into which special magical dust is inserted (whatever this dust is I can vouch for the energy it produces and the technicolor dreams). All of these are visible reminders of the power of the supernatural and the ways in which it is omnipresent and can be used for good or ill and, if for ill, it can be countered through expert knowledge.

Religion, of course, is no less separated from politics and is deeply conscious of the play of powers in the visual imagery of saints, sadhus, flags and colour. One moment in this is the rise of the BJP (Bharata Janata Party) in India, now holding together a fragile coalition. It is an avowedly Hindu Nationalist party in which the saffron robes of its followers remind the people of India of the temples and the saffron flags that fly from them. The ideological power house of the BJP is the RSS (Rashtriya Swayamsevak Sangh), which is located with the doctrines of a Hindu past and present for India rather than the complex intermingling of peoples that is India. Highly organised on a military model, the RSS uses young male militants who, within the temples, train traditionally in martial arts and are currently seen parading in martial arts uniforms, as in any army. But they work, they insist, with the 'sword of truth' rather like the much earlier crusades with their Christian rhetoric. Given this masculinist turn, it is not surprising that the most militant BJP supporters are young urban men, many with higher education, who are opposed to positive action for the lower castes, and are convinced of their privileged place in India (van der Veer, 1993; Bhatt, 1997; Vanaik, 1997).

To speak of these as representations is to invoke the power of signs and thereby language. As the late Cardinal Hume, English Roman Catholic Primate, made clear when he suggested in a recent interview that the Church would be making a video, 'We have to tell our story in pictures', because the times have changed and people are used to a visual message. Representation is the production of meaning through language. Languages use a system of signs that stand in for, symbolise or reference the world. Meaning is produced by the practice, the work of representation, and it is constructed through signifying practices; that is, meaning producing practices (Hall, 1997). I use the notion of a language here in a broad sense to mean all forms of representation because they 'speak' or, rather, communicate to the viewer/listener. It is a conversation in which viewers decode messages and read meanings and in which subjects are not dumb receptacles of all images that come their way. These are related to biography, cultures, life experience and re-organised within these constituting 'mediations', to use Martin-Barber's (1993) term, or forms of framing, to put it another way.

Consumption

The seductions of capitalism, as suggested in the discussion of sexualities in Chapter 5, rely on powerful visual signs to persuade us of the pleasures of consumption, and the worlds of the media, marketing and advertising exploit semiotic powers and use them to create a world of endless desires. Advertising understands desire as productive, and what it produces in relation to consumption is not only profits but 'lifestyles', and with that identities bound to consumption patterns. In fact, the marketing and advertising agencies have used considerable resources in analysing and understanding what has happened to 'the haves' of post-war capitalism. The most sophisticated advertising uses productive desire in tandem with current fears and longings and through this heady mix is able to seduce. It is the power of seduction that is at work in the visual imagery of product management.

The power of the visual to promote sales is set within the context of a social formation in which 'I shop therefore I am', which has become a major motif of life. Shopping is no longer securing the things we need in life but is now called 'retail therapy', the major leisure pursuit and a pastime that can lead to addiction producing shopoholics. Shopping has become the metaphor of our age. It has come to symbolise the power of money, the infinite capacity for consumption beyond need and the exchange, money for goods, which symbolises the way in which we now live our lives – throwaway culture, instant fixes, fashion today – out of time tomorrow. This view, while not endorsing the more fanciful of Baudrillard's claims, does endorse the sense that he made of consumption when he wrote, 'Consumption, in so far as it is meaningful, is a systematic act of the manipulation of signs.' (Baudrillard, 1988: 22). Thus, commodities are no longer valued in terms of their use-value but in terms of what they signify, and this creates an economy of signs that is fuelled by advertising on the understanding that representations are signs without depth – that is, they do not stand in for anything, they are just what they are. It is because of this understanding that

Baudrillard uses the term hyper-real, and argues that it is within this world that we live every bit as much as within a world of economics and commodities. The hyper-real is every bit as material in its effects. Clearly, this is borne out by the attention to television programmes and the self-referring media in which soap operas now provide forms of gossip rather than the streets where we live. Similarly, advertising plays on the anxieties of the time and offers solutions: like the advertisement for Fox's biscuits, which is set in a community hall and in blocks of flats. The alienated urban landscape of loneliness and dread is transformed, the elderly are befriended, the stranger becomes welcome, racism, fear of the other are all solved by a packet of biscuits between friends. Advertising on this model offers a narrative with a happy ending, a seduction no less, like a primary school text on multi-culturalism, a realist drama amid all the surreal lager adverts that tap into the subconscious with their clever dream-like sequences of sex and death. The impact is visual, and its power is to seduce us, the viewer/consumer, into buying beer or biscuits!

Consumption has become a world of style, of surfaces which should be pleasurable for consumers; consequently shops and shopping malls are designed with desire and fantasy to the fore. Meadowhall, for example, outside the northern city of Sheffield, is a shopping mall but as you work your way through the covered streets towards the oasis at the centre, the design unfolds to match the global products available. Other malls are like huge conservatories, products of artifice designed to bring nature and the feel-good-factor back into shopping because shopping is a pleasure and a pastime. As Jon Goss (1997: 268) comments, 'Developers readily employ the glitz and showcraft of entertainment – literally "learning from Las Vegas" (Venturis *et al.*, 1972); the iconography of advertising (Frampton, 1983: 19) – "learning from Madison Avenue"; and the "imagineering" of North American theme parks – "learning from Disney".' How else would it be possible to have so many shopping centres with names from the rural – Meadowhall, The Shires, Bluewater – which resonate with the place of the rural in English culture. Whether minimalist with white walls and stainless steel or awash with colour, shops are designed to increase the pleasures of spending – play areas that rely on visual stimuli and are, at the same time, the materials of visual surveillance. The power of the image in the context of shops and shopping malls as pleasure domes is enormous, just like the part they play in advertising. Williamson's (1981) seminal work on advertising, which used structuralist analysis in order to decode advertisements and the ways in which they are a play of power and desire, re-cycling underlying binaries like nature/culture, is a very telling analysis of advertising. This type of analysis, and those that have followed which relate advertising to the broader concerns of consumption using Bourdieu's (1984) work, have analysed the ways in which consumption has come to order class and status hierarchies located with money and taste, and to differentiate these by region, gender and ethnicity. Such analyses begin to reconceptualise the social in ways that, like Baudrillard (1988), emphasise signs, sign systems and signifying practices. For De Certeau (1984), consumption is one key to everyday life because it is not passive but productive, every encounter between consumers and commodities changes people, things and everyday life. Thus, there is a constant play of powers within consumption that are diffused throughout the encounters and the ways in which consumers understand and act upon their desires and the commodities they are offered. As an understanding of the role of consumption in relation to identities and social interaction, this is akin to Foucault's account of the dispersal of powers within social life. This is, in part, because we belong to a televisual age in which the visual imagery of advertising is one part of a vast stock of visual images that constitute worlds for viewers and consumers. Our knowledge of the world and most especially the social, I want to argue, is powerfully constructed through the visual images of the global telecommunications networks.

Televisual powers

To address televisual powers is not to reiterate an account of dumb viewers into whom messages are poured. It is quite clear that images, messages and the power of television are mediated by the encounter between televisual worlds and viewers. Martin-Barbero (1993) describes this as the processes of mediation whereby viewers have an active engagement with the material or an active disengagement – they switch channels or turn-off (one study suggests that up to 25 per cent of viewers surf other channels during the advertisement breaks). Lewis (1994) emphasises both the ambiguities and polysemic world of televisual signs while acknowledging the routinised ways in which people watch television. Given these ongoing engagements and disengagements, the importance of television as a global network that constructs a vision of the world cannot be underestimated. The vision it constructs of peoples, politics, architecture, history, etc., is a constitution of the social, and as television moves around the globe and crosses the boundaries of the public and the private it has an ever growing impact upon the way in which the social is configured. For some writers, such as Silverstone (1994), the world constructed involves a suburbanisation of the life-world and he notes (ibid.: 52), 'I want to suggest that television is both historically and sociologically a suburban medium'. In part, he relates this to the issue of the private and public spheres but also to the content of television with its situation comedies and the more complex soap operas that provide an account of family life and relationships. I prefer the term domesticating for this genre of television and the ways in which television can mediate disaster and war into the living room of suburban homes. It has always been one of the great mysteries of the construction of sociology that representations have been understood through fields that have developed separately from sociology–media studies, mass communications and latterly cultural studies. Fortunately, the 'cultural studies' turn (it says it all) in sociology has gone some way to rectify this.

We revision our world through the medium of television; especially 'other worlds', for they are framed by television programmes such as wildlife programmes, holiday shows and 'exotic' locations for advertisements. Many of these types of programme turn nations and their visual symbols into spaces of consumption, often differentiated for the complex variety of tourists that now prevail. In this sense, there is an articulation between the world of shopping and the imaginary lands and peoples with which we are acquainted through television. This is not to understand television in the old discourse of cultural imperialism in which it was understood as all powerful, homogeneous and lacking in the mediations to which I have referred. Television and its visual impact are much more complex and although it may domesticate, it may also politicise in novel ways. The power of the drama/documentary in British television to raise issues and debate across the national space is coupled with the power of television to sustain the visibility of politics and politicians, the monarchy and areas of the state. Television had a huge impact on the development of the anti-Vietnam war movement (the first televised war) and has, more recently, brought the full horror of Bosnia and Rwanda into peoples homes alongside countless tragedies. But, suggest the critics, these are constructed representations that may make a spectacle out of suffering and leave viewers inured to violence and pain. One contradictory consequence may well be that the way in which the social is constructed is more sensitised to violence and this feeds the sense of danger, risk and uncertainty for those people in parts of the world where it is most safe to be, fuelling the sense of unease that is inherent in the human psyche.

Reporting the news has been researched and debated by the Glasgow University Media Research Group (Eldridge, 1993) through an analysis of the ways in which the ideologies of professionals and the constraints of production and government have an impact upon the news as it is constructed and represented. This is especially important in relation to national events, including war, when the issue of national security and the whole panoply of state powers is involved. The Falklands War and the ways in which it was reported and commented upon caused considerable debate, as did the more recent intervention in Kosova and the bombing of Iraq. The Conservative Party ministers and the tabloid newspaper, *The Sun*, were incensed by the more critical television reporting on the Panorama programme which *The Sun* dubbed 'Traitorama' (ibid.: 10). The Gulf War, it is said by Baudrillard (1995), was designed for the media with the emphasis upon technologies and not upon bodies, death and guns in the old sense. Only when there was coverage of the Baghdad bombing of people in a shelter did the real sense of a war with its violence and death become certain through the visual images presented on television. This is part of the ways in which the media is contested space, and one in which different interests seek to exercise power in relation to agenda-setting roles. There is an ongoing contestation, which involves journalists, production technologies, government and consumers.

So important is television that Rowe and Schelling (1991: 137) claim that 'modernity arrived in Latin America with television'. Perhaps an exaggeration, but in the sense that this medium allowed for national space/time to be engineered, for the worlds beyond the local to be viewed and for stories from all sectors to be told, very often through the powerful 'telenovela' format, it produced a novel account and, in relation to modernity, it did so through visual representations. Globo television from Brazil is now the fourth largest media company in the world and sells products across the globe. As Morley and Robins (1995: 141) write:

> The screen is a powerful metaphor for our times: it symbolises how we now exist in the world, our contradictory condition of engagement and disengagement', and they are willing to acknowledge that television can be 'liberating' because it can extend knowledge and experiences in a vicarious way.
>
> But it can also be very problematic...The spectator-self can rove almost at random from one visual sensation to the next: a cruising voyeur. The screen exposes the ordinary viewer to harsh realities, but it also tends to screen out the harshness of those realities.
>
> (ibid.)

This is, in part, the processes of mediations to which I have referred, but it is also in the production values of journalists and editors who are 'making the news'.

None of this devalues the notion that visual images are powerful and, in fact, crucial to the construction of the social at a commonsense level. In short, social processes are seen, imagined or real, they are in the mind's eye and part of the cognitive maps with which people plot their paths through the social. The extraordinary worlds that we can see, past, present and future, through televisual media suggest the limitless quality of the social, which is reinforced through the power of the internet where the worlds of community and chat rooms have been created as forms of social interface through cyberspace. They rely on the visual medium of the screen and the creative energies of World Wide Web users, giving a new meaning to the local and the global as subjects put their own personal spaces, bedrooms, living rooms, on the web and create new identities, names, locations, etc. against the backdrop of the global. The constitution of this as a social world is the subject of debate, and the recent papers by Burrows (1997) and McBeath and Webb (1997) suggest differing views. Burrows invokes not simply cyberspace but the hard-edged, futuristic novels of William Gibson as a form of sociological understanding that offers an account of the social (one may not like it much but that is beside the point). Webb, on the other hand, offers a critique of the 'virtual community' of web surfers and chat room encounters as existing without the texture of embodied encounters. However, in so far as forms of connection and mutuality are developed within these modes, I do not see these virtual communities as any less 'communal' for their virtuality.

The discussion has already drawn upon the power of the image within photography in the work of Deborah Poole (1997) on Lima and similar studies in relation to the construction of 'the other'. The responses from 'other worlds' have become famous for their re-readings of the photography of the mad, and photography portraying criminality and race – such as Sander Gilman's (1991) work *The Jew's Body* and Chris Pinney's re-reading of the *Royal Anthropological Institute Archive*. Quoting Heidegger, '...the fact that the world becomes a picture at all is what distinguishes the modern age' (Pinney, 1997: 130). Pinney (1997) links these developments, located with pressure to dominate the world, with current vogues and practices of Western travel. These are related to the early anthropological ways of framing the world and recoding space and the impact that this and orientalist practices had on the West, to the extent that unless 'the Orient' was packaged like the pictures it was unrecognisable.

The paintings and the photographs have become so much a part of the West and European imaginaries that the real becomes the imaginary. But, the arrival of 'virtual reality' is another story, especially in relation to the carefully 'framed' world, as Pinney (1997: 303) comments:

> In the short term, virtual reality dramatically intensified the metropolitan world's oppression of, and indifference to, the 'Third World', but it contained within it the seeds of its own destruction. Virtuality was uniquely different from other forms of representation inasmuch as it 'unframed'. Unlike paintings, photographs, books, fruit machines and cinema, it had no apparent frame or window. Now, at least, the person who experiences virtuality does not spectate but is immersed within, and part of, the visual and experiential field.

Art and power

This is, of course, a development from the pleasures of looking that are part of the joy of art, photography or spectacle. Virtuality offers a total, sensational experience, something which abstract art has tried to generate. Art disrupts, disturbs and is experienced, but not innocently because it too is read even though it can refuse to be representational. This lack of representation has been crucial to the definition of 'modern' or 'abstract' art, which seeks to offer an experience, to be conceptual and suggest that a plurality of readings is possible. Colour speaks, shapes speak and the combinations speak again. More recently, art has included the use of video and music, looped slides that are presentations and events rather than the more static canvasses and sculptures of previous eras. However, this was the basis of the art movements in France in the early twentieth century, which sought to disrupt the division between art and life, high culture and popular culture, dream and lived reality. Many of these themes were central to the Surrealists, and have been developed latterly within the critique of modernism by post-modernist writers and artists, seeking novel ways in which to disrupt art and life-worlds. These disruptions have been concerned primarily with the power of art and culture and the ways in which art defines the social. In other ways too, art is conceived as offering a vision of power in relation to specific ideological moments as captured in the Art and Power exhibition, held in London at the Hayward Gallery in 1995, as a facsimile of the 1937 Paris Exhibition, where the art and architecture born of the two major political ideologies of the twentieth century and realised in the socialist and fascist states met. The exhibition offered a glimpse of the 'heroic' art and architecture of Albert Speer in Berlin and Mussolini in Rome, plundering, as it does, images from the past as expressive means to the glorification of a fascist future. Equally powerful are Moscow's designs for the Metro and the Commissariat buildings and the Palace of the Soviets, buildings on a huge scale reaching into the sky complete with statues to patriots, workers and leaders, marking the end of the Avant-Garde Movement of the twenties. It is a powerful vision, demonstrating the use of art in relation to the glorification of a specific ideology and political system. It is also a reminder of why the grand narrative – whether of the city or the nation – is now so negatively assessed. The critique of the fascist vision is found within the exhibition, manifest in the shape of the Spanish Pavilion, a deceptively light structure which boasts no columns or imposing massive statues and certainly no pretensions to grandiose scale. Instead, the pavilion is a seductively simple building, sporting a curved totem pole capped by a stylised heart. It reminds the worlds of the thirties and today that celebrations through art and architecture can be very different from those designed to evoke the intimidating power and ambitions of the state. Elliot (1995: 31), in his introduction to the exhibition, suggests, persuasively, that, 'The dictators of the thirties were the apotheosis of modernity. By looking simultaneously at both the past and the future, they were able to sustain the fantasy of being able to stand outside their own time'. This is, of course, the ultimate power in which the past was erased and the future lay in their hands. That future was not only in art and architecture, with their heroic canvasses and massive buildings, but in the ways in which this defined the social and the subjects of the new world order.

While such political dictators sought to stand outside time, there were other interwar social commentators who used art and film effectively to provide a critique of modern urbanism, the most famous being the Austrian-born sceptical modernist film director and writer, Fritz Lang. Lang's social and political concerns were already apparent in *Dr Mabus, the Gambler*, made in Berlin in 1922, which contained pointed allusions to post-First World War social and economic conditions in Germany. But in *Metropolis* (1927) Lang used images of high-tech landscapes and routinised and dehumanised workers cast against mechanistic and steeled cityscapes to inscribe a futuristic vision of the urban–industrial world of capitalist development and authoritarian politics; it was a terrain theatrically re-visioned, of course, through the lens of scientism and the mutant chaos of the late twentieth century in Ridley Scott's 1981 seminal film *Blade Runner*.

The monumentalism of the Art and Power exhibition in which whole cities were envisioned with monuments to dictators and the nation, contrasts sharply with the disruptive powers of the art of the Surrealists or later post-modern artists like Keith Piper, whose exhibition Relocating the Remains visually deconstructed the power/knowledge complex in relation to academic subject divisions, especially those in social sciences, which have become naturalised and part of the commonsense of the era. The exhibition poster showed a hand with a globe within, 'the whole world in his hands', signifying the ways in which power has come to be exercised by Western modernity in relation to the peoples and cultures of the globe. Piper's work is a powerful statement about the ways in which histories, cultures and geographies can be re-visioned once the centre is de-centred. The world falls into different patterns and ways of expressing itself against the categorisations of subject disciplines built upon a Eurocentric foundation. This type of destabilisation has a profound effect on the ways in which the social is understood and the most powerful tool in this new understanding is the visual, the re-representation and re-framing of a world that does not begin and end with a European standpoint. This is also important because it alerts us to the malleability of the social.

The social and the visual

The malleability of the social exists not only in the ways that it is constantly reinvented through the social practices of everyday life, in interaction and the performative work of social lives, but also in the ways in which it is envisioned and seen as the social. This notion of the reflective social is one part of an ongoing mirror dance between individual subjects and a world conceived of as beyond the self, although the self is productive of this world. Visual imagery and the whole panoply of imaginings are a crucial constituent of the social, and cannot be separated from the sociological account of social worlds. This multi-textured world is a de-centred one in which the ties of the social are various and variable, involving a reflexivity which constructs and destroys simultaneously the 'ontological security' of which Giddens (1990) writes. The spaces of the social are traversed by the visual and its imaginary, providing limitless ways in which social life can be constructed, 'the stuff of dreams' or of nightmares, which can be fuelled or challenged by art, photography, television and film but also react again on these visions to revise them. This endless world of signs and signifiers is no more or less the social than the world of interpersonal relations and kinship, which cannot be conducted without an ability to read the signs. Thus, there is a crucial link between semiotics and power in all its forms, from the coercive architecture of Albert Speer to the seductions of consumption and television advertising which become the patents, the templates for the ways in which we understand the world as curiously 'real'.

Elizabeth Chaplin (1994) in her book *Sociology and Visual Representation* moves from the world of art history through cultural studies, and relates the development of visual literacy to the attempts within sociology to provide a more visually conscious account of social phenomena. In part, as she suggests, this is a response to the growing importance of 'representation' within the discipline and, as will be clear from this chapter, the contestations over representations are power relations in which images are fought over. This has been explored, for example, in relation to photographic records and the myriad of ways in which photography is used by the police and employers as part of the exercise of surveillance of citizens and workers. It is estimated that over 50 per cent of workers in Britain work in settings where cctv is used. As we have also seen, studies of visual media, aesthetics and taste all imply greater attention to the visual world. But it also means that the actual presentation of sociological materials will be more creative using a variety of textual and visual modes. This is already apparent in recent anthropological work discussed previously but also in texts like George McKay's

(1998) *DIY Culture*, which presents recent social movements and the work of activists seeking ways in which they can exercise the power to define their lives and concerns. The text includes photographic and cartoon material articulated with written text in accounts of road protestors, rave culture and environmentalist actions as examples of direct action movements in which people have claimed the power to define the political agenda.

Importantly, this is part of a re-assessment of the 'ocular' as the basis for the discipline and relates not simply to sociology but, more generally, to Western thought and the rise of modernity.

From Platonic philosophy onwards, vision was privileged as the road to truth, distanced and distinguished from religious visionary encounters. The search for truth was located with seeing the truth and this became the central paradigm of science, including the development of social science. Contained in the language of 'seeing is believing' and reproduced through a whole technology of experimentation and empiricist approaches to knowledge, the power of this frame, in which accounts of the world have been generated, has also been constantly critiqued. Latterly, it is the critiques from Nietzsche and Husserl (Foucault re-organised these understandings in relation to an understanding of modernity as a series of technologies and disciplinary modes) that have at their core visual power. Nietzsche contributed much to this understanding through his critique of monovision, suggesting instead a plurality of visual positions and celebrating the variety of ways of seeing the world.

Modernity produced a hegemony of vision, demoting diverse forms of knowing and using this privileged mode as a basis for organising social life in a systemic and binary account: reason/religion, science/magic, self/other. It is this organisation of social life through the hegemony of vision that is explored in Foucault's account of the rise of medicine and the birth of the prison as exemplars of an imperial gaze that ordered and objectified the world through the power of looking. As Flynn (1993: 281–2) so neatly expresses the shift, 'For modernity, vision has become supervision. The "hegemony" of vision in Foucault's modernity is the hegemony of power – a redundancy!…The vehicles of this disciplinary economy are surveillance, normalization and their synthesis, the examination.' While acknowledging the power of Foucault's analysis, Flynn is ever conscious of the paradox generated by the attempt to undermine the visual by the visual, and although it is suggested that Foucault sidesteps this in developing a diacritical vision, his work is replete with spatial imagery that also signals the visual. Instead, Flynn suggests indeterminacy that uses 'narrative vision' and undermines 'totalising consciousness and subjectivity' but 'Without a utopian heaven, one cannot have a hell: for Foucault, the light-footed positivist, that's just the way it is. If this is not a victory for the visual, it is at least the triumph of the Other'.

What Foucault's analysis offers is a way of understanding the dispersal of the totalising vision of the sovereign to 'governmentality organised by surveillance, panopticism, the normalising gaze dispersed throughout the social system, maintaining civil order' (Levin, 1993: 21). Thus, we now live with a myriad of forms of technological-tooled ocular-centrism, expressed in the increasing use of cctv and surveillance mechanisms, which seem to suggest that the constant surveillance under which subjects keep themselves is not enough for the maintenance of social order. Delinquency has not disappeared and disobedient subjects of the state seem to be less susceptible to the internal enforcement of discipline or the law. Instead, the law has come to the populace and the power of the visual in relation to this is neatly summed up in an article entitled 'Here's looking at you' (*The Guardian*, 28 July 1998), which draws upon a number of reports on surveillance techniques used in Britain and the human rights implications of some of these. The most common, which has become part of the landscape, is the use of cctv in shopping malls and car parks, on public buildings and in workplaces. It is everywhere, in the interests of security, and provides visual records of movements, meetings, social interaction and, more generally, social life. This is spatially organised to provide an all-seeing eye that monitors the general public living their everyday lives. Mobile phones, e-mail and car licence plates provide additional means through which individuals can be tracked. Smart cards will soon provide another means to individuals and as Richard Norton-Taylor, the author of the article comments, 'But the Justice Report also highlights a curious trust of government in Britain about the potential threats posed by new technology. For this reason the Cabinet Office has pressed ahead, with no complaints, to promote smart cards to enable people to obtain services, such as a car tax or benefit payment, more easily and efficiently. It is the other side of the coin – not the State covertly compiling personal data but the individual voluntarily offering the data. The first steps, perhaps, to a universal identity card.' And identity cards are a mark of visibility and the power of government to insist upon the visibility of citizens.

Visibility is not, however, only about governmentality and the power of the state in relation to the citizen; citizens also demand visibility in relation to claims on the state and state agencies. Visible politics is a central tenet of democratic politics in which citizens have the right to assemble, march and protest in ways that attempt to usurp the authorities' control over public space. The Red Star activists took their protest to the city and county council buildings, making visible their claims as black citizens to move beyond the inner city and into the seat of power and decision-making. This is reproduced countrywide with protestors, whether farmers or gay activists, taking over the streets of London and making themselves visible and with this their political agenda.

Recent celebrated visibility has been afforded to the environmental campaigners who have used novel ways in which to circumnavigate trespass and land laws. Living in trees, making caves in the ground, the eco-warriors are often involved in dangerous measures and direct confrontations with bailiffs and police in the interests of the environment. Campaigns in Britain have been fought against the extension of Manchester Airport, the Newbury By-pass and the M11 Link Road. Opposition to these projects was a complex mixture of a politics of the environment with claims by citizens to be consulted and the attempt to generate 'free spaces' within civil society. The context for these activities was a widespread campaign against a bill introduced to curb the rights of assembly, the Criminal Justice Bill of 1994. The official discourse of the bill saw the eco-warriors and their politics, alongside the development of rave culture – huge parties as forms of spectacle – as a threat to public order. Those involved in these activities were mostly young people for whom dance culture, notions of autonomy and pleasure were the mainstay of a politics removed from party politics, a cultural emphasis in politics, designated by George McKay (1998) as *DIY Culture* against the culture of passivity. It is a politics of direct action in which non-violence is emphasised and it has had an impact beyond its youth base. The Countryside March on London, organised by the National Union of Farmers, brought together a coalition of workers and owners, suburbanites and country people in a march on London that brought the countryside to London and government in ways not seen before. As the marchers made clear, the attempt was to puncture the construction of the countryside as inert and as a landscape against which Englishness is constructed and, instead, to present the reality of the rural. This was organised in the context of farmers who had suffered through the loss of cattle in the BSE (bovine spongiform encephalopathy) crisis; the televisual image of the countryside in the city was very powerful and based on the visibility of country folk, including elderly farmers in Barbour coats threatening to starve the city folk! There is no doubt that this constitutes a form of collective performative power which, like the eco-warriors, transgressed hegemonic notions of the rural and constituted a form of spectacle.

Visual power

Visibility is a key moment in our understanding of power but, as the direct action politics discussed briefly in this chapter suggests, visibility is used to undermine visual power. Surveillance is a key element in relation to the management of populations within modern states, from the cartography of territorial claims that police borders with the use of military and police powers, to the increasing use of cctv to monitor the daily activities of citizens. To be a citizen is to be visible through documentation, taxation and in everyday life, but in a deeper sense it is the visibility of the self that marks the modern period with its reflexivity and the myriad of forms of self-discipline that constitute the technologies of self. This self is a visible self that can be watched, monitored, policed, and activated in a counter to the hegemony of vision. The lifestyle politics which has fuelled so much of the direct action politics of the eighties and nineties is fuelled by a 'culture of immediacy' with an emphasis upon spectacle rather than history or theory (McKay, 1998). Although it is visionary, the emphasis upon non-violence and dialogue also moves it towards the attempt to engage in 'conversations' in an attempt to re-frame understandings of social and political life.

Visibility in these moments of resistance is afforded through technological mediations, both television and the internet, as powerful constitutive elements of civil society, echoing the views of Alexander and Jacobs (1998: 24) who write: '…civil society must be conceived not only as a world of voluntary associations, elections, or even legal rights, but also, and very significantly, as a realm of symbolic communication.' They suggest a narrative structure to civil society which is represented through the media coverage of political events which consists of a plot and characters. Thus, in relation to politics, it is a romantic genre with heroes and villains within the overall 'utopian genre' of civil society. This is an interesting and relevant reading of the place of television, especially in the political life of nation-states. Contestations are bound up with the level of media coverage that can be marshalled and the ways in which it can be used to insist upon the visibility of claims against the state or employers. Recent examples are the use by the Zapatistas in Mexico of both the major media companies and the internet in their struggles with the Mexican Government, and Aung San Suu Kyi, leader of the opposition in Burma, who when stopped en route to meet members of her party refused to leave her car. The photograph of her car on a bridge travelled the global media and once again placed the Burmese military in the headlines of news programmes and newspapers worldwide. The power of the image has become an essential tool of politics and the fight against repression expressed in the actions of peoples throughout the world, from the earlier attempts by women in Chile and Argentina to recover 'the disappeared', those who had been taken by the military never to be seen again and who constituted an erasure in national consciousness were, in part, recovered through the actions of women protesting this erasure. The lessons learned from this form of political action have been repeated again and again in relation to the power of television as a global medium. In this way, the visual, as I have suggested, is imbricated in the construction of the power relations of the social; it can no longer be thought as a reflection of the social. Rather, media forms, most especially television, are also makers of the social, practices that construct imagination, stories that are part of the commonsense, traversing hegemonic and counter-hegemonic resistances, designed to coerce and to seduce as forms of power.

8   Conclusion

Power and the social

Theorising and defining power has consistently been one of the major preoccupations within sociology. Similarly, constituting the social as the object of sociological enquiry has been an ongoing concern recently foregrounded in work on the body, sexualities and the revisioning of the binaries natural/social and virtual/real. This book has sought ways in which to bring these together in the basic argument that one invokes the other and that power and the social exist co-extensively. Having made this argument, however, the preceding chapters have sought ways in which to embroider and elaborate the ways in which power and the social are intertwined. Both remain contested areas of analysis within sociological work, theoretically and substantively, but, in conclusion, I want to suggest that there are ways in which these contestations can be ordered.

One way in which the preceding pages have sought to do this is by presenting an account of modalities of power in relation to sites. Thus, power has not been understood to be simply a capacity, a thing like a football over which different teams seek control. Instead, this book has been much more interested in the strategies and tactics of the team, suggesting an account of power as fluid and diffused throughout social life. Conceptually, power and the social are seen as enmeshed, the one within the other, and the task of sociology is to find appropriate ways in which to analyse and understand this confluence.

This book began with 'A brief history of power' in which an account was given of the major ways in which philosophical and sociological accounts have sought to answer the question: What is power? It was clear from this brief overview that to ask: 'What is power?' is less useful than to view power as relational and part of social life in all its diversity. But, it was also clear that the writings of Hobbes and Machiavelli still exercise an influence over the conceptualisation of power, in part, because their writings appear to answer the questions: 'What is power?' and 'Who has power?'. Sociological accounts have emphasised the relational aspects of power, especially the work of Weber, but this too has underscored the notion of power as 'power over' and the imposition of one person's will on another. However, it is clear from this, that writing about power invokes social relations. Indeed, Weber developed his account by discussing different forms of power and relating these to specific historical periods and social structures, outlining forms of power like charismatic power and, most importantly for modern societies, legal–rational power. Legal–rational power developed in response to the rise of modern forms and the role of the state in securing cohesion and order in capitalist social formations. Like Marx, Weber was impressed by the ways in which the state claimed to hold legitimacy in the use of force and violence. But, for Marx, there were clear disjunctures in capitalism organised on the basis of class and the great contradiction between the proletariat and the bourgeoisie. While examining capitalism as both an economic and social force, Marx was aware of the role of both violence and of ideas in changing the world and organising the collective strength with which to do that in terms of the revolutionary potential of the working class. The subtleties in Marx's analysis were often overridden as his ideas became entrenched in revolutionary movements throughout the world. As Communist parties developed, the economics of capitalism and the inevitability of class warfare became a mantra, and one against which members of these parties struggled. One of the most well known was Gramsci who re-introduced the power of the ideological sphere and the impact of cultural forms in shaping the power relations of modern societies. Gramsci promoted an alternative to the economistic accounts that had become the commonsense of the socialist movements. These different moments produced differing and sometimes allied conceptions of power and power relations. However, there is no doubt that for all these writers to enter the social world is to enter power relations.

This is precisely the starting point for Foucault's analysis in which power is not a thing, nor the end point of the individual will, nor the property of a class or a revolutionary party. Instead, Foucault sought ways in which to analyse the confluence of the social and power by examining specific modes of the operation of power in modern societies. One of these was the way in which power/knowledge produced one another. Thus, the bureaucracies analysed by Weber were more than legal–rational entities; these forms of order were ways in which power was exercised through the population. What was important about the rise of welfarist societies was that through the record keeping and accounting practices which are central to modern states, citizens were both individuated and objectified simultaneously. For Foucault, this was central to 'the management of populations' within liberal democracy. And it did not begin and end with record-keeping and the organisation of specific institutions like the prison. The keepers of these institutions produced an account of the self that became part of the subjectivities of citizens so that, while policed, citizens also policed and disciplined themselves. Foucault also analysed the ways in which the development of medicine was archetypal for the formation of the power/knowledge complex, and that it exercised an overarching surveillance upon forms of organisation and moral questions in modern societies. Thus, for Foucault, to be part of the social is to be enmeshed in power relations and the power/knowledge complex. But, the social is not a single entity, as this book has tried to argue; instead, it is a myriad of socials that coalesce in specific ways.

The introduction to this book also suggested that discourses on power are not the preserve of philosophy or sociology but are part of the immense body of myth and stories, religious texts and dramas that contribute towards our understanding of power, from the Hindu epics to Shakespeare and, latterly, modern televisual drama. I am sorry that constraints of space have not allowed for more analyses of these accounts of power and the subject because these address many of our concerns about the relationship between social worlds and power plays. Instead, the first chapter of the book sought ways in which to draw out of the multiplicity of accounts of power, a 'grammar' of power in which specific forms of power were emphasised. I used the term modalities of power for these differentiated forms.

The modalities of power that I foregrounded as ways of understanding power were: repression/coercion, power as constraint, hegemony and counter-hegemony, power as manipulation and strategy, power/knowledge, discipline and governance and, finally, seduction and resistance. Repression, coercion and constraint were allied with the zero-sum view of power – the football that one side has and the other does not and in which one group, or class, or gender is power-full and the other is power-less. The accounts of power framed by the notions of hegemony and counter-hegemony offer a very different view from the zero-sum view of power and are primarily concerned with the process of power and the ways in which alliances are forged and processes of legitimation are secured. Importantly, this is a mobile notion in which the securing of hegemony is never fixed but is constantly in process. This coupled with the notion of the social as fractured offers ways in which to understand the social as power-filled. Power as manipulation and strategy crosses over with sociological accounts of actions and institutions and also the ways in which alliances are formed as part of a rational process in order to secure the best outcomes. This is also much in evidence at a commonsense level in which power is understood, much as a game of tactics and strategies, and it was, of course, central to the Machiavellian ethnography of power as he observed and analysed it in the time of the princes and their states in what is now Italy. This way of understanding power is located with the rational actor of Weber's model who locates a goal and through planning and action moves through a process of analysis to action in pursuit of the goal, as an individual or member of a collectivity. The assumption, therefore, is that power is a capacity that can be invoked by people in pursuit of their goals. This assumes that power is outside waiting to be mobilised in specific circumstances allied with the social context. Power becomes a variable and can be caught, held, bowled or lost just as in the game of cricket. Contrary to this view was the Foucauldian sense of power imbricated in all social relations, discourses and institutions. Power is imminent and always present in social life and, thus, there is a dispersal of powers, but these do come to rest in specific ways and places. This book has used these insights in a variety of ways throughout the chapters. Similarly, and importantly, the last modalities of power, seduction and resistance, are, I have suggested, two of the most important ways in which power is imbricated in social life. It is clear from the chapters on sexualities and visual power that these forms of power are crucial to the reproduction of capitalism in the new era. These forms invoke the Foucauldian notion that wherever there is power there is resistance, and these resistances take place in a myriad of disorganised and spontaneous ways on a daily basis. Resistance is also the basis of much political mobilising from which strategies may be generated. But, it is, I have tried to argue, seduction that plays such a crucial role in late modernity because it offers a vision away from the zero-sum game, and suggests that subjects are willing, knowing subjects in the seductions of consumption and all that it implies for the politics of identities. These, therefore, are the modalities of power with which we began, which suggest that there might be ways of understanding power that use the insights from Foucault on the dispersal of powers but are also able to understand that this dispersal does not negate understandings of power in multiple forms.

Similarly, the understanding that the social is de-centred, fractured and should be thought of and analysed in this way does not prevent an analysis that suggests that there are sites in which specific fractures coalesce that are central to our understanding of the multiplicities of social life. Thus, although working with the modalities of power, this book has sought ways in which to explore specific sites that are of key concern for sociology – but not sociology alone. These sites are racialised power, engendered power, class and power, sexualised power, spatial power and visual power. My contention is that together these form a grammar of power and one way in which we can better understand the social as multiple but having, we might want to suggest, critical mass in relation to power in these areas. In my explorations of these sites, I have also sought to travel widely in relation to the examples and the substantive material that I have used. This is, in part, a reflection of my own research biography but also one further attempt to shift the ground beneath our feet in sociology, away from a eurocentric, North American focus to the concerns of a globalising world, a trans-national world in which there is increasing cross-border concern. Sociology has also become a cross-border endeavour in which cultural and media forms, art and visual stimuli are more likely to be part of the analysis and the forms of methodology used in the construction of sociological knowledge.

Despite the attempt to provide an account of power and the social using the conception of modalities and sites I am still left wondering about power, and I would like to close the book by suggesting that the fluidity and dispersal of powers that constitute the social in the post-modern world have strong resonances with the ways in which knowledge is being organised and thought of in many disciplines. Quantum physics offers a mirror of the ways in which sociology is beginning to conceive social life, away from the solidity produced in the reification of 'institutions' and mechanistic notions of the ordering of relations between individuals and 'society', to an understanding of an uncertain world. Danah Zohar and Ian Marshall (1994: 26) describe this in the following way, 'Each possible journey and each eventual destination is associated with a probability, but nothing is ever determined. Indeterminacy – the lack of any physical basis for predicting the outcome of events – characterises the quantum realm.' As the writers explain, what is revolutionary about quantum physics is that it has abolished the binaries of either/or and works instead with both/and, which has major implications, they suggest, for the ways in which we can seek to live with the diversity and uncertainty that constitutes post-modern societies.

Reflecting upon what this will mean for the politics of democratic societies,

Zohar and Marshall (1994: 273) suggest that rather than perpetuating the older notions that there is either consensus and community or fragmentation, we are learning to see pluralism and diversity in different ways, '...to explore how we might both celebrate our diversity and at the same time find some creative unity in our differences'. This theme has been taken up in the recent literature on the politics and possibilities of post-modern societies. For some, such as Beck (2000) and Held (2000), the possibilities lie in a genuinely cosmopolitan social and political sensibility and forms of governance that will place diversity not at the margins of social life but at the core. The uncertainty with which we are living has produced calls for a 'sociology beyond societies' from John Urry (2000), which also suggests that sociology will have to think the social in different more mobile ways, and that includes the impact of globalisation and the development of trans-national spaces. Thus, the social as conceived in sociology can no longer be country-specific but needs to shift its gaze beyond the boundaries while recognising the historical and cultural specificities of social formations. This call is now commonplace and has led Beck (2000) to suggest that sociology is carrying too many 'zombie' categories; that is, categories from some past time that have outlived their conceptual viability.

While Giddens (1984, 1991) emphasises the empowering qualities of changing times and seems to suggest that individuals do have power in their own hands as a means to engage in transformative projects, Bauman (2000) is more circumspect and more willing to press for changes in sociological paradigms. Bauman, like Dana Zohar, uses the metaphors of light and heavy, solid and liquid, in relation to the changes between modern and post-modern times. Thus, he notes (ibid.: 113) that modernity was the era of 'hardware' or 'heavy' modernity, comprising armies, factories and machinery, all in the interests of conquering space. As he notes, 'territory' and its domestication was the crucial marker of this period, suggesting, as this book has done, the central relationship between power and space. However, in the new liquid modernity, power and space are no simple couplet; the relations are more elusive. It is the era of software rather than hardware in which capital can travel at speed and in which the power of money and its circulation sustains the circuits of power. Bauman writes of 'liquid modernity' in part as a metaphor for the seeming lack of solidity in the present era, and Castells (1997) writes of flows and circuits. Both enunciations are ways of trying to name the insight from Marx in the era of solidity, 'All that is solid melts into air'.

For Bauman (2000: 213), the implications for sociology are clear, and he concludes his discussion with a call to sociology:

> For the denizens of modern society in its solid and managed phase, the major opposition was one between conformity and deviance; the major opposition in modern society in its present liquefied and de-centred phase, the opposition which needs to be faced up to in order to pave the way to a truly autonomous society, is one between taking up responsibility and seeking a shelter where responsibility for one's own actions need not be taken by the actors.

Bauman emphasises this against the call to fixity and the 'primordial' claims of belonging that can be seen in the racial, national and religious identities that work within the simple binary of 'them' and 'us'.

Interestingly, it is precisely the software world of global communications in which the work of trying to fix identities is being carried out. The number of 'hate sites' on the internet grows daily and their rhetoric more convoluted and fiercely condemnatory of a world of hybridity and deterritorialisation. Many of these groups, such as White Pride World Wide, certainly existed before the internet, but the net has given a global impetus beyond the national legal confines of nation-states to groups and individuals who are determinedly anti-global. For sociology, cyberspace presents another way in which the social can be decoupled from the nation or simple conceptions of society as a network of institutions. Indeed, sociology has to find ways in which to integrate the virtual with the social in forms of cybersociology.

The literature on virtual worlds grows daily, but it is interesting that the accounts from sociology and cultural studies place power and the virtual together, producing collections such as Brian Loader (1997) on governance and divisions and David Holmes (1998) on *Virtual Politics*. In a recent intervention, Tim Jordan (2000) directly addresses the issue of cyberpower through an analysis of the role of the individual, the social and the imaginary of cyberspace. The social in cyberspace is an online society and, although it has been suggested that this is an egalitarian one, it is clear that forms of community and the relationship between the online society and the individual are, suggest Jordan, structured by the technology available and through which information flows can be accessed. No less than other worlds and the myriad of socials that have been the subject of this book, virtual worlds are constituted in power relations. Jordan (2000: 218) concludes:

> Cyberpower points not to the ultimate dominance of elites, though it clearly identifies the burgeoning power of elites, nor does it predict the libertarian ideal of individual empowerment, though it makes conspicuous the ongoing creation of powers for individuals in cyberspace. Cyberpower points to these processes continuing, driven by dreams and nightmares.

The emphasis on processes and the imaginary worlds of dreams and nightmares shares with Castells and with Bauman a vision of a world in flux but which has moments when the overlapping of power and the social is constituted as a site. These concerns are not those of sociologists alone but have been explored in literatures that range from poetry to popular management manuals. There are clear fashions in management gurus and ideas. In the recent past, understanding charismatic leadership was the key to competitive edge and, therefore, it was important to secure charismatic managers. On the other hand, encouraging flexible, creative workers in a non-hierarchical, flattened management structure was deemed to secure success on the basis of winning companies like IKEA and NOKIA. However, solidity and the search for laws has reasserted itself in relation to discourses on power and Robert Greene and Joost Elffers (1999) have enjoyed success with their small book *The 48 Laws of Power*. The book plunders a variety of texts, from the work of Machiavelli to that of Wilhelm Reich, in order to produce 'the 48 Laws', which include, 'conceal your intentions' at number 3. The book provides recipe knowledge for corporate managers and, it suggests, for life beyond the corporation and is another version of the self-help manuals that are now so popular. The underlying conception, however, remains committed to the notion of power as capacity, a tool or a weapon that needs to be invoked and used in the corporate sphere. This is also reflected in the way in which the authors discuss flexibility and 'formlessness', which is presented as the injunction, Law 48. 'Assume formlessness' and they note, 'Power can only thrive if it is flexible in its forms...The formlessness of power is more like that of water, or mercury, taking the form of whatever is around it. Changing constantly, it is never predictable' (Greene and Elffers, 1999: 180–81). They conclude:

> Rigidity will only make you look uncannily like a cadaver. Never forget, though, that formlessness is a strategic pose...Remember: Formlessness is a tool...You use formlessness, not because it creates inner harmony and peace, but because it will increase your power.

This is the model of the game and of the strategic and tactical encounter that secures power and makes you a winner. Included within this tactical repertoire is the notion of flux and change. and this is integrated as part of the recipe for success. But, it is interesting that even in this 'text' the idea of malleability and flow is incorporated as the major trend within which power plays have to be elaborated.

'Go with the flow' has, however, been reinvented by a generation of activists who are computer literate and who have discovered the power of the internet as an organising tool for direct action. The recent protests in Seattle, Prague and The Hague against the increasing power of the IMF (International Monetary Fund), the World Bank and the WTO (World Trade Organisation) are fuelled by a populist rhetoric which sets itself against the increasing impoverishment of large sections of the less developed world and in which the slogan 'Power to the People' has been recast for a globalised world. Using the internet to organise and staging demonstrations with the appearance of spectacles, this is activism for the media age in which visibility on television is coupled with control of space on the ground. The meetings of these global institutions were indeed disrupted, although the work of these agencies continues apace. However, it is interesting that the World Bank now wishes to consider cultural forms as modes of development and not simply the commodification of cultures within the tourist industry.

Power is here, there and everywhere, legally and militarily organised in the Criminal Justice System and the armed forces, but it is also in the workplace, on the streets, in our interactions and in our subjectivities. Given the ubiquity of power it seems appropriate, therefore, to close with the quotation with which I began: 'Power is the shadow of freedom and, as an Arab proverb says, one cannot jump outside one's own shadow' (Laclau, 1996: 52).

Appendix
Major theorists of power

The following provides chronologically organised short notes on some of the major theorists of power.

Plato (*c*. 428–347 BC) sought to outline the conditions of the ideal republic in which a learned cadre of intellectuals would govern. The vision was a very authoritarian one in which power was held by a few.

Ibn Khaldun (1332–1406) was a Muslim statesman who, following a career in politics, turned to the study of the ways in which politics and society are inter-related. His work prefigured many sociological concerns and he related power to cultural and social forms.

Machiavelli, Niccolò (1469–1527) was one of the most innovative theorists of power and his name has become synonymous with power relations and power struggles. His work presents an ethnography of power in the ways that tactics are employed to secure outcomes.

Hobbes, Thomas (1588–1679) was a key figure in the development of moral and political philosophy. Hobbes sought to understand power relations between subjects and the sovereign and the ways in which stability and order in society could be secured.

Locke, John (1632–1674) analysed the ways in which popular consent was developed within societies and how far rulers have justifiable power in relation to their subjects. Locke was interested in the means by which power is legitimated and suggested that if it was not legitimate people had grounds for resistance.

Baron de Montesquieu, Charles de Secondat (1689–1755) was noteworthy for his attempt to integrate environmental and social factors in the development of societies. For Montesquieu, laws were the expression of the power relations between the governed and those who governed, and it was laws that provided the basis for social control in societies.

Rousseau, Jean-Jacques (1712–1778) is famous for the epigram, 'Man is born free; and everywhere he is in chains': society does not offer freedom but constraints. Rousseau was concerned with developing an account of power relations in which people would be self-governing in conditions of equality.

Marx, Karl Heinrich (1818–1883) is recognised as the key analyst of capitalism and radical inspiration to people's movements worldwide. Marx sought to make the power relations of capitalism transparent and to link political, economic and ideological forms of power in relation to the lives of working people.

Nietzsche, Friedrich Wilhelm (1844–1900) remains a controversial figure who suggested that life should be lived in relation to 'the will to power', which he conceived as the creative and productive impulse of people. For Nietzsche, power was productive and existed beyond government and institutional arrangements.

Weber, Max (1864–1920) developed an account of power through his analysis of forms of domination which were located with different forms of legitimacy: traditional, charismatic and legal–rational. Modern nation-states were characterised by growing bureaucratic forms that provided the means whereby citizens were managed.

Gramsci, Antonio (1891–1937) was an Italian Marxist imprisoned by the Fascists during which time he wrote an extensive collection of pieces gathered together as *The Prison Notebooks*. Gramsci contested the singular emphasis upon economic relations in Marxism and re-asserted the power of ideological and cultural forms in contributing towards the generation and reproduction of liberal democracy.

Arendt, Hannah (1906–1975) distinguished between power and violence and dismissed the notion that violence could be legitimised through the ends to which it was directed. Arendt sustained an active account of power and emphasised empowerment.

Fanon, Frantz (1925–1961) was a psychiatrist working in Algeria who articulated the violence of racism and the colonial encounter and its embeddedness within the colonial psyche. He suggested that violent means were a cathartic necessity for the emancipation of those colonised and subjugated.

Foucault, Michel (1926–1984) provided a major impetus to the theorisation of power through his analyses of modern societies in which power is dispersed throughout social life. He used the example of the development of the prison in order to explore disciplinary power and its impact on modern life, but was equally concerned to understand the ways in which power is central to the constitution of subjectivities.

Bauman, Zygmunt invokes power relations throughout his work and suggests that power is both constraining and a source of emancipation. Bauman acknowledges the disciplinary state and state interventions in individual lives, but reasserts the necessity of public power as central to a revisioned public sphere.

Bourdieu, Pierre focuses attention upon the importance of cultural consumption as a means to securing class and status distinctions in society. These forms interact with 'symbolic power' which is founded on the authority of experts, trained and certificated and able to exercise power over others.

Butler, Judith concentrates attention upon the power of heterosexuality to define the body and sexuality in society, and the ways in which this generates forms of resistance. For Butler, gender/sexual identities are infinitely malleable and it is the attempt to fix the body in one mode which is a product of power relations then subverted by forms of performative power using parody, masquerade and transgressive styles.

Giddens, Anthony understands power as 'transformative capacity' and this is allied with an account of the reflexive self within democracy. However, power coalesces in specific ways allied with bureaucratic forms and locales, most especially cities and nation-states.

Habermas, Jürgen developed a theory of communicative action as a basis for outlining the conditions under which a participatory public sphere could be sustained. This would enable the widest possible debate on public issues within the power relations of society.

Hall, Stuart emphasises power as practice in a great variety of contexts, from academic debates concerning the role of culture to interventions in the politics of race. Hall has sought ways in which to redefine the terms in which we construct the social world, emphasising the power of naming and its role in re-visioning contemporary metropolitan urban spaces.

Lukes, Steven defined power in relation to interests and whose interests were served in relation to the outcomes of power. This was one attempt to remove the discussion of power from an individualist account and emphasise the social embeddedness of power relations.

Further reading

For an extended discussion of the relationship between sociology and modernity:

Swingewood, A. (2000) *A Short History of Sociological Thought*, 3rd edn, London: Macmillan.

Giddens, A. (1990) *The Consequences of Modernity*, Cambridge, UK: Polity Press.

Hall, S. and Gieben, B. (eds) (1993) *Formations of Modernity*, Cambridge, UK: Polity Press, (especially Chapters 1 and 6).

Texts by Foucault

Foucault, M. (1977) *Discipline and Punish: The Birth of the Prison*, London: Allen Lane.

Foucault, M. (1979) *The History of Sexuality: Volume 1 An Introduction*, London: Allen Lane.

Texts on Foucault

McNay, L. (1994) *Foucault: A Critical Introduction*, Cambridge, UK: Polity Press.

McHoul, A. and Grace, W.A. (1995) *A Foucault Primer: Discourse, Power and the Subject*, London: UCL Press.

Sawicki, J. (1991) *Disciplining Foucault: Feminism, Power and the Body*, London: Routledge.

Texts on power

Clegg, S. (1989) *Frameworks of Power*, London: Sage.

Fanon, F. (1965) *The Wretched of the Earth*, London: Allen Lane.

Gilroy, P. (2000) *Between Camps*, London: Allen Lane.

Hall, S. (1993) 'The West and the rest: discourse and power', in Hall, S. and Gieben, B. (eds) *Formations of Modernity*, Cambridge, UK: Polity Press, 275–332.

Hindess, B. (1996) *Discourses of Power*, Oxford: Blackwell.

Laclau, E. and Mouffe, C. (1985) *Hegemony and Socialist Strategy: Towards a Radical Democratic Politics*, London: Verso.

Lukes, S. (1974) *Power: A Radical View*, Basingstoke: Macmillan.

Lukes, S. (ed.) (1986) *Power*, Oxford: Blackwell.

Bibliography

Adkins, L. and Lury, C. (1996) 'The cultural, the sexual and the gendering of the labour market', in Adkins, L. and Merchant, V. (eds) *Sexualising the Social: Power and the Organisation of Sexuality*, London: Macmillan, 204–24.

Adkins, L. and Merchant, V. (eds) (1996) *Sexualising the Social: Power and the Organisation of Sexuality*, London: Macmillan.

Alexander, J.C. and Jacobs, R.N. (1998) 'Mass communications, ritual and civil society', in Liebes, T. and Curran, J. (eds) *Media, Ritual and Identity*, London: Routledge.

Althusser, L. (1969) *For Marx*, London: Verso.

Althusser, L. (1972) *Lenin and Philosophy*, London: Verso.

Alvarez, S. (1990) *Engendering Democracy in Brazil*, Princeton, NJ: Princeton University Press.

Anderson, B. (1991) *Imagined Communities*, 2nd edition, London: Verso.

Ansell-Pearson, K. (1994) *An Introduction to Nietzsche as Political Thinker: The Perfect Nihilist*, Cambridge: Cambridge University Press.

Appadurai, A. (1996) *Modernity at Large: Cultural Dimensions of Globalisation*, Minneapolis, MN: Minnesota University Press.

Arendt, H. (1969) *On Violence*, London: New Left Books.

Augé, M. (1995) *Non-Places: Introduction to an Anthropology of Supermodernity*, London: Verso.

Balibar, E. (1991) 'Is there neo-racism?', in Balibar, E. and Wallerstein, I. (eds) *Race, Nation and Class*, London: Verso.

Barnes, T.J. and Duncan, J.S. (eds) (1995) *Writing Worlds*, London: Routledge.

Bartky, S.L. (1988) 'Foucault, femininity and the modernization of patriarchal power', in Diamond, I. and Quinby, L. (eds) *Feminism and Foucault: Reflections on Resistance*, Boston: Northeastern University Press, 61–86.

Baudrillard, J. (1988) *Selected Writings* (Poster, M. ed.) Cambridge, UK: Polity Press.

Baudrillard, J. (1995) *The Gulf War Did Not Take Place*, Sydney: Power Publications.

Bauman, Z. (1987) *Legislators and Interpreters*, Cambridge, UK: Polity Press.

Bauman, Z. (1992) *Intimations of Postmodernity*, London: Routledge.

Bauman, Z. (1993) *Modernity and the Holocaust*, Oxford: Oxford University Press.

Bauman, Z. (1996) 'From pilgrim to tourist', in Hall, S. and du Gay, P. (eds) *Questions of Cultural Identity*, London: Sage, 18–37.

Bauman, Z. (1998) *Globalization*, Cambridge, UK: Polity Press.

Bauman, Z. (2000) *Liquid Modernity*, Cambridge, UK: Polity Press.

Bayliss, V. (1998) *Redefining Work*, London: RSA.

Beale, J. (1982) *Getting it Together: Women as Trade Unionists*, London: Pluto Press.

Beck, U. (1992) *Risk Society: Towards a New Uncertainty*, London: Sage.

Beck, U. (2000) 'Rethinking the Cosmopolitan Manifesto' Plenary delivered at the Cosmopolis Conference, Helsinki, September 2000.

Beechey, V. (1979) 'On patriarchy', *Feminist Review*, 3: 66–82.

Beetham, D. (1985) *Max Weber and the Theory of Modern Politics*, Cambridge, UK: Polity Press.

Beetham, D. (1991) *The Legitimation of Power,* London: Macmillan.

Berman, M. (1983) *All that is Solid Melts into Air: The Experience of Modernity*, London: Verso.

Bhatt, C. (1997) *Liberation and Purity: Race, New Religious Movements and the Ethics of Postmodernity*, London: UCL Press.

Bogue, R. (1989) *Deleuze and Guattari*, London: Routledge.

Bourdieu, P. (1973) 'Cultural reproduction and social reproduction', in Brown, R. (ed.) *Knowledge, Education and Cultural Change*, London: Tavistock.

Bourdieu, P. (1977) *Outline of a Theory of Practice*, Cambridge: Cambridge University Press.

Bourdieu, P. (1984) *Distinction: A Social Critique of the Judgement of Taste* (trans. Nice, R.), Cambridge, MA: Harvard University Press.

Breckenridge, C. and van der Veer, P. (eds) (1993) *Orientalism and the Postcolonial Predicament*, Philadelphia, PA: University of Pennsylvania Press.

Breughal, I. (1989) 'Sex and race in the labour market', *Feminist Review*, 32: 49–68.

Brod, H. (ed.) (1987) *The Making of Masculinities: The New Mens Studies*, London: Allen Unwin.

Brod, H. (ed.) (1988) *A Mensch Among Men: Explorations in Jewish Masculinities*, Freedom, CA: Crossing Press.

Burchill, J. (1999) *Diana*, London: Oram Press.

Burke, A. (1986) 'Racism, prejudice and mental illness', in Cox, J. (ed.) *Transcultural Psychiatry*, London: Croom Helm, 139–57.

Burrows, R. (1997) 'Cyberpunk as social theory: William Gibson and the sociological imagination', in Westwood, S. and Williams, S. (eds) *Imagining Cities: Scripts, Signs Memory*, London: Routledge, 235–48.

Butler, J. (1990) *Gender Trouble: Feminism and the Subversion of Identity*, London: Routledge.

Butler, J. (1993) *Bodies That Matter: On the Discursive Limits of 'Sex'*, London: Routledge.

Campbell, B. (1998) *Diana, Princess of Wales: How Sexual Politics Shook the Monarchy*, London: The Women's Press.

Carrier, J.G. (1995) *Gifts and Commodities: Exchange and Western Capitalism Since 1700*, London: Routledge.

Cassell, P. (1993) *The Giddens Reader*, London: Macmillan.

Cassirer, E. (1932) *The Philosophy of the Enlightenment* (trans. Koelln, F.C.A. and Pettegrove, J.P.), Princeton, NJ: Princeton University Press, 1951.

Castells, M. (1997) *The Power of Identity*, Oxford: Blackwell.

Cavendish, R. (1982) *Women on the Line*, London: Routledge.

Chaplin, E. (1994) *Sociology and Visual Representation*, London: Routledge.

Clegg, S. (1989) *Frameworks of Power*, London: Sage.

Cockburn, C. (1983) *Brothers: Male Dominance and Technological Change*, London: Pluto Press.

Cockburn, C. (1991) *In the Way of Women: Men's Resistance to Sex Equality in Organizations*, London: Macmillan.

Cohen, P. (1988) 'The perversions of inheritance: studies in the making of multi-racist Britain', in Cohen, P. and Bains, H. (eds.) *Multi-Racist Britain*, London: Macmillan.

Cohn, B.S. (1996) *Colonialism and its Forms of Knowledge: the British in India*, Princeton, NJ: Princeton University Press.

Connell, R.W. (1987) *Gender and Power*, Cambridge, UK: Polity Press.

Connell, R.W. (1995) *Masculinities*, Cambridge, UK: Polity Press.

Corcoran-Nantes, Y. (1993) 'Female consciousness or feminist consciousness: women's consciousness raising in community-based struggles in Brazil', in Radcliffe, S. and Westwood, S. (eds) *Viva: Women and Popular Protest in Latin America*, London: Routledge, 136–55.

Craib, I. (1997) *Classical Social Theory*, Oxford: Oxford University Press.

Crain, M. (1996) 'The gendering of ethnicity in the Ecuadorian Andes', in Melhuus, M. and Stølen. K. (eds) *Machos, Mistresses, Madonnas: Contesting the Power of Latin American Gender Imagery*, London: Verso.

Crompton, R. (1998) *Class and Stratification: an Introduction to Currrent Debates* (2nd edition) Cambridge, UK: Polity Press.

Cruz, J. and Lewis, J. (eds) (1994) *Viewing, Reading, Listening: Audiences and Cultural Receptions*, Boulder, CO: Westview Press.

Curtis, B., Rose, N. and Miller, P. (1995) 'Taking the state back out: Rose and Miller on political power', *British Journal of Sociology*, 46 (4): 575–97.

Dahrendorf, R. (1987) 'The erosion of citizenship and its consequences for us all', *New Statesman*, 12th June: 12–15.

Das, V. (ed.) (1990) *Mirrors of Violence: Communities, Riots and Survivors in South Asia*, Delhi: Oxford University Press.

Davis, C. (1996) *Levinas: An Introduction*, Cambridge, UK: Polity Press.

Davis, M. (1990) *City of Quartz*, London: Verso.

Davis, M. (1998) *Ecology of Fear*, London: Picador.

De Certeau, M. (1984) *The Practice of Everyday Life* (trans. Rendall, S.F.), Berkeley, CA: University of California Press.

Deleuze, G. (1983) *Nietzsche and Philosophy* (trans. Tomlinson, H.), Minneapolis: University of Minnesota Press.

Deleuze, G. (1986) *Foucault* (trans. Séanttand), Minneapolis: University of Minnesota Press.

Deleuze, G. (1988) *Spinoza: Practical Philosophy* (trans. Hurley, R.), San Francisco, CA: City Lights.

Deleuze, G. and Guattari, F. (1983) *Anti-Oedipus: Capitalism and Schizophrenia* (trans. Hurley, R., Seem, M. and Lane, H.), Minneapolis: University of Minnesota Press.

Deleuze, G. and Guattari, F. (1986) *Nomadology: The War Machine*, New York: Semiotext.

Dennis, N. Henriques, F. and Slaughter, C. (1956) *Coal is our Life*, London: Eyre and Spottiswoode.

Derrida, J. (1978) 'Violence and metaphysics: an essay on the thoughts of Emmanuel Levinas', in Derrida, J. (ed.) *Writing and Difference*, London: Routledge, 79–154.

Derrida, J. (1992) *The Gift of Death* (trans. Wills, D.), Chicago, IL: University of Chicago Press.

Derrida, J. (1996) *Specters of Marx: The State of the Debt, The Work of Mourning and the New International* (trans. Kamuf, P.), London: Routledge.

Dews, P. (1986) 'The nouvelle philosophie and Foucault', in Gane, M. (ed.) *Towards A Critique of Foucault*, London: Routledge, pp. 46–61.

Dowding, K. (1996) *Power*, Milton Keynes: Open University Press.

Dyrberg, T.B. (1997) *The Circular Structure of Power*, London: Verso.

DuBois, W.E.B. (1989) [1903] *The Souls of Black Folk*, New York: Bantom.

Eldridge, J. (1993) *Getting the Message: News, Truth and Power*, London: Routledge.

Elliot, D. (1995) 'The battle for art', in Elliot, D. (ed.) *Art and Power: Europe Under the Dictators 1930–1945*, London: Hayward Gallery.

Engels, F. [1845] (1987) *The Condition of the Working Class in England in 1844*, Harmondsworth: Penguin.

Epstein, D. (1996) 'Keeping them in their place: hetero/sexist harassment, Gender and the enforcement of heterosexuality', in Holland, J. and Adkins, L. (eds) *Sex, Sensibility and the Gendered Body*, London: Macmillan, 202–22.

Escobar, A. and Alvarez, S.E. (eds) (1992) *The Making of Social Movements in Latin America: Identity, Strategy and Democracy*, Boulder, CO: Westview Press.

Evans, D.T. (1993) *Sexual Citizenship*, London: Routledge.

Featherstone, M (1987) 'Lifestyles and consumer culture', *Theory, Culture and Society*, 4: 55–70.

Featherstone, M. (1992) *Consumer Culture and Postmodernism*, London: Sage.

Featherstone, M., Hepworth, M. and Turner, B. (1991) *The Body – Social Process and Cultural Theory*, London: Sage.

Featherstone, M., Lash, S. and Robertson, R. (eds) (1995) *Global Modernities*, London: Sage.

Fernando, S. (1988) *Race, Culture and Psychiatry*, London: Croom Helm.

Field, F. (1989) *Losing Out: The Emergence of Britain's Underclass*, Oxford: Blackwell.

Flores, J. (1997) 'Qué assimilated, brother yo soy asimilao', in Romero, M., Hondagneu-Sotelo, P. and Ortiz, V. (eds) *Challenging Fronteras: Structuring Latina and Latino Lives in the US*, London: Routledge, 175–87.

Flynn, T.R. (1993) 'Foucault and the eclipse of vision', in Levin, D.M. (ed.) *Modernity and the Hegemony of Vision*, London: University of California Press.

Fog Olwig, K. and Haserup, K. (eds) (1997) *Siting Culture: The Shifting Anthropological Object*, London: Routledge.

Foucault, M. (1967) *Madness and Civilisation: A History of Insanity in the Age of Reason* (trans. Howard, R.), London: Tavistock.

Foucault, M. (1970) *The Order of Things* (trans. Sheridan, A.), New York: Random House.

Foucault, M. (1973) *The Birth of the Clinic* (trans. Sheridan, A.), New York: Vintage.

Foucault, M. (1977) *Discipline and Punish* (trans. Sheridan, A.), London: Allen Lane.

Foucault, M. (1978) *The History of Sexuality*, Vol. 1, *An Introduction* (trans. Hurley, R.), New York: Pantheon. (First published in 1976 as *Histoire de la Sexualitié 1 la Vonte de savoir*, Paris: Gallimard.)

Foucault, M. (1980) *Power/Knowledge: Selected Interviews and Other Writings, 1972–1977*, London: Harvester Press.

Foucault, M. (1989) *Foucault Live. Interviews, 1966–1984*, Lotringer S. (ed.), New York: Semiotext.

Frampton, K. (1983) 'Towards a critical regionalism: six points for an architecture of resistance', in Foster, H. (ed.) *Postmodern Culture*, London: Pluto, 16–56.

Fraser, N. (1989) *Unruly Practices: Power, Discourse and Gender in Contemporary Social Theory*, Cambridge, UK: Polity Press.

Frisby, D. (1984) *Georg Simmel*, Chichester: Horwood.

Gagnon, J.H. and Simon, W. (1974) *Sexual Conduct: The Social Sources of Human Sexuality*, London: Hutchinson.

Game, A. (1991) *Undoing the Social: Towards a Deconstructive Sociology*, Milton Keynes: Open University Press.

Giddens, A. (1973) *The Class Structure of the Advanced Societies*, London: Hutchinson.

Giddens, A. (1979) *Central Problems in Social Theory: Action, Structure and Contradiction in Social Analysis*, London: Macmillan.

Giddens, A. (1984) *The Constitution of Society*, Cambridge, UK: Polity Press.

Giddens, A. (1985) *A Contemporary Critique of Historical Materialism, Volume II: The Nation, State and Violence*, Cambridge, UK: Polity Press.

Giddens, A. (1990) *The Consequences of Modernity*, Cambridge, UK: Polity Press.

Giddens, A. (1991) *Modernity and Self-Identity: Self and Society in the late Modern Age*, Cambridge, UK: Polity Press.

Gilman, S.L. (1988) *Disease and Representation: Images of Illness from Madness to AIDS*, New York: Cornell University Press.

Gilman, S.L. (1991) *The Jew's Body*, London: Routledge.

Gilroy, P. (1993) *The Black Atlantic*, London: Verso.

Gilroy, P. (2000) *Between Camps: Nations, Cultures and the Allure of Race*, Harmondsworth: Penguin.

Goldberg, D.T. (1993) *Racist Culture*, Oxford: Blackwell.

Goldthorpe, J.H. (1980) *Social Mobility and Class Structure*, Oxford: Clarendon Press.

Goodchild, P. (1996) *Deleuze and Guattari: An Introduction to the Politics of Desire*, London: Sage.

Goss, J. (1997) 'The "magic of the mall": an analysis of form, function and meaning in the contemporary retail environment', in McDowell, L. (ed.) *Undoing Place: A Geographical Reader*, London: Arnold, 264–84.

Gramsci, A. (1971) *Selections from the Prison Notebooks*, London: Lawrence Wishart.

Greene, R. and Elffers, J. (1999) *The 48 Laws of Power*, London: Profile Books.

Grimshaw, J. (1993) 'Practices of freedom', in Ramazanoglu, C. (ed.) *Up Against Foucault: Explorations of some Tensions between Foucault and Feminism*, London: Routledge, 51–72.

Guha, R. (ed.) (1982–1989) *Subaltern Studies*, Vols. 1–4, Dehli: Oxford University Press.

Guy, D.J. (1991) *Sex and Danger in Buenos Aires: Prostitution, Family and Nation in Argentina*, London: University of Nebraska Press.

Hall, S. (1997) 'The work of representation', in Hall, S. (ed.) *Representation: Cultural Representations and Signifying Practices*, London: Sage, 13–74.

Hall, T. and Hubbard, P. (1998) *The Entrepreneurial City: Geographies of Politics, Regimes and Representations*, New York: John Wiley.

Hand, S. (ed.) (1989) *The Levinas Reader: Emmanuel Levinas*, Oxford: Blackwell.

Harrison, G., Owens, D., Holton, A. and Boot, D. (1988) 'A prospective study of severe mental disorder in Afro-Caribbean patients', *Psychological Medicine*, 18: 643–57.

Harvey, D. (1996) *Justice, Nature and the Geography of Difference*, Oxford: Blackwell.

Harvey, P. and Gow, P. (1994) *Sex and Violence: Issues in Representation and Experience*, London: Routledge.

Hawthorn, G. (1987) *Enlightenment and Despair* (2nd edition), Cambridge: Cambridge University Press.

Hearn, J. (1987) *The Gender of Oppression Men, Masculinity and the Critique of Marxism*, Brighton: Wheatsheaf.

Heidegger, M. (1977) 'The age of the world picture', in Heidegger, M. (ed.) *The Question Concerning Technology and Other Essays*, New York: Harper Row.

Held, D. (2000) Keynote address: Conceiving Cosmopolitanism, University of Warwick, UK.

Held, D., McGrew, A., Goldblatt, D. and Perraton, J. (2000) *Global Transformations: Politics, Economics and Culture,* Cambridge, UK: Polity Press.

Hennessy, R. (1995) 'Queer visibility in commodity culture', in Nicholson, L. and Seidman, S. (eds) *Social Postmodernism: Beyond Identity Politics,* Cambridge: Cambridge University Press, 142–83.

Henriques, F. and Slaughter, C. (1956) *Coal is Our Life,* London: Routledge

Hepple, L.W. (1992) 'Metaphor, geopolitical discourse and the military in South America', in Barnes, T. and Duncan, J. (eds) *Writing Worlds: Discourse, Text and Metaphor in the Representation of the Landscape,* London: Routledge: 136–55.

Hesse, B. (1997) 'White governmentality: urbanism, nationalism and racism', in Westwood, S. and Williams, J. (eds) *Imagining Cities: Scripts, Signs, Memory,* London: Routledge, 86–103.

Hindess, B. (1996) *Discourses of Power: From Hobbes to Foucault,* Oxford: Blackwell.

HMSO (1991) *The Citizens Charter,* London: HMSO.

Hobbes, T. (1994) [1650] *The Elements of Law: Human Nature and De Corpore Politico,* (ed. Gaskin, J.C.A.), Oxford: Oxford University Press.

Hobbes, T. (1966) [1651] *Leviathan,* (ed. Gaskin, J.C.A.), Oxford: Oxford University Press.

Holland, J. and Adkins, L. (eds) (1996) *Sex, Sensibility and the Gendered Body,* London: Macmillan.

Holmes, D. (ed.) (1998) *Virtual Politcs: Identity and Community in Cyberspace,* London: Sage.

Howes, D. (ed.) (1996) *Cross-Cultural Consumption,* London: Routledge.

Husserl, E. (1970/1954) *The Crisis of European Sciences and Transcendental Phenomenology: an Introduction to Phenomenological Philosophy* (trans. Carter, D.), Evanston, WY: Northwestern University.

Hutnyk, J. (1997) *The Rumour of Calcutta: Tourism, Charity and the Poverty of Representation,* London: Zed Press.

Hutton, W. (1995) *The State We're In,* London: Jonathan Cape.

Inden, R.B. (1990) *Imagining India,* Oxford: Blackwell.

Jackson, S. (1996) 'Heterosexuality as a problem for feminist theory', in Adkins, L. and Merchant V. (eds) *Sexualising the Social: Power and the Organisation of Sexuality,* London: Macmillan, 15–35.

Jacobs, J.M. (1996) *Edge of Empire: Postcolonialism and the City,* London: Routledge.

James, C.L.R. (1963) *Beyond A Boundary,* London: Hutchinson.

Jamieson, L. (1996) 'The social construction of consent revisited', in Adkins, L. and Merchant, V. (eds) *Sexualising the Social: Power and the Organisation of Sexuality,* London: Macmillan, 55–77.

Jawardena, K. and de Alwis, M. (eds) (1996) *Embodied Violence: Communalising Women's Sexuality in South Asia,* London: Zed Books.

Jordan, T. (2000) *Cyberpower: The Culture and Politcs of Cyberspace and the Internet,* London: Routledge.

Kakar, S. (1996) *The Colors of Violence: Cultural Identities, Religion and Conflict,* Chicago: University of Chicago Press.

Keane, J. (1996) *Reflections on Violence,* London: Verso.

Kerr, M. (1958) *The People of Ship Street,* London: Routledge.

Laclau, E. (ed.) (1994) *The Making of Political Identities,* London: Verso.

Laclau, E. (1996) 'Deconstruction, pragmatism, hegemony', in Mouffe, C. (ed.) *Deconstruction and Pragmatism*, London: Routledge, 47–67.

Laclau, E. and Mouffe, C. (1985) *Hegemony and Socialistist Strategy: Towards a Radical Democratic Politics*, London: Verso.

Laclau, E. and Zac, L. (1994) 'Minding the gap: the subject of politics', in Laclau, E. (ed.) *The Making of Political Identities*, London: Verso, 11–39.

Lacquer, T.W. (1992) 'Sexual desire and the market economy during the Industrial Revolution', in Stanton, D.C. (ed.) *Discourses of Sexuality: From Aristotle to AIDS*, Ann Arbor, MI: University of Michigan, 185–215.

Latin American Subaltern Studies Group (1993) 'Founding statement', in Aronna, M., Beverley, J. and Oviedo, J. (eds) *The Postmodernism Debate in Latin America*, *Boundary*, Durham, NC: Duke University Press, 110–21.

Lefebvre, H. (1974) *La Production de l'espace*, Paris: Anthropos.

Lefebvre, H. (1991) *The Production of Space* (trans. Nicholson-Smith, D.), Oxford: Basil Blackwell.

Lefebvre, H. (1995) *Introduction to Modernity*, London: Verso.

Levin, D.M. (ed.) (1993) *Modernity and the Hegemony of Vision*, Berkeley, CA: University of California Press.

Levinas, E. (1987) *Collected Philosophical Papers* (trans. Lingis, A.), Dordrecht: Martins Nijhoff.

Lewis, J. (1994) 'The meanings of things: audiences, ambiguity and power', in Cruz, J. and Lewis, J. (eds) *Viewing, Reading, Listening: Audiences and Cultural Receptions*, Boulder, CO: Westview Press, 141–57.

Lewis, R. and Rolley, K. (1998) '(Ad)dressing the dyke: lesbian looks and lesbians looking', in Niva, M., Blake, A., MacRury, I. and Richards, B. (eds) *Buy this Book: Studies in Advertising and Consumption*, Routledge: London, 291–308.

Leys, S.N. (1991) *'The Hour of Eugenics': Race, Gender and Nation in Latin America*, Ithaca, NY: Cornell University Press.

Leyshon, A. and Thrift, N. (1997) *Money/Space: Geographies of Monetary Transformation*, London: Routledge.

Loader, B. (ed.) (1997) *The Governance of Cyberspace: Politics, Technology and Global Restructuring*, London: Routledge.

McAlpine, A. (1998) *The New Machiavelli: Renaissance Real Politik for Modern Managers*, London: Aurum Press.

McBeath, G.B. and Webb, S.A. (1997) 'Cities, subjectivity and cyberspace', in Westwood, S. and Williams, S (eds) *Imagining Cities: Scripts, Signs, Memory*, London: Routledge, 249–60.

McClintock, A. (1995) *Imperial Leather: Race, Gender and Sexuality in the Colonial Context*, London: Routledge.

McDowell, L. (1997) *Capital Culture: Gender at Work in the City*, Oxford: Blackwell.

Machado, L.M.V. (1993) 'We learned to think politically: The influence of the Catholic Church and the Feminist Movement on the emergence of the health movement of the Jardim Nordeste area in Sao Paulo, Brazil', in Radcliffe, S.A. and Westwood, S. (eds) *Viva: Women and Popular Protest in Latin America*, London: Routledge, 88–111.

Machiavelli, P. (1984) [1513] *The Prince*, Oxford: Oxford University Press.

McKay, G. (ed.) (1998) *DIY Culture: Party and Protest in Nineties Britain*, London: Verso.

McNay, L. (1992) *Foucault and Feminism: Power, Gender and the Self*, Cambridge, UK: Polity Press.

McNay, L. (1994) *Foucault: A Critical Introduction*, Cambridge, UK: Polity Press.

Macpherson, C. B. (1962) *The Political Theory of Possessive Individualism: Hobbes to Locke*, Oxford: Clarendon Press.

Macpherson, C. B. (1973) *Democratic Theory: Essays on Retrieval*, Oxford: Clarendon Press.

Malik, K. (1996) *The Meaning of Race*, Oxford: Blackwell.

Mama, A. (1989) 'Violence against black women; gender, race and state responses', *Feminist Review*, 32: 30–49.

Marcuse, H. (1968) *One Dimensional Man*, London: Sphere.

Martin-Barbero, J. (1993) *Communication, Culture and Hegemony: From Media to Mediations*, London: Sage.

Marx, K. (1974) [1887] *Capital: a Critical Analysis of Capitalist Production*, London: Lawrence and Wishart.

Marx, K. and Engels, F. (1967) [1848] *Manifesto of the Communist Party*, Moscow: Progress Publishers.

Massey, D. (1994) *Space, Place and Gender*, Cambridge, UK: Polity Press.

Massey, D. (1995) 'Rethinking radical democracy spatially', *Environment and Planning a Society and Space*, 13: 283–8.

Marshall, T.H. (1950) *Citizenship and Social Class*, Cambridge: Cambridge University Press.

Menon, R. and Bhasin, K. (1996) 'Abducted women, the state and questions of honour: three perspectives on the recovery operation in post-partition India', in Jayawardena, K. and De Alwis, M. (eds) *Embodied Violence: Communalising Women's Sexuality in South Asia*, London: Zed Press, 1–31.

Miller, D. (1998) *A Theory of Shopping*, Cambridge, UK: Polity Press.

Mitchell, J. (1974) *Psychoanalysis and Feminism*, Harmondsworth: Penguin.

Montesquieu, C. (1952) [1784] *The Spirit of the Laws*, Chicago: William Benton.

Morley, D. and Robins, K. (1995) *Spaces of Identity: Global Media, Electronic Landscapes and Cultural Boundaries*, London: Routledge.

Morris, L. (1994) *Dangerous Classes*, London: Routledge.

Mouffe, C. (1992) *Dimensions of Radical Democracy: Pluralism, Citizenship, Community*, London: Verso.

Mouffe, C. (1993) *The Return of the Political*, London: Verso.

Murray, C.A. (1984) *Losing Ground*, New York: Basic Books.

Murray, C.A. (1990) *The Emerging British Underclass*, London: IEA Health and Welfare Unit.

Nanda, S. (1990) *Neither Man Nor Woman: The Hijras of India*, Belmont, CA: Wadsworth Publishing.

Nandy, A. (1990) 'The politics of secularism and the recovery of religious tolerance', in Das, V. (ed.) *Mirrors of Violence: Communities, Riots and Survivors in South Asia*, Delhi: Oxford University Press, 69–93.

Niva, M., Blake, A., MacRury, I. and Richards, B. (eds) (1998) *Buy this Book: Studies in Advertising and Consumption*, Routledge: London.

Nuckolls, C.W. (1995) Motivation and the will to power: ethnopsychology and the return of Thomas Hobbes', *Philosophy of the Social Sciences*, 25(3): 345–9.

Outhwaite, W. (1994) *Habermas: A Critical Introduction*, Cambridge, UK: Polity Press.

Pateman, C. (1998) *The Sexual Contract*, Cambridge, UK: Polity Press.

Phillips, A. (1991) *Engendering Democracy*, Cambridge, UK: Polity Press.

Pieterse, J. (ed.) (1992) *Emancipations: Modern and Postmodern*, London: Sage.

Pieterse, J. and Parekh, B. (eds) (1995) *The Decolonization of the Imagination: Culture, Knowledge and Power*, London: Zed Press.

Pile, S. and Thrift, N. (eds) (1995) *Mapping The Subject: Geographies of Cultural Transformation*, London: Routledge.

Pinney, C. (1997) 'Future travel: anthropology and cultural distance in an age of virtual reality or, a past seen from a possible future', in McDowell L. (ed.) *Undoing Place: A Geographical Reader*, London: Arnold, 294–311.

Piper, K. (1997) *Relocating the Remains,* London: Royal College of Art.

Plummer, K. (1996) 'Intimate citizenship and the culture of sexual story telling', in Weeks, J. and Holland, J. (eds) *Sexual Cultures: Communities, Values and Intimacy*, London: Macmillan, 34–53.

Polanyi, K. (1957) *The Great Transformation*, Boston: Beacon Press.

Pollert, A. (1981) *Girls, Wives, Factory Lives*, London: Macmillan.

Poole, D. (1997) *Vision, Race and Modernity: A Visual Economy of the Andean Image World*, Princeton, NJ: Princeton University Press.

Poulantzas, N. (1973) *Political Power and Social Classes*, London: New Left Books.

Poulantzas, N. (1975) *Classes in Contemporary Capitalism*, London: New Left Books.

Radcliffe, S. and Westwood, S. (1996) *Remaking the Nation: Place, Identity and Politics in Latin America*, London: Routledge.

Radford, J. and Russell, D.E.H. (eds) (1992) *Femicide: The Politics of Woman Killing*, Buckingham: Open University Press.

Ramazanoglu, C. (ed.) (1993) *Up Against Foucault: Explorations of some tensions between Foucault and Feminism*, London: Routledge.

Rattansi, A. (1982) *Marx and the Division of Labour*, London: Macmillan.

Rattansi, A. and Westwood, S. (eds) (1994) *Racism, Modernity and Identity: On the Western Front*, Cambridge, UK: Polity Press.

Rousseau, J.J. (1968) [1762] *The Social Contract*, Harmondsworth: Penguin.

Rousseau, J.J. (1974) [1762] *Émile*, London: Dent.

Rowbotham, S. (1973) *Woman's Consciousness, Man's World*, Harmondsworth: Penguin.

Rowbotham, S. (1983) *Dreams and Dilemmas*, London: Virago.

Rowe, W. and Schelling, V. (1991) *Memory and Modernity: Popular Culture in Latin America*, London: Verso.

Rubin, H. (1998) *The Princessa: Machiavelli for Women*, London: Bloomsbury.

Runnymede Trust (1994) *Neither Unique Nor Typical*, London: Runnymede Trust.

Said, E.(1978) *Orientalism*, London: Routledge.

Sayyid, B.S. (1997) *A Fundamental Fear: Eurocentrism and the Emergence of Islam*, London: Zed Books.

Schirmer, J.G. (1989) '"Those who die for life cannot be called dead", Women and Human Rights Protest in Latin America', *Feminist Review*, 32: 3–29.

Schirmer, J.G. (1993) 'The seeking of truth and the gender of consciousness: the comardres of El Salvador and the Conavigua widows of Guatemala', in Radcliffe, S. and Westwood, S. (eds) *Viva: Women and Popular Protest in Latin America*, London: Routledge, 30–64.

Sciorra, J. (1996) 'Return to the future: Puerto Rican vernacular architecture' in King, A.D. (ed.) *Re-Presenting the City: Ethnicity, Capital and Culture in the 21st Century Metropolis*, London: Macmillan, 60–92.

Scott, J. (1996) *Stratification and Power: Structures of Class, Status and Domination* Cambridge, UK: Polity Press.

Seidman, S. (1995) 'Deconstructing queer theory or the under-theorization of the social and the ethical', in Nicholson, L. and Seidman, S. (eds) *Social Postmodernism: Beyond Identity Politics*, Cambridge: Cambridge University Press, 116–41.

Sennet, R. (1970) *The Uses of Disorder*, Harmondsworth: Penguin.

Sennett, R. and Cobb, J. (1972) *The Hidden Injuries of Class*, Cambridge: Cambridge University Press.

Sibley, D. (1995) *Geographies of Exclusion*, London: Routledge.

Silverstone, R. (1994) *Television and Everyday Life*, London: Routledge.

Sivanandan (1990) 'All that melts into air is solid: the hokum of New Times', *Race and Class*, 31: 1–31.

Skinner, Q. (1981) *Machiavelli*, Oxford: Oxford University Press.

Skocpol, T. (1979) 'France, Russia, China: a structural analysis of social revolutions', *Comparative Studies in Society and History*, 18 (2): 104–29.

Skocpol, T. (1994) *Social Revolutions in the Modern World*, Cambridge: Cambridge University Press.

Smart, C. (1996) 'Desperately seeking post-heterosexual women', in Holland, J. and Adkins, L. (eds) *Sex, Sensibility and the Gendered Body*, London: Macmillan, 222–42.

Soja, E. (1989) *Postmodern Geographies: The Reassertion of Space in Critical Theory*, London: Verso.

Soja, E. (1996) *Third Space: Journeys to Los Angeles and Other Real-and-Imagined Places*, Oxford: Blackwell.

Spivak, G.C. (1993) 'Can the subaltern speak?', in Williams, P. and Chrisman, L. (eds) *Colonial Discourse and Post-Colonial Theory: a Reader*, London: Harvester Wheatsheaf, 66-111.

Stanton, D. (1992) *Discourses of Sexuality: from Aristotle to AIDS*, Ann Arbor, MI: University of Michigan Press.

Stanworth, M. (ed.) (1987) *Reproductive Technologies: Gender, Motherhood and Medicine*, Cambridge, UK: Polity Press.

Stepan, N. (1991) *"The Hour of Eugenics" Race, Gender and Nation in Latin America*, Ithaca, NY: Cornell University Press.

Stoler, A. (1995) *Race and the Education of Desire: Foucault's History of Sexuality and the Colonial Order of Things*, Durham, NC: Duke University Press.

Swingewood, A. (1980) *Marx and Modern Social Theory*, 2nd edn, London: Macmillan.

Taussig, M. (1987) *Shaminism, Colonialism and the Wild Man*, Chicago: Chicago University Press.

The Industrial Society (1998) *20 20 Vision*, London: IS.

Thompson, E.P. (1971) 'The moral economy of the crowd in eighteenth century England', *Past and Present*, 50 (1):76–136.

Tolson, A. (1977) *The Limits of Masculinity*, London: Tavistock.

Touraine, A. (1981) *The Voice and The Eye: An Analysis of Social Movements*, Cambridge: Cambridge University Press.

Touraine, A. (1995) *Critique of Modernity*, Oxford: Blackwell.

Urry, J. (2000) *Sociology Beyond Societies: Mobilities for the Twenty First Century*, London: Routledge.

van der Veer, P. (1993) '"The foreign hand": orientalist discourse in sociology and communalism', in Breckenbridge, C. A. and van der Veer, P. (eds) *Orientalism and the Postcolonial Predicament: Perspectives on South Asia*, Philadelphia, PA: University of Pennsylvania Press, 23–44.

van der Veer, P. and Asad, T. (1995) 'Genealogies of religion: discipline and reasons of power in Christianity and Islam', *Social History*, 20 (3): 365–72.

Vanaik, A. (1997) *The Furies of Indian Communalism: Religion, Modernity and Secularization*, London: Verso.

Venturis, R., Scott-Barown, D. and Izenour, S. (1972) *Learning from Las Vegas*, Cambridge: MIT Press.

Walby, S. (1990) *Theorising Patriarchy*, Oxford: Blackwell.

Walzer, M. (1989) *The Company of Critics: Social Criticism and Political Commitment in the Twentieth Century*, London: Peter Halban.

Ward, P.M. (1999) *Colonias and Public Policy in Texas and Mexico: Urbanization By Stealth*, Austin: University of Texas Press.

Weber, M. (1958) [1904-5] *The Protestant Ethic and the Spirit of Capitalism*, New York: Scribner.

Weeks, J. (1986) *Sexuality*, London: Tavistock.

Weeks, J. (1989) *Sexuality and its Discontents: Meanings, Myths and Modern Sexualities*, London: Routledge.

Weeks, J. and Holland, J. (eds) (1996) *Sexual Cultures: Communities, Values and Intimacy*, London: Macmillan, 88–111.

Werbner, P. (1997) 'Essentialising essentialism, essentialising silence: ambivalence and multiplicity in the constructions of racism and ethnicity', in Werbner, P. and Modood, T. (eds) *Debating Cultural Hybridity: Multi-Cultural Identities and the Politics of Anti-Racism*, London: Zed Books, 226–54.

Werbner, P. and Modood, T. (1997) *Debating Cultural Hybridity: Multi-Cultural Identities and the Politics of Anti-Racism*, London: Zed Books.

Westwood, S. (1984) *All Day Every Day: Factory and Family in the Making of Women's Lives*, London: Pluto Press. (1985, Chicago: University of Illinois.)

Westwood, S. (1990) 'Racism, black masculinities and the politics of space', in Hearn, J. and Morgan, D. (eds) *Men, Masculinities and Social Theory*, London: Unwin Hyman.

Westwood, S. (1991) 'Red Star over Leicester: racism, the politics of identity and black youth in Britain', in Werbner, P. and Anwar, M. (eds) *Black and Ethnic Leaderships: The Cultural Dimensions of Political Action*, London: Routledge, 146–70.

Westwood, S. (1992) 'When class became community: radicalism in adult education', in Rattansi, A. and Reader, D. (eds) *Rethinking Radical Education: Essays in Honour of Brian Simon*, London: Lawrence and Wishart, 222–48.

Westwood, S. (1994) 'Racism, mental illness and the politics of identity', in Rattansi, A. and Westwood, S. (eds) *Racism, Modernity and Identity: On the Western Front*, Cambridge, UK: Polity Press, 247–65.

Westwood, S. (1996) 'Feckless fathers: masculinities and the British State', in Mac an Ghaill, M. (ed.) *Understanding Masculinities: Social Relations and Cultural Arenas*, Buckingham: Open University Press, 21–35.

Westwood, S. (1997) 'Imagining cities', in Westwood, S. and Williams, J. (eds.) *Imagining Cities: Scripts, Signs, Memory*, London: Routledge, 1–16.

Westwood, S. (1998) 'Nationalism and the politics of national identities in Latin America', *The Eastern Anthropologist,* 50: 3–4.

Westwood, S. (2000) 'Imagining America remembering home: Latina/o cultures in urban America', in Westwood, S. and Phizacklea A., *Trans-Nationalism and the Politics of Belonging*, London: Routledge.

Westwood, S. and Radcliffe, R. (1993) 'Gender, racism and politics of identities in Latin America', in Radcliffe, S. and Westwood, S. (eds) *Viva: Women and Popular Protest in Latin America*, London: Routledge, 1–30.

Westwood, S. and Williams, J. (eds) (1997) *Imagining Cities: Scripts, Signs, Memory*, London: Routledge.

Westwood, S., Couloute, J., Desai, S., Matthew, P. and Piper, A. (1989) *Sadness in My Heart: Racism and Mental Illness*, Leicester: Black Mental Health Group/Leicester University.

Williams, P. (1997) *Seeing a Color-Blind Future*: *The Paradox of Race (BBC Reith Lecture Series)*, London: Virago Press.

Williams, R. (1983) *Towards 2000*, London: Chatto and Windus.

Williamson, J. (1978) *Decoding Advertisements*: *Ideology and Meaning in Advertising*, London: Boyars.

Willmot, P. and Young, M. (1957) *Family and Kinship in East London*, London: Routledge.

Winant, H. (1995) *Racial Conditions*, Minneapolis, MN: University of Minnesota Press.

Witz, A., Halford, S. and Savage, M. (1996) 'Organised bodies: gender, sexuality and embodiment in contemporary organisations', in Adkins, L. and Merchant, V. (eds) *Sexualising the Social*: *Power and the Organisation of Sexuality*, London: Macmillan, 173–91.

Young, R. (1995) *Colonial Desire*: *Hybridity as Theory, Culture and Race*, London: Routledge.

Young, M. and Willmott, P. (1962) (revised edition) *Family and Kinship in East London*, Harmondsworth: Penguin.

Young, M. and Willmott, P. (1974) *The Symmetrical Family*, New York: Pantheon.

Zohar, D. and Marshall, I. (1994) *The Quantum Society: Mind, Physics and the New Social Vision*, London: Flamingo.

Index

and power 126–8; capitalism 121–3; Catholicism 119–20; community of nations 116–19; consumption 121–3; environmental campaigns 130–1; Ecuador 116–17; governance and 129–30; image, crucial nature of 125–6; interwoven with spatial 115; language, meaning and 120–1; miracles 119–21; modernity and television 124–5; modernity and visual hegemony 129; monumentalism 127–8; nature of 115; news reports 124; perspective on 131–2; Peru 118–19; religion 119–21; semiotics of power 116; social and the visual 128–31; spatial interwoven with 115; televisual powers 123–6; violence and 124; visibility undermining 131; visible nations 116–19

Walby, Sylvia 64
Walzer, M. 73
Ward, P.M. 112
Webb, S.A. 125
Weber, Max 14–15, 45, 48–9, 72, 133–4, 142
Weberian model of power 2
Weeks, J. 89
welfare to work 53–5

Werbner, P. 22, 42, 43
Westwood, *et al.* 37
Westwood, Sallie: citizenship, visions of 53; city life 113; engendered power 65; 'feckless' fatherhood 77; land rights and power 105; Marxist underpinning of studies 57; masculinity, plurality of 74; national interest, contradictions on 102; Red Star youth project 40; resistance, on analysis of 73
Williams, Patricia 35–6
Williams, Raymond 112
Williamson, J. 122
Wilmott, P. 63
Winant, H. 26, 35
Witz *et al.* 95
woman, disrupting force of 68–71
working class, making the 49–50
Working for Ford (Benyon, H.) 57
Wright, Richard 29, 31, 38
WTO (World Trade Organisation) 139

Young, M. 63
Young, R. 32

Zac, L. 24, 25
Zohar, Danah 136–7